Attachment,
Intimacy,
Autonomy

Attachment, Intimacy, Autonomy

USING ATTACHMENT THEORY IN ADULT PSYCHOTHERAPY

Jeremy Holmes, MD, MRCP, FRCPsych

JASON ARONSON INC.
Northvale, New Jersey
London

Production Editor: Elaine Lindenblatt

This book was set in 11 pt. Berkeley Book by Alpha Graphics of Pittsfield, New Hampshire, and printed and bound by Book-mart Press of North Bergen, New Jersey.

Library of Congress Cataloging-in-Publication Data

Holmes, Jeremy.
    Attachment, intimacy, autonomy : using attachment theory
in adult psychotherapy / by Jeremy Holmes.
      p.   cm.
    Includes bibliographical references and index.
    ISBN 1-56821-872-9 (s/c : alk. paper)
    1. Attachment behavior.   2. Object relations (Psychoanalysis)
   3. Psychotherapist and patient.   4. Intimacy (Psychology)
   5. Autonomy (Psychology)   I. Title.
    [DNLM: 1. Object Attachment.   2. Psychotherapy. WM 460.5.O2
H751a 1996]
RC455.4.A84H65 1996
616.89'14—dc20
DNLM/DLC
for Library of Congress   96-5660

For information and catalog, write to Jason Aronson Inc., 230 Livingston Street, Northvale, New Jersey 07647. Or visit our website: http://www.aronson.com

Manufactured in the United States of America. Jason Aronson Inc. offers books and cassettes. For information and catalog write to Jason Aronson Inc., 230 Livingston Street, Northvale, New Jersey 07647.

For the grandchildren:

Floyd

and Rosy, Zenta, and Marcus

Contents

Part III
Wider Implications

Acknowledgments

In 1982, thanks to the generosity of the Welcome Foundation, I was able to devote the best part of a year to reading, thinking, and writing about attachment theory (Holmes 1993). Since returning to my clinical work in the National Health Service I have tried to apply attachment concepts in the various clinical situations in which, as a psychotherapist and psychiatrist, I find myself. This volume is an attempt to communicate these efforts. This process could not have come about without the help of the "attachment community"—that invisible college of researchers, theorists, and clinicians who have found in attachment theory a congenial meeting point and source of inspiration. In different ways, I am greatly indebted to Ursula and Richard Bowlby, John Birtchnell, John Byng-Hall, Morris Eagle, Peter Fonagy, Paul Griffiths, Victoria Hamilton, Dorothy Heard, Peter Hobson, Sebastian Kraemer, Mary Main, Mary Sue Moore, Brian Lake, Pat Sable, and Felicity de Zulueta, although, of course, I alone am responsible for the infelicities, unwarranted speculations, and howlers that this work no doubt contains.

I must also thank the wider circle of like-minded psycho-
therapists and psychoanalysts whom I see as committed to a tol-
erant and eclectic psychotherapeutic perspective and who have
also influenced and supported me over many years: John Adey,
Sidney Bloch, Sidney Crown, Anthony Bateman, Pat Gall-
wey, Frank Margison, Russell Meares, Joan and Julian Raphael-
Leff, Richard Lindley, Pat Millner, Roy Muir, Anton Obhotzer,
Jonathan Pedder, Anthony Ryle, Nigel Simpson, Anthony Storr, Nick
Temple, Joy Tompson, Lorraine and Robert Tollemache, and
Charles Rycroft.

Communicating psychotherapeutic ideas and experience
while at the same time respecting confidentiality is a thorny ethical dilemma that troubles the psychotherapy profession and can
be a source of unnecessary distress to its clients. This book is mainly
based on case histories, all of which have been disguised in the
interests of confidentiality, and are perhaps best seen as "true fictions." I have asked permission to publish, wherever possible.
Where the patient is still in treatment, such a request inevitably
has a big impact on the transference. I am enormously indebted to
my patients, without whom both my livelihood and this work
would not have been possible.

I live and work in a situation of comparative intellectual isolation. Lecturing, though daunting at times, is a wonderful stimu-
lus to thought; discussions with colleagues provide essential feed-
back and correctives. There is thus for me a reciprocal relationship
between lecturing and writing—lecturing stimulates ideas, which
are often first tried out verbally and only later committed to print.
I am grateful to the various conference organizers, editors, and
peer reviewers who have invited me to lecture or accepted my
offerings.

Writing and practicing is also only possible with the support
of one's immediate colleagues and family. In our "periphery of
excellence" my immediate colleague Glenn Roberts has been un-
complainingly tolerant of my lecturing and writing commitments
—albeit on a quid pro quo basis! My secretary, Pat Bartlett, con-

tinues to provide indispensable backup, efficiency, and cheerfulness. Matthew Holmes compiled the index, and offered his characteristically skeptical and perceptive comments. Last, but definitely not least, as ever, none of this would have been possible without the support, interest, and tolerance of Ros and Joshua Holmes, on whose final judgments I always rely.

Introduction

Psychotherapy has reached a critical phase in its hundred-year history. Psychoanalysis, the founding parent, is under threat—philosophically, scientifically, and fiscally—and yet continues to fascinate each new generation of thinkers, and to generate vigorous new ideas. Psychotherapies abound, and there is an urgent search for common ground. The assault on welfare spending in the West means that publicly funded psychotherapy is under intense scrutiny. There is an urgent need to bring psychotherapeutic ideas to bear on the needs of the seriously mentally ill.

Within this confusion—often creative, sometimes destructive—attachment theory has increasingly come to be seen as a possible paradigm for clarification and unification. Since John Bowlby's death in 1991, interest in attachment theory has continued to grow apace (Holmes 1993, Karen 1994). Perhaps the greatest contribution of attachment theory is its integrative potential, bringing together ideas from evolutionary biology (Slavin and Kriegman 1992), psychoanalysis, ethology (Kraemer 1992), and cognitive science, as well as providing a meeting point for researchers and clinicians from around the world (Goldberg et al. 1995). There is a growing feeling in the psychological sciences of the need for a "new paradigm" that can synthesize the best ideas from psychoanalysis, cognitive science, and neurobiology into a more coherent whole (Holmes 1994c). Attachment theory is on the leading edge of the search for such a conceptual revolution. With its emphasis on relationships, attachment theory is determinedly humanistic, while retaining the scientific rigor of Darwinian ethology.

Attachment theory has also provided a major impetus to psychotherapy research, recently through the use and further refinement of Mary Main's Adult Attachment Interview (AAI) (Main and Goldwyn in press). The AAI has great potential as a reliable instrument for measuring psychodynamic change, using language as an index of patterns of security and insecurity of inner objects. In Britain it is being used in several major outcome studies looking at the treatment of borderline personality disorder. The work of Bartholomew (1990), Hazan and Shaver (1994), and Birtchnell (1993) also provide important examples of attachment theory–influenced research on relationships and their impact on the patterns of neurotic disorders.

While attachment theory's place as a research paradigm is secure, its influence on clinical practice has, up to now, been less clear. Clinical attachment theory is the central focus of this book. Clinicians are increasingly recognizing the overwhelming importance of the therapeutic alliance—or attachment bond—as a basis for successful psychotherapy. Several models of psychotherapy based on attachment theory now incorporate this finding into their training procedures. Some acknowledge an explicit debt to attachment theory, especially Klerman and Weissman's interpersonal therapy (Klerman et al. 1984), and Ryle's (1990, 1995) cognitive analytic therapy. For Meares (1993), as for Winnicott, the essence of psychotherapy is "learning to play"—the emergence of an inner language within the context of a secure, attuned relationship. The salience of attachment may well underlie the general finding of the *equivalence paradox* in psychotherapy research—different psychotherapeutic approaches producing roughly similar outcomes (Stiles et al. 1986)—and provides a rationale for the undervalued field of supportive psychotherapy (see Chapter 5).

Attachment theory also has an important contribution to make to sociology (see Epilogue). In her movingly entitled book, *From Pain to Violence*, de Zulueta (1994) brings Bowlby's ideas to bear on the increasing violence in modern society, which she attributes to "attachment gone wrong." The angry destructiveness of modern youth, seen also in borderline personality disorders—in which violence is often directed against the self—as well as psychopathic disorders, can be understood, as in Bowlby's original formulation, as the protest of children separated from, or deprived of, a secure base.

These broad themes form the background to this book, whose main aim is to persuade the busy but inquiring practitioner of the relevance of attachment ideas to the everyday practice of psychotherapy, psychology, and psychiatry. It is divided into three parts. Part I starts with an overview of recent research in attachment theory and shows how these findings can inform psychotherapeutic work. Chapter 2 goes on to look at the history of attachment theory, and especially its relationship with psychoanalysis, with detailed clinical examples—continued in Chapter 3—of the application of attachment ideas to individual psychotherapy with adults. Part II consists of three clinical topics approached from an attachment point of view: splitting, suicide, and supportive psychotherapy. In a wider perspective, Part III looks at the relationship between psychiatry and psychotherapy, psychotherapeutic ethics, and social policy, all from the angle of attachment theory. I have tried to give vivid clinical examples and to draw on my personal experience throughout, which means that the style varies from the objective to the more personal, polemical, and, in places, poetic.

There is increasing interest in generic and integrative approaches to psychotherapy. Attachment theory has much to offer the various branches of psychiatry and psychotherapy. One only has to work daily with patients suffering from schizophrenia and their families to see how the distress of having a mentally ill relative activates intense attachment behavior, which may in turn contribute to the severity of the patient's disablement (cf. Doane and Diamond 1994). The focus of this book, however, is that of individual psychotherapy, which is the bedrock of my psychotherapeutic, as opposed to psychiatric, work. My basic reference point is psychoanalysis and psychodynamic psychiatry. This is unashamedly eclectic "UK-style" dynamic psychotherapy in which, alongside psychoanalytic theory and technique, supportive and cognitive therapies also have their place (Holmes and Crown 1996). It is practiced in the setting of a publically funded health system, in which patients are for the most part seen once weekly, or less, for periods usually not more than 2 to 3 years.

Attachment theory is not just another brand name in psychotherapy. An interest in attachment ideas does not mean abandoning tried and tested techniques. Successful psychotherapy depends on the capacity to hold to a secure technical base *and* to be open to the exploration of new ideas. That is one of the essential, and possibly deceptively simple, messages of attachment theory.

Part I

Theory and Practice

From Attachment to Intimacy

The overall aim of this book is to explore the contribution of attachment theory to everyday clinical psychotherapeutic practice. In this chapter I shall review some current themes in contemporary attachment theory and their implications for psychotherapy. Like secure attachments, sound theory liberates. Good maps facilitate exploration of unknown and potentially dangerous territory. But a bad map can be a trap, leading us deeper into labyrinths of confusion, as we cling all the more to our theories. The contemporary psychotherapist is faced with a plurality of models and theories. How is she to choose between them, reconcile them, select what is useful, and discard the inessential?

Attachment theory can help since it is not so much a single theory as an overall framework for thinking about relationships, or, more accurately, about those aspects of relationships that are shaped by threat and the need for security. These themes are centrally relevant to the work of psychotherapy. But so far, for reasons I shall explore, attachment theory has had relatively little direct impact on the practice of psychotherapy with adults. One reason is to be found in its language, which tends to be "external" and descriptive rather than "internal" and experiential. Yet this very drawback contains also one of the great strengths of attachment theory—its capacity for scientific evaluation and refutation (Holmes 1993).

Before considering these themes in more detail, I shall trace the evolution of contemporary attachment theory from its origins in the ideas and research of John Bowlby and Mary Ainsworth in the 1950s (see Figure 1–1).

BOWLBY

Attachment theory arose from the encounter between the new science of ethology and that phase in the history of psychoanalysis in which it was moving from drive theory toward the relational perspective embodied in the work of Balint, Winnicott, Fairbairn, and Melanie Klein (Greenberg and Mitchell 1983). From ethology and evolutionary biology came the idea that social as well as intrapsychic behavior could be instinctive and that relationships could be observed experimentally without necessarily doing violence to their complexity and humanity. From object relations came the notion of an internal world comprising not so much a mechanistic "psychic apparatus" but representations of people, of the self, and its significant others and their mutual relationships, however distorted by immaturity or phantasy.

Bowlby based his psychology on the opposing themes of attachment and separation/loss. He saw loss and separation as psychologically very similar, loss being an irrevocable case of separation. For the psychotherapist, several key features of Bowlby's original formulation of attachment theory stand out. First, he saw the biological function of attachment as protection from predation. Thus the principal role of the attachment bond is to provide security. Second, there is a reciprocal relationship between secure attachment and creative or playful exploration; only when attachment needs are assuaged (Heard and Lake 1986) can the individual turn away from her attachment figure toward the world, whether inner or outer. This immediately suggests that the function of the

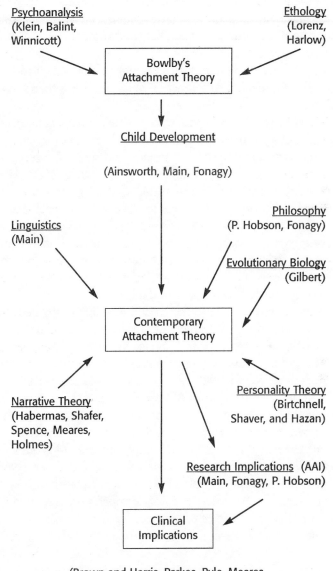

Figure 1–1. The evolution of contemporary attachment theory.

psychotherapeutic setting is to provide a secure base (Ainsworth 1969) or safe haven from which the patient can reach out to and explore both her inner world and her environment. Third, Bowlby believed that attachment is not a childish need that is outgrown, but persists, albeit in latent form, throughout life. Adult relationships can be understood in attachment terms no less than those of children.

Then there is the powerful relationship between attachments, and their disruption, and the emotions: "The psychology and psychopathology of emotion is . . . in large part the psychology and pathology of affectional bonds" (Bowlby 1979b, p. 130). Affects are motivators and reinforcers in the psychology of attachment. Attachment theory provides a relational context in which disturbing feelings—fear of separation; sadness about loss; anger and protest about separation; terror, rage and guilt in reaction to trauma; jealousy of those whose attachment potential one imagines to be greater than one's own; envy of a withholding attachment figure; and so on—can be located and understood.

Separation/loss is the other great theme in Bowlby's dualistic picture of relationships. Initially he was concerned with the traumatic impact of separation itself, hence his much-challenged view that continuous uninterrupted maternal care for at least the first five years of life was the precondition of psychological health. Later, partly under the influence of Ainsworth's research, and informed by Rutter's (1981) magnificent review, he took a more subtle position, in which, rather than loss per se, it is the response to separation and the way it is handled within the family that becomes central to the genesis of neurosis. The capacity of the caregiver to recognize and accept protest is as much a foundation of psychological health as the absence of major separation. The denial of trauma and suppression of protest were seen by Bowlby as crucial determinants of neurosis, summarized in the title of one of his last papers: "On Knowing What You are Not Supposed to Know, and on Feeling What You are Not Supposed to Feel" (Bowlby 1979a). This paper is important because it represents a movement beyond the behavioral manifestations of grief to the meaning and significance of loss and thus to the narrative structures that surround them. These are themes that, as we shall see, have been central to post-Bowlbian research.

AINSWORTH AND THE POST-BOWLBIANS

Although Bowlby was primarily a theoretician, his ideas founded a new school of empirical research in developmental psychology, much of which is highly relevant to the practice of psychotherapy. The co-founder of attachment theory was Mary Ainsworth. Apart from her role as a teacher and inspirer of subsequent generations of attachment researchers, she made two major contributions.

The first was her invention of the *strange situation* as a measure of attachment status in 1-year-olds (Ainsworth 1982). This simple but replicable test enables us to classify infants as securely or insecurely attached to a caregiver. Strange-situation status is based on the response of the infant to the mild stress of being brought to a strange room in a clinic and then separated from her caregiver for a series of 3-minute periods. Children who protest on separation and can be pacified on reunion, after which they return to exploratory play, are deemed to be *secure*. About two-thirds of children behave in this way in normal populations. Those who do not show this pattern are classified as insecure, in all of whom there is inhibition of exploration.

Three patterns of insecure attachment are now recognized: *Insecure-avoidant* children protest little on separation, and on reunion with the caregiver hover nervously nearby. *Insecure-ambivalent* children protest, but cannot be pacified when their caregiver returns, burying themselves in her lap or clinging furiously to her. The *insecure-disorganized* pattern was established after reexamination of videotapes of children who could not easily be classified as avoidant or ambivalent. These children show no coherent pattern of response; they "freeze" or collapse to the ground, or lean vacantly against a wall on reunion. In average populations about one-fifth of children are avoidant, one-sixth ambivalent, and one in twenty disorganized, although the proportion of the latter goes up dramatically in vulnerable groups, such as the socioeconomically disadvantaged and those whose mothers have been abused as children (Crittenden 1988).

Ainsworth's and her students' second great contribution was to study the links between the parent–infant relationship in the first year of life and subsequent classification in the strange situation. The kernel of their findings was that parental responsiveness to infant affect is a key determinant of secure attachment. In summary, environments may be consistently responsive, consistently unresponsive, or inconsistently responsive. The mothers of the secure infants pick their babies up more quickly when they show signs of distress, play with them more, and generally seem more aware of them and their needs than the parents of insecure children. Parents of children who show the avoidant pattern are more brusque and functional in their handling, while parents of those who show the ambivalent reaction tend to be less attuned to their children's needs, often ignoring them when they are obviously distressed and intruding upon them when they are playing happily. As mentioned, mothers of the disorganized group tend to be greatly stressed and to have a high incidence of abuse in their own childhood.

Insecure attachment patterns can be seen as defensive strategies designed to maintain contact with rejecting or inconsistent parents (Hamilton 1985). This contrasts with the classically Freudian notion of defense (Bateman and Holmes 1995) in which inner pain, rather than outer threat, is warded off, but clearly the two are related, especially in Bowlby's environmentalist model of psychopathology. In the hierarchy of priorities, exploration is sacrificed for the sake of security. Put crudely, avoidant children cling to things because they find people are threatening, while ambivalent children cling to people to compensate for their perceived inconsistency. Both patterns contrast with the "fluid attentional gaze" (Main 1995) of the securely attached child, who can move from things to people and back to herself with confidence and poise.

It should be noted that the attachment-based approach to research and clinical practice adopted throughout this book is highly dependent on this four-fold typology of behaviors and psychological states. Leiman (1995) argues strongly against typological classifications, stating that human psychology is far more complex and multidimensional than can be captured by a few "ideal types." Without denying the force of his argument, I believe that the paradigmatic approach is heuristically useful in practice and research, but it is important to remember that character is far more subtle than the labels "avoidant," "ambivalent," "borderline," or even "secure type" can possibly convey.

Significantly from a psychotherapeutic perspective, Stern (1985) and Trevarthen (1984) and their students have moved on from these behavioral descriptions to the inner worlds of parent and child. Trevarthen writes of *primary intersubjectivity*, the empathic bond that connects baby and parent from the early days of life through mutual gaze, imitation, and affective responsiveness. Stern writes about nascent *sense of self* in the developing child. He emphasizes parental *attunement* as the precondition of a stable and coherent sense of self. Both Stern and Trevarthen use musical metaphors to describe the preverbal interactive patterns between parents and children: tone, pitch, timbre, and rhythm all contribute to the eventual security or insecurity of the relationship. For example Stern speaks of *cross-modal attunement*, in which the parent pats the baby (tactile mode) in time to the child's rhythmic cooing (vocal mode), suggesting that in the "dance" of this shared play is to be found the basis for the child's sense of herself in relation to others. These shared meanings form the foundations of the capacity for intimacy.

Parental attunement on the one hand and the ability to accept protest without retaliation or excessive anxiety on the other form the basis for secure attachment. In Winnicott's (1971) terminology the parental environment must be sufficiently responsive to give a child a sense of both healthy omnipotence *and* vulnerability. First, through parental attunement, the child must be able to feel she has "created" the object, that the world is her oyster. This is the basis of healthy narcissism and self-esteem. Second, the child needs to be able to feel that her parents can survive her rage, and so be able, after an angry outburst, to say, "Hello object, I destroyed you!" (Winnicott 1971). As we shall see, these primary attachment and separation experiences provide a nucleus for the development of the capacities for intimacy and autonomy, respectively.

Longitudinal Studies of Attachment

It is not possible to summarize here the vast amount of important research that has flowed from Ainsworth's original work. I will discuss only those points that are relevant to the main thread of my argument. First is the familiar question of the respective roles of temperament and handling in the origins of security or insecurity. Attachment theory is essentially a nurturant hypothesis about psychological development, developed by Bowlby partly in response to his conviction that psychoanalysis had underestimated the role of environmental trauma in generating neurosis. Early strange-situation studies tended to confirm this in that attachment status with one parent is uncorrelated, at least at 1 year of age, with that of the other. What is being measured appears to be an inter-active pattern, rather than an intrinsic property of the infant. The separate representation of attachment patterns with each parent provides a greater chance of psychological robustness than would be the case if only one—the mother's—influence counted. However, newborn infants undoubtedly differ markedly in temperament, so that attachment status presumably depends on the "goodness of fit" between a particular parent with her own attachment history and capacities and the unique inborn temperament of her particular child.

Second, much research has pointed to the predictive power of attachment status in infancy for subsequent behavior. Long-term follow-up studies have shown that children classified as secure at 1 year of age will, on the whole, still be showing signs of security at school entry, interacting well with their peers and teachers

(Bretherton 1991a). By contrast, the insecure-avoidant children are more likely to be loners, given to unprovoked aggression, while those classified as insecure-ambivalent tend to be potential victims, unable to ask for help appropriately and clinging to their teachers. Attachment patterns are self-perpetuating developmental tracks that maintain some predictability in an uncertain interpersonal world.

However, despite the stability of attachment patterns, attachment status can change over time. Children classified as insecure may become secure if their mother's circumstances improve, or if she receives successful psychotherapy (Murray and Cooper 1994).

MAIN, FONAGY, AND THE
ADULT ATTACHMENT INTERVIEW

The development of the Adult Attachment Interview (AAI) by Mary Main and her colleagues (Main and Goldwyn in press) in the mid-1980s gave a new impetus to attachment research, moving it even closer to the clinical realities of adult psychotherapy. The AAI is an audiotaped semistructured psychodynamic assessment session, whose aim is to "surprise the unconscious" into revealing itself by asking detailed questions about relationships with parents and significant others, and about losses and separations and how the subject coped with them.

The AAI is original in that its scoring system is based not so much on content as on the form and structure of the subject's narrative style. Paralleling the strange-situation classification, narratives are classified as secure-autonomous, insecure-dismissive, insecure-enmeshed (or preoccupied), and disorganized (or unresolved). In *secure-autonomous* narratives the subject speaks coherently, logically, and concisely about her past and its vicissitudes, however problematic these may have been. *Insecure-dismissive* narratives are unelaborated and unrevealing; the subject may state that she has no memories of her childhood before the age of 11, or that her parents were "brilliant," without being able to amplify or produce relevant examples. By contrast, in *insecure-*

enmeshed narratives the subject appears bogged down in her history, telling rambling and inconclusive stories as though past pain was still alive today. The *unresolved* category is rated separately and coexists with the others; it refers to points in a narrative where the logical flow is interrupted, broken, or disjointed. Main suggests that these narrative fractures may represent the emergence of previously repressed traumatic memories.

The AAI was developed within a theoretical framework that predicted that there would be connections between attachment status in childhood and narrative style in later life. This hypothesis has been supported by at least two sets of recent studies. First, Main and others have shown that, along with other measures looking at what I have called "narrative competence" (Holmes 1992) such as picture completion and tell-a-story tasks, attachment patterns in infancy are remarkably predictive of adolescents' AAI status when measured some fifteen years later (Benoit and Parker 1994, Warn and Carlson 1996). Perhaps even more striking are the findings of Fonagy and his co-workers (1991), who showed that the outcome of the AAI administered to prospective parents was a good predictor of attachment status of their subsequent 1-year-old children 20 months later. Mothers with secure-autonomous narratives tended to have children who were found to be secure in the strange-situation, while dismissive parents tended to have insecure-avoidant infants.

Even more significantly, Fonagy and his co-workers (1994) found that the capacity to think about oneself in relation to others, which he calls the *reflexive self function* (RSF), is a key determinant of whether mothers whose own childhoods were traumatic will have infants who turn out to be insecure in the strange situation. The capacity for RSF is a vital protection against psychological vulnerability in the face of environmental difficulty—a highly significant finding for psychotherapists, since a large part of their work could be seen as enhancing RSF (*insight* in a researchable guise) in their patients. These studies demonstrate the continuity of attachment across time. Looking backward we see how parental attachment patterns influence security, or its lack, in their infants; looking forward, those early infant attachment patterns seem to predict behavior in school, and later the ways in which individuals talk and think about themselves, and perhaps how they relate intimately to others.

These are large claims and much research needs to be done to fill in the details and to understand exceptions to these general trends. Nevertheless it is hard not to be impressed by these vivid illustrations of the links between a preverbal psychobiological phenomenon—attachment status in infancy—and verbal, meaning-saturated psycholinguistic phenomena—the attachment narrative in adult life. This is a link, so to speak, between the supersonic squeak of the newborn rat separated from its mother and the plaintive wail of the funeral bagpipe. The existence of such links is a central theoretical tenet of psychodynamic psychotherapy.

Play, Self-Awareness, and a Theory of Mind

Given their stability and predictive power it is reasonable to assume that attachment status and AAI classification are tapping into some meaningful psychological configuration. This might in the various languages of psychotherapy be described as a representational world, state of object relations, set of basic assumptions, or the balance between paranoid-schizoid and depressive positions. Attachment status seems to relate to patterns of parental handling in the first year of life, and is thus clearly an interpersonal phenomenon. The strange situation measures the *enactment* of the child's relationship to her parents. The AAI by contrast defines individuals' *description* of their relationship to their own life—a movement from mechanism to meaning.

While attachment emerges from parental handling, narrative style has to do with the individual's relationship to herself. Between the strange situation and the AAI a process of internalization has taken place, which comprises an individual's awareness of herself, her significant others, the relationships between them, and her awareness of, and ability to report on, these phenomena.

What then can we say about the origins of these kinds of awareness, and their relationship to security and insecurity? Here Meares (1993) has developed a hypothesis based on what he calls "self-narrative." He starts from Winnicott's (1971) notion of the child's need to be able to play "alone in the presence of the mother" if a stable "true" (in attachment terms "secure") sense of self is to emerge. By providing a quiet background presence, the mother, in a typical Winnicottian paradox, enables the child to forget her and to concentrate on the self-exploration that is the essence of solitary play. If, on the other hand, the mother is unavailable, or inconsistent, or unattuned, the child will be forced to think about her parent, and so be liable to forget herself.

Meares (1993) studied tape recordings of the type of speech used by 3- to 4-year-olds during this solitary play. This, following Vygotsky (1962), he calls *inner speech*, although at this particular stage in linguistic development it is audible, and therefore available for scientific study. Inner speech has specific features that differentiate it from social speech. Rather like Freud's (1911) contrast between primary and secondary processes, inner speech is disconnected and incomplete, words flowing into one another by association rather than following a logical progression. Audible inner speech stops rather abruptly around 5 to 6 years of age. It is reasonable to speculate that self-awareness, which is so bound up with a sense of self, privacy, awareness of emotional truth and falsehood, the ability to plan and to reflect on emotions, and on the capacity for both autonomy and intimacy, is a continuation of this play talk described by Meares. What started as an interaction, shaped by the attachment dynamic, has become internalized, so that the child now has within herself (a) the vigilant yet nonintrusive maternal function, (b) the generative playful function, and (c) the capacity to put feelings into words. Acquiring inner speech means becoming intimate with oneself; knowledge of oneself goes hand in hand with knowledge of others. If required, the playing child can report on the goings on of her inner world: "I was pretending the Mommy had gone away and the baby was sad." As an adult, perhaps during an AAI, she might be able to say: "When my parents separated I used to pretend that my doll's mother had gone away and then returned." Analytic psychotherapy re-creates the childhood situation of being "alone in the presence of another"; free association is, perhaps, none other than inner speech externalized once more.

The acquisition of inner speech is a developmental function. We can imagine how it could be disrupted in ways that might correspond with insecure patterns on the AAI. If the parent is unavailable the child may be so concerned with maintaining proximity to her that she will unable to play and so find her inner voice, leading to dismissive narratives and difficulty with intimacy. Preoccupied narratives may reflect unmetabolized pain that has not been transmuted into the metaphor of play, as though the child-in-the-adult is still searching for a safe container and using whoever happens to be at hand for that purpose. Here, unable safely to protest, the sufferer will have difficulties with autonomy. If the parent has been intrusive, the child may also have compromised her autonomy, her self-narrative being contaminated with the parental narrative, always thinking and feeling what is expected, rather than what she otherwise might if a less-intrusive or less-neglectful parent (or a good psychotherapist) were available. Finally, if the environment is traumatizing the whole containment/self-narrative envelope may be obliterated, leaving lacunae and discontinuities in the texture of inner reality and its representation in inner speech.

These ideas can be linked with the notion of a child's *theory of mind*, as developed in the psychoanalytic literature by Fonagy and colleagues (1994), Hobson (1993), and Leiman (1995). Fonagy and colleagues argue that traumatized children lack a theory of mind in the sense that they have difficulty in seeing others as having feelings, intentions, and desires, any more than they can accurately define their own inner world.

Faced with aggressive or sexually intrusive parents, the normal process of *secondary intersubjectivity,* in which a child shares her experiences of the world with her caregivers via visual cuing, imitation, and so on, is inhibited. Leiman (1995) sees this in terms of inhibition of the normal mediating function of the parent, who, under favorable conditions, helps to create shared meanings in the transitional or interactive space between the child and her objects. To perpetrate his cruelty, the abuser has to remove from his consciousness the knowledge that the child can experience fear, pain, disgust, and so on. The child grows up in a world in which her feelings—and meanings—are discounted or obliterated. At the same time the child is dependent on the abuser, and may indeed be strongly attached to him. Here we have attachment without intimacy. By destroying the child's autonomy, the abuser also destroys the possibility of intimacy.

There is often a vicious circle, based on the attachment dynamic, in which the more the child is traumatized, the more she clings to her attachment figure, who thereby is encouraged to perpetrate further abuse, and so on. The abused child is likely also to deny the existence of her abuser's mind, since not to do so would be to face the unacceptable fact that those one loves and on whom one depends have malevolent intentions. In his work on autism, Hobson (1993) similarly postulates an interruption in the development of a theory of mind, presumably in this case biologically based, via inhibition of intersubjective experience.

Attachment Patterns in Adult Relationships

Fonagy's argument suggests the need for a radical distinction between intimacy and attachment. Intimacy is based on intersubjectivity, the knowledge that one has a mind like that of others, particularly one's intimates. Attachment is a necessary but not sufficient condition for intimacy. Indeed too much attachment, in the sense of clinging relationships, inhibits intimacy no less than the reverse.

Hazan and Shaver (1994), in their individual differences research (individual differences being the very lifeblood of psychotherapy), have used the attachment typology of infant–parent relationships to explore intimate relationships between adults. They see Bowlby's key elements of secure parenting—proximity and responsiveness—as equally applicable to successful adult intimate relationships. By translating Ainsworth's strange-situation classification into a series of statements about intimate relationships, they have found that adults readily identify with one of a number of descriptions of relationship patterns. For secure adults, proximity and responsiveness is easily achieved and assumed to be available when needed. Those who are troubled by ambivalence may fall in love frequently, be excessively jealous, reveal themselves too readily and too early in relationships, and see their partners as fickle. A contrasting pattern is found among avoidant individuals who tend to find close relationships problematic, to dissociate sexual from emotional commitment, and are uncomfortable about intimate self-revelation.

Narrative in Psychotherapy and Psychoanalysis

This brings us to the contribution that attachment theory can make to the theme of narrative in psychotherapy, which has been the subject of much recent debate. This has come from several diverse sources: empirical, political, and philosophical. First, research on common factors in psychotherapy suggests that, in the assimilation of warded-off problematic experiences (Shapiro 1995), all effective therapies offer patients a rationale, or story, within which their difficulties can be located and helped to make sense, and that this in itself produces an enhanced sense of mastery. Second, an influential contribution to contemporary ideas in family therapy has been the work of White and Epston (1990), who, based on Foucault's polemical rehabilitation of the forgotten voices of "the clinic," see neurosis as the "insurrection of subjugated knowledge" and the task of psychotherapy as that of "restorying" unassimilated experience. Third, a long-running dispute continues between those who claim for psychoanalysis a scientific status and those, like Rycroft (1985) and Shafer (1992), who see it as an hermeneutic discipline, concerned more with meaning than mechanism, coherence rather than correspondence (Cavell 1994), with narrative rather than historical truth (Spence 1982, 1987), or with, in Freud's (1937b) terms, constructions rather than reconstuctions.

Attachment theory can contribute usefully to this debate. It helps to cut across the often sterile dichotomy between historical truth and narrative truth. By focusing on the form as much as the content of narratives, Main's work suggests that the stories that patients tell are based on both historical experience and retrospective constructions, and are influenced by defensive processes. Patients who cannot remember the details of their childhood are repressing painful memories. Those who are bogged down in past history may be clinging to their pain in the hope of evoking protective attachment behavior in potential caregivers. Patients who tell us neat packaged, psychologically aware narratives may equally be avoiding the pain of disruption, chaos, and intrusion typical of disorganized attachment and abuse.

The task of the therapist becomes, in Rycroft's (1985) words, that of an "assistant autobiographer," helping the patient toward more authentic self-narratives, not for aesthetic reasons—a beautifully crafted self-narrative is just as likely to be defensive as a chaotic one—but as a primary expression of secure selfhood and relatedness. Narrative is not in itself the issue. It is merely a marker of emotional health; but it is the only one we have: "I gotta use words when I talk to you" (Eliot 1952, p. 32). The AAI confirms clinical experience that suggests that therapists do best to attend as much to the *way* their patients talk as to what they talk about. The typology of insecure attachment—avoidant, ambivalent, disorganized—provides a useful framework for considering different narrative styles as they present to clinicians.

Intimacy and Autonomy

What is the relevance of all this to the work of psychotherapists? If adult intimate relationships are shaped according to varying patterns of attachment, is it not likely that the same will be true of therapist–patient relationships (Mallinckrodt et al. 1995)? If psychotherapy is based on self-narratives, and the form of the stories people tell about themselves can be related to attachment motifs, can we approach therapeutic narratives with an attachment focus? The word *intimate* implies both closeness and communication. We know about our loved ones by what is said, and what is not said, and the same is true in psychotherapy. A narrative is a *gnarus*, a knowing. How can knowledge of attachment theory help us to know our patients better?

Let us summarize the main points of the argument so far. Attachment theory is based on the poles of attachment and separation. The goals of psychotherapy can be summarized as those of intimacy and autonomy. Secure attachment provides a foundation for both intimacy and autonomy. Non-intrusive responsiveness allows for the development of inner speech and thus of an inner world, a self that can recognize the existence of other selves. Acceptance of separation-protest enables the inevitable separations and losses inherent in development to be negotiated. Autonomy and intimacy are reciprocally related. Autonomy is possible on the basis of a secure inner world—we can go out on a limb, stand our ground, make our own choices, and tolerate aloneness if we can be sure that attachment and intimacy are available when needed. Conversely, intimacy is possible if the loved one can be allowed to be separate; we can allow ourselves to get close if we feel autonomous enough not to fear engulfment or attack, and also know that separation does not mean that our loved one will be lost forever.

How does this apparent paradox—autonomy based on intimacy, intimacy a prerequisite for autonomy—come about? It is the job of the self to carry out this integrative task, to produce a coherent sense of the continuity of an individual across time and place. The secure child has, by the time of school entry, developed the rudiments of autonomy, the capacity for intimacy, and the sense of a coherent self. These early shoots will be consolidated by early adulthood into the autobiographical competence of an individual who knows who she is and can ask for closeness, assert independence, and make sense of the variety of her experiences.

If intimacy and autonomy, like attachment and exploration, are reciprocally related, insecure attachment can be seen as an unbalancing of this reciprocity. The avoidant person—and this is a pathology particularly of men—is detached but not autonomous. He longs for intimacy but fears he will be rejected; he hovers on the shores of intimacy, ever fearful to take the plunge. The ambivalent individual—this is typical of insecure women—is attached but cannot be intimate. She longs for autonomy, assertion, and independence but is fearful that if she strikes out on her own she will lose her secure base forever. In psychiatric terms the avoidant is the obsessional or the schizoid individual, the ambivalent is the anxiety-driven or hysterical type.

These relationships can be visualized in the triangle of attachment (see Figure 1–2). The base of the triangle (the apex can be ignored for the moment) forms the attachment axis, each corner of which has, in an Eriksonian dichotomy (Erikson 1968), a defensive, insecurity-avoiding and a positive, exploratory-creative facet. At the center of detachment is autonomy, which carries within it the seeds of avoidance and isolation, and fear of engulfment. At the corner of attachment is intimacy, which is shadowed by the possibility of ambivalence and clinging as an avoidance of irreparable loss.

Clinical Applications: Avoidance and Ambivalence

Attachment ideas can inform therapy in assessment, in thinking about transference, and in devising therapeutic strategies.

Assessment

Attachment themes often stand out more clearly at assessment than in the creative confusion of the therapy that follows. The following vignettes illustrate how dismissive and enmeshed narratives manifest themselves in clinical practice. Each case centered around the threat to a relationship—in the first two cases because intimacy was lacking, in the third because autonomy was compromised.

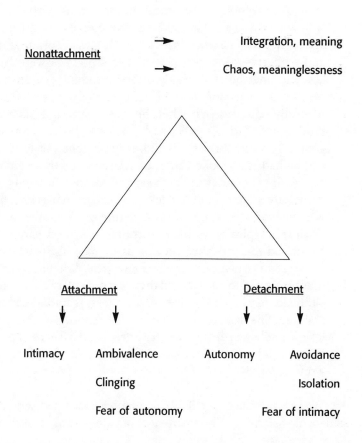

Figure 1–2. The triangle of attachment.

Bob: An Avoidant Narrative

Bob, a 40-year-old vehicle maintenance fitter, presented with classic features of morbid jealousy, probably in the context of mild depression. He became irrationally convinced that his wife was having an affair and was troubled by intrusive images of her with her imagined lover. He was deeply ashamed and embarrassed to reveal this. His sentences were hesitant and unelaborated. He described his childhood as "normal," and it was only toward the end of the session that it painfully emerged that when he was 1 year old his older brother had died, his father had developed tuberculosis and gone into a sanatorium, his mother had gone out to work, and he had been looked after for several years by an elderly aunt with Victorian attitudes toward childcare. The family was eventually reunited, but Bob felt alienated from his father and was unable to paint any kind of picture of his mother at all. With this typically avoidant narrative style and pattern of childhood relationships, it came as no surprise that, while casual affairs came easily, he had had great difficulty in committing himself to his wife and they had only married recently, although they had been together for fifteen years and had two children. She described herself as a "scuba widow": his great love was subaqua diving, which he described in terms of peace and tranquillity and the absolute trust needed to go down with a diving buddy.

We can speculate that Bob's avoidant strategy had served to insulate himself from early experiences of pain, rejection, and loss. With depression, long-buried yearnings for intimacy came to the surface in the shape of his jealous fantasies, yearnings manifest previously only in the almost intrauterine although highly restricted and controlled closeness of diver and partner. Bob's hesitant, unelaborated, dismissive narrative style was typical of unassuaged attachment needs. He could barely allow himself to be attached, let alone become intimate.

The next case illustrates how anxious attachment patterns are not in themselves pathological; they may be compatible with success, especially where striving type A personalities are required.

Charles: The Loneliness of the Long-Distance Sailor

Charles, another typical avoidant patient, had achieved considerable success as headmaster of a large secondary school and as a solo deep-sea sailor, but one day he simply lay down on the floor of his office sobbing, feeling that he could not "go on." He felt that those responsible for educational administration had no idea of what their "reforms" meant in practice, especially for those like himself who tried to be sensitive to children's emotional as well as narrowly academic needs. In a striking image he described his whole life as a bright "storefront" that belied everything that lay behind, which was "shriveled and dying." The storefront represented success, the face he presented to the world; behind it lay his thwarted desires for closeness and freedom. Predictably, he described a childhood in which he had felt close to neither of his parents—both were active in local government and "good works" but had had little time for their children—and a stable marriage, but one in which there was little intimacy or sexual closeness.

Avoidant attachment should be seen as a predisposition to pathology rather than as a disorder in itself—a rigidity that may mean that when circumstances change difficulties come to the surface. This is equally true of ambivalent patterns of attachment.

Jane: An Enmeshed Narrative

In contrast to the previous cases, Jane, a lawyer in her mid-thirties, was in tears throughout her session as she described her overwhelming feelings of grief and rage when she discovered that her partner had been having an affair and had asked him to leave. They had been inseparable during the whole of their five-year relationship, which she described in great and painful detail. She needed to be near her partner at all times and now that he was gone she felt in a state of continuous terror. She was particularily troubled by violent fantasies toward him and his new girlfriend, and felt it was very likely she might attack them physically. She was the youngest of six children, and described how as a child she felt that her mother did not "like" her, and yet Jane was constantly cling-ing to her, frightened to go to school or away on holiday—a typical ambivalent pattern of clinging and inhibition of anger. As an adult she had had several affairs with older married men in which she had always been rather passive, and her current partner was the first with whom she felt more equal, which added to the poignancy of the separation.

Jane's main problems were her inability to assert herself and her tendency to cling to people. Her autonomy was compromised, based on ambivalent attachment, in which she could allow nei-ther her partner nor herself to relate as separate, free individuals. In the avoidant cases the longing for intimacy had never found expression in the interpersonal field, and so erupted as an all-powerful but unwanted fantasy. Jane's similarly unacknowledged and so unmodulated separation protest manifested itself as mur-derous fantasies, there never having been a safe container for her anger during her childhood. Her tragedy was that, in driving her partner away with her anger, she was confirming her lifelong fan-tasy that protest inevitably leads to rejection.

Transference and Therapeutic Strategies

The basis of successful therapy is a positive therapeutic bond. The patient will attach him- or herself, in one way or another, to the person of the therapist. The nature of this attachment, the trans-ferential feelings that it engenders, and the therapeutic strategies required will differ markedly according to the nature of this primary attachment link.

In working with avoidant patients the first task is to establish some kind of emotional contact—often through tears or anger. The therapist may feel she and the patient are warily circling one another; the sessions may seem vacuous and difficult to recall afterward when writing notes. The patient may provoke the therapist to be rejecting, or assume a pseudo-intimacy that does not correspond with the therapist's experience. All this may need to be interpreted, but not in such a way that it repeats the rebuffs that would have been the patient's experience of her early childhood attempts at closeness. Any evidence of real intimacy—the recognition that therapist and patient have separate yet shared mental space—must be reinforced and welcomed.

Ambivalent patients are usually highly dependent. The therapist may feel stifled, or crowded out, or coerced into helping the patient rather than listening to him or her, overwhelmed by the patient's distress, and invaded by a sense of helplessness. There may be an ancient mariner–like sense of being caught in the grip of a narrative that must simply be listened to until it is played out.

The avoidant patient will respond to breaks in the therapy by retaliatory missed sessions, or insisting that the gaps are of no consequence. The ambivalent patient, by contrast, will become highly distressed around any separation and may require special "babysitting" arrangements from other mental health workers during long breaks. The key issue here is the expression of appropriate anger at separation. According to attachment theory, this would have been missing in the origins of ambivalent separation, the child never daring to bite the hand that feeds, for fear of losing it altogether. The patient needs to learn that she can protest and therapy will survive. As the patient begins to detach herself from her past, her pain, and, when necessary, her therapist, she discovers that she does not actually lose them. They are there, in her inner world. She can begin to speak about herself with detachment. This point is illustrated by Raymond, a patient to whom I shall return in Chapter 3.

Raymond: Overcoming Ambivalent Attachment

Raymond, a factory manager in his mid-fifties, had a major depressive breakdown, precipitated by his factory, to which he had devoted his whole life, going into receivership. In therapy he constantly ruminated on his past mistakes and how things might have turned out differently, omnipotently blaming himself for everything that had gone wrong. In a typically ambivalent-enmeshed way, he always arrived early for his appointments, and in sessions the therapist felt slightly trapped and stifled by his controlling monologues. On one occasion Raymond described how, after leaving a session, he had suddenly felt furious with the therapist for his inconsistency and insensitivity. Having gotten this off his chest, Raymond visibly relaxed. To become angry rather than controlling or sulky was a new experience for him, and for the therapist to respond without retaliation or withdrawal but with acknowledgment was equally novel. Exercising his autonomy had not, as he feared, compromised his attachment. Stronger in himself, he could now look at how he had contributed to his downfall. He started to say, "Perhaps that job really was too much for me," and to value his enforced idleness, which had enabled him at last to devote some time to his much-neglected family and garden. He had moved, some way at least, from ambivalent clinging to autonomy.

Disorganized Narratives

What about the third pattern of insecure attachment? So far we have said little about the disorganized attachments and their equivalent on the AAI—narratives that are incoherent or show breaks and fissures. Much less is known about the subsequent developmental history of this group but it is tempting to speculate that some of these children will go on to develop borderline personality disorder. Seen from an attachment perspective, the security of borderline patients is both qualitatively, through trauma, and quantitatively more compromised than that of the avoidant or ambivalent patients we have been describing. Borderline patients are likely to have difficulties with both autonomy and intimacy. Instability of attachment or oscillations between dependency and detachment are typical. It could be said that some of these patients at least are attached to chaos and disorder—actively seeking it out even when things are going reasonably well. The consequences of stability are to experience unbearable feelings of depression or emptiness. One feature that has been identified in the subsequent histories of children with disorganized attachment patterns is *parentification*, in which they strive always to be in a caregiver role, thereby, presumably, avoiding the confusion associated with being the recipients of chaotic or abusive care. All these phenomena are familiar to psychotherapists who work with these patients. Indeed the Kohut (1977)–Kernberg (1984) debate—about whether what these patients need is acceptance and empathy or limit-setting and interpretation of negative transference—can be reframed in attachment terms as a discussion about whether the primary problem is with intimacy, in which case empathy is the main need, or autonomy, which is fostered best when aggression is acknowledged and firmly contained.

Katherine, a borderline patient to whom I shall refer several times in the course of this book, serves to illustrate some of these points. More details of her history will emerge in the subsequent two chapters.

Katherine: Disorganized/Incoherent Attachment

Katherine was a divorced teacher in her fifties with one grown daughter. Her childhood had been chaotic and painful. She was sexually abused by a tyrannical father, and neglected by her depressed mother. She showed features of both avoidance and ambivalence. Her avoidance showed itself in the way she had had frequent unreciprocated love affairs, followed by disillusionment and despair, and had never felt close to any-

one except perhaps to her daughter, whom she had nevertheless sent to boarding school from an early age. In a typically
ambivalent pattern, she had clung to her mother throughout
her life, and was constantly trying to be the sort of person
she imagined her mother would want her to be. She showed
features of disorganized narrative, seeming at times illogical,
assuming the therapist knew things of which he was unaware,
and occasionally drifting off into brief trance-like states. During the early period of therapy she showed much improvement compared with her previously chaotic and unhappy life,
but her problems with the therapist became more intense; the
transference neurosis became more and more salient. Her adherence to therapy was absolute, but the therapist rarely felt
a sense of reciprocity or mutual interchange; Katherine was
too terrified to allow either herself or her therapist autonomously to think thoughts or feel feelings. She complained con-
tinually about the therapist's indifference, demanding tokens
of his esteem and approbation: "Do you *like* me?" "It's a good
thing I am finally able to cry about my feelings of abandonment and neglect as a child, isn't it?" At the same time she
devoted herself unflaggingly to troubled friends and pupils
whom she saw as damaged and desperately in need of her
help. After several weeks in which she had become increasingly distressed in the sessions, while the therapist felt drowsy
and detached and unable to help, the therapist began to see
himself in the position of the patient's mother, who, on one
occasion in Katherine's childhood when the patient, desperate for attention, had announced that she had swallowed a
nail, had vaguely said, "Go and eat some bread or something."

The therapist could at this point have interpreted the
mother-transference, but chose instead a more simple clarifi-
cation/confrontation, having found with this patient that interpretations tended to perpetuate rather than dispel confusion,
since Katherine tended compliantly (and ambivalently) to
reply by offering the responses she thought the therapist was
seeking. He said, therefore, that although he recognized her

intense distress, he did not really understand what exactly was troubling her. The patient was initially furious: "How can you say that—your *job* is to understand me." But then she began to see how this reaction was similar to her feelings for her mother. The patient then explored her fantasy that somehow therapy would put all to rights; her wish that the therapist would "re-parent" her as she deserved and that all her pain and misery would be resolved. Now she felt she could not win; only therapy could help her, and yet that was exactly what therapy could not do. But somehow *seeing* that made her feel better, enabled her to detach herself from her desires a little. The therapeutic space—not just the physical space but the shared mental space of therapist and patient—had given her a glimpse of intimacy. She could begin to see her mother in more compassionate terms, could laugh at her demandingness, tease her therapist, show appropriate resentment about his holidays, and value what he did have to offer rather than simply bemoan what he could not. She then told a story about her rickety garden shed. She had been advised to remove the ivy that covered it, since this was infiltrating the roof and destroying the mortar. However,when she did so it became clear the ivy alone was holding the building together, which was now in imminent danger of collapse. It was only when firm supports were introduced that the building became secure again. The movement from her clinging, infiltrating, parasitic self to one more soundly grounded was symbolized by this anecdote. Achieving secure foundations had proved to be a costly business, she remarked, although not half so expensive as psychotherapy!

Casement (1985) describes his dilemma as a therapist when confronted by a severely traumatized patient who demanded reassurance in the form of physical holding. Knowing the severity of her history he was tempted to acquiesce, but refrained, thereby repeating the trauma itself in which the patient's mother had been unable to hold her when she was badly burned as a child. He analyzes this case, which had a good outcome, in terms of Winnicott's (1965) notion of "bringing the trauma into the area of omnipotence." An unpredictable and indifferent world impinges on a defenseless child, who then has to seal off feelings of psychic pain, rage, and guilt. In therapy the trauma is repeated, but this time the patient can see how she and the therapist contribute to this repeated trauma and so can begin to integrate and master a previously warded off experience, which could not have happened if the patient had been reassured. Similarly the therapist's incomprehension of Katherine's distress, repeating the childhood trauma of indifference and heartlessness, seemed to open the door to greater maturation and acceptance.

A borderline patient, so familiar with chaos, through therapeutic moments like these may begin to come to terms with her powerlessness, seeing how much of life is the result of accidents of history, and move from helpless impotence, through therapeutically engendered omnipotence, to mature acceptance. Thus the borderline patient, in a paradoxical way, may be able to see beyond both attachment and loss to a deeper truth in which attachments are seen to be inevitably transient, and losses, through their cyclical nature, ultimately recoverable.

Nonattachment

This brings me to the third point of the attachment triangle (Figure 1–2), which I call *nonattachment*. This term, derived from Buddhism, seems to me to capture the equidistant position based on awareness of the different aspects of the self and the world that is needed if experience is to be coherently integrated. But it also implies the inherent fragility of the self, as both a necessity and ultimately a fiction. We have many selves, and we live in a world that is at times chaotic and indifferent. To survive we must integrate as best we can, and find as much meaning as we are able in the world that surrounds us. Nonattachment underlies narrative or autobiographical competence, the search for meaning, reaching toward a sense of self, and an ability to observe and accept things as they are without being overwhelmed with envy or destructiveness. It can clearly be related to psychoanalytic ideas such as Anna Freud's picture of the balancing ego equidistant from id and superego; the Kleinian image of the depressive position, in which destructiveness and loss are accepted and others related to as whole objects despite their inherent unreliability; Bion's *alpha-function*, in which preconceptions are creatively transmuted into conceptions, which might be compared with the movement from attachment to intimacy (Bateman and Holmes 1995); and, as already discussed, to Fonagy's RSF.

Like avoidance and ambivalence, nonattachment also contains the possibilty of both health and disorder. Where nonattachment cannot be achieved, the individual is at the mercy of different aspects of the self that cannot be integrated into a coherent whole. The chaos and meaninglessness of the environment invades the self, which is part of the core experience of borderline personality disorder. The breakdown of the parental containing function, in whole, or more usually in part, leads to this failure of nonattachment; one has no space into which to go to get a perspective on oneself and one's environment. I have introduced the term *nonattachment* to convey the idea that in negation there is always a positive—an experience that seems to me to be near the heart of psychotherapy, or at least of analytic psychotherapy. (For further discussion of nonattachment, see pp. 84 and 191.)

CONCLUSION

To summarize, recent attachment research supports the view that the development of a healing narrative—the Shakespearean injunction to "give sorrow words"—is the key task of psychotherapy. This work can be usefully informed by attachment ideas and research findings.

As stated at the outset, attachment theory is not so much a new theory as an overall framework for thinking about relationships, which is compatible with many existing and evolving theoretical perspectives. In addition to its obvious research potential, I have suggested that attachment theory can help the clinician in a number of different ways.

First, it provides a theoretical basis for the research finding that a good therapeutic alliance is the best predictor of good outcome in therapy. The prime task of the therapist is to offer a secure base for the patient, one that is likely to have been lacking in the past. Only from this base can she begin to explore her inner and outer worlds.

Second, attachment theory offers a picture of the therapeutic process as a microcosm of attachment and separation, with its rhythm of regular sessions punctuated by endings and breaks. This is analogous to the strange situation, in which the patient is subjected to minor stresses and their resolution and which can be examined in the "laboratory" of therapy.

Third, with its emphasis on bonds—their formation, threatened rupture, and/or severance—and the affective responses that accompany these processes, attachment theory is consistent with the view, now rapidly gaining support, of an "assimilation model" of psychotherapy (Shapiro 1995). This puts problematic experience at the heart of psychotherapy. Previously warded-off, or repressed, affect is evoked, focused on, turned into narrative, experimented with, and finally mastered in the course of a therapy. The AAI provides the possibility of making scientific links in this chain from the biology of parent-child interaction to the narrative paradigms of psychotherapy.

Finally, I have proposed a "triangle of attachment," which implies a typology of attachment narratives, and the kinds of progress that can be expected to take place in the course of a therapy. I have suggested a movement from attachment to intimacy, from detachment to autonomy, and from disorganization through both attachment and detachment to nonattachment.

These kinds of ideas can enable the discipline of psychotherapy to advance, to hold firmly to its core beliefs and sound ideas, and to modify or discard those that have outlived their usefulness, in short, to be as nonattached to itself as, ultimately, it requires its patients to be to themselves.

I shall now step back in time from these contemporary concerns and consider in more detail the origins of attachment theory in the life of John Bowlby, focusing particularly on his relationship with the institutions and ideas of psychoanalysis.

2

Attachment Theory and Psychoanalysis

At Trumpan on the Waternich peninsula of the Scottish island of Skye there stands a remote and wild hillside graveyard. There John Bowlby lies buried, among the hills and coast where for half a century he loved to walk, and where he spent his holidays, and, after retirement, the spring and summer months of the year. Much of his writing was done there, and he and his wife, Ursula, were familiar figures on the Kyle of Lochalch ferry, their car filled to the brim with books, a few personal possessions perched precariously in suitcases on the roof rack. The contrast with the busy sophistication of Hampstead and the Tavistock Clinic in London where Bowlby spent the other half of his year could hardly be greater, and this split—or creative tension—between town and country, wildness and civilization, culture and nature, forms the background to this chapter.

Bowlby's headstone is a simple granite slab, with the inscription "To be a pilgrim," taken from John Bunyan's famous hymn *The Pilgrim's Progress*. The choice was apt: Bunyan, the puritan, the dissenter, the rebel, who spent many years imprisoned for his radical views, who used simple, profound, and powerful words:

> There's no discouragement
> Shall make him once relent
> His first avowed intent . . .

Bowlby had a stubborn, determined streak, which meant that he was prepared to follow his ideas, however unpopular, to their logical and detailed conclusion.

> Who so beset him round
> With dismal stories
> Do but themselves confound
> His strength the more is . . .

The pilgrim's prescription "gainst all disaster" is to "follow the Master." Whatever his difficulties with the psychoanalytic world and especially with the "dismal stories" of Kleinian psychoanalysis, Bowlby's admiration for Freud never wavered. But his first and most abiding master was Darwin, with whom I believe he strongly identified. At a time when most men or women of achievement might have been resting on their laurels, Bowlby devoted the final years of his life to writing his biography of Darwin, perhaps his most personal and accessible work.

This chapter starts by picking out some of the key strands of Bowlby's early years, and from there continues to consider the three interrelated themes of *psychobiography, psychobiology,* and *psychoanalysis* that preoccupied Bowlby for most of his working life. The quest for Bowlby has for me centered on three main issues: first, the attempt to understand the origins of attachment theory in Bowlby's own character and life history; second, to look at Bowlby's break with psychoanalysis, which meant that attachment theory was for two decades virtually airbrushed out of the psychoanalytic record—rather like some dissident in Stalinist times—given Bowlby's avowed intent to direct his theoretical work "primarily towards my colleagues in the International [Psychoanalytic] Association" (Bowlby 1991, p. 11); and third, and this is the main focus of this book, to track the reattachment of Bowlbian and post-Bowlbian ideas within psychoanalytic psychotherapy, and to show

how they can contribute to and enrich the emergence of a new relational perspective within psychoanalysis in both theory and practice (Mitchell 1988).

PSYCHOBIOGRAPHY

Born in 1907, Bowlby was contemporary with the younger Darwin grandchildren. Good family therapist that he was, Bowlby begins his Darwin story with the grandparental generation, and I shall follow his example (cf. Holmes 1993). Bowlby's paternal grandfather was a successful journalist, "Bowlby of the Times," who was killed in 1861 in Beijing during the opium wars, which he was covering as a foreign correspondent, leaving a widow and several children, of whom Bowlby's father, Anthony, was the eldest. Anthony, able, single-minded, and very hard-working, eventually became a fashionable London surgeon, and, having successfully operated on one of Queen Victoria's numerous children and spent World War I almost entirely at the front as a surgeon general, was duly knighted, becoming President of the Royal College of Surgeons in 1920. He died in 1927, late enough to sanction Bowlby's career switch from naval cadet to medical student, early enough not to oppose his choice of psychiatry and psychoanalysis as a career.

Sir Anthony felt his duty was to support his widowed mother, and it was only after her death, when he was 40, that he felt free to marry. May Mostyn's wedding dress was embroidered with violets in deference to her mother-in-law for whom the statutory year of mourning had not yet passed. May herself was not young, 30 years old, the oldest daughter of a country parson, the Honorable Hugh Mostyn, who, as "Grampy," was to play an important part in the lives of the Bowlby children. He loved country pursuits—walking, shooting, fishing, hunting—and, during the long Bowlby holidays would join them in Scotland, teaching them his skills with infectious enthusiasm.

John Bowlby's parents were thus both well into middle age by the time he, the fourth child, arrived. His father worked very hard, and John was to see little of him during his childhood, but perhaps enough to alert him to the way in which childhood be- reavement can lead to emotional avoidance—Sir Anthony's remote and rather frightening manner being no doubt in part typical of his class and occupation, but also perhaps connected with the loss of his father at an early age. Bowlby appears to have grieved little when he died; it was the death of his closest friend, the Labor politician Evan Durbin, in a drowning accident in the 1940s that put him in touch with his feelings of sadness and loss. The nega- tive effects of suppressed mourning were a central theme for Bowlby. His theory about Darwin's mysterious illness centers on the death of his mother when he was 8 and on the refusal of the family— especially his workaholic doctor father—to speak about this, so much so that when Darwin was playing a Victorian word comple- tion game he insisted there was no such word when his fellow player added the letter M to Charles' s OTHER (Bowlby 1990)!

Bowlby's mother was also a product of her era. The oldest of numerous children, she was released by her marriage from look- ing after her younger brothers and sisters. She seems to have rather despised her own mother, but revered her father, and "Grampy's" views were adduced as the final word in any discussion. She cer- tainly favored boys; her youngest daughter, Evelyn, recalled in her eighties with miserable and furious tears the feelings of neglect and favoritism of her early years, while her older brother Tony remem- bered "a generally happy childhood"—each respectively perhaps illustrating the enmeshed and avoidant narrative styles outlined in the previous chapter.

A possible explanation for this different perception lies in the pattern of family holidays that played a very important part in the Bowlby household (as they were to for John's family in the next generation). May Mostyn had vowed that she would never marry a "city man," and, when she did, insisted that they spend long holidays away from her husband's practice in Manchester Square in the West End of London. In London May saw little of her chil- dren, whose care was left mainly to nannies and nurserymaids. The children were ushered into the drawing room from five until six o'clock in the evening where May would sometimes read to them her favorite adventure stories, *Children of the New Forest* and *Treasure Island*. But things were very different when they were on holiday. Each year they would spend the Easter holidays in the New Forest and long summer holidays in Scotland. Here May would share her love of nature and country activities with the children. A boyhood naturalist and beetle collector, John became a lifelong hill walker, and clearly understood Darwin's ecstatic feeling that "No poet ever felt more delight at seeing his first poem published that I did at seeing in Stephen's *Illustrations of British Insects* the magic words 'captured by C. Darwin esq.'" (Bowlby 1990, p. 167).

John was sandwiched between two brothers. Tony, like himself, was a highly intelligent and vigorous little boy with whom there was an intense but generally amicable rivalry; only thirteen months separated them and they were dressed and treated almost as twins. Jim, his younger brother, was by Bowlby standards considered backward, which worried John and may well have influenced his eventual choice of career. He was very excited when in his teens he read about monkey gland extract (thyroxine), hoping that the answer to Jim's difficulties had been found.

John started his training as a naval cadet, but chafing against the narrow intellectual and political service horizons, just as he was to feel constrained within the psychoanalytic society three decades later, as well as suffering badly from seasickness, changed to studying medicine at Cambridge. But the naval values of probity, order, punctuality, and a love of the sea remained with him for a lifetime.

Prematurely self-possessed, John knew his own mind and, his preclinical studies completed, decided to take a year off to work in a progressive school for maladjusted boys, much influenced by the ideas of the Reichian A. S. Neil. There he found his vocation as a child psychiatrist, and when he returned to his medical studies in London (which he found desperately dull; he alleviated his boredom by running a highly successful sandwich stall, "Bogey's

Bar," for fellow students) simultaneously started his training in psychoanalysis.

The impact of Bowlby's psychoanalytic training is something of a mystery. Bowlby himself was deeply reticent, eschewed gossip, and could well have been classified as "avoidant" on the Adult Attachment Interview. The British Psychoanalytic Society that Bowlby joined in the 1930s was in turmoil, riven between Melanie Klein and her mostly British followers, and the Viennese refugees who clustered around Anna Freud and her father after their arrival in London in 1938. Freud was clearly not immortal, and the question of who was to succeed him was on everybody's mind. Bowlby's analyst was the leading Kleinian Joan Riviere, who was also Winnicott's analyst, and one of his supervisors was Klein herself. Bowlby, like everyone else, was caught up in this struggle. He emerged from his training as a non-Kleinian Kleinian, which stood him in good stead when, after the gentleman's agreement between Klein and Anna Freud in 1944, he became training secretary of the psychoanalytic society—in part a recognition of his exceptional organizational skills, but also by virtue of being a compromise candidate who was acceptable to both sides (Grosskurth 1986).

How then did Bowlby resist the force field of the polarization between the Kleinians and the Anna Freudians? How did he keep his head while all about him were losing theirs? An obituarist stated, "It is a tribute to his independence to point out that neither of these two formidable ladies [Riviere and Klein] appear to have had the slightest effect on his subsequent development" (Storr 1992, p. 396). This is not entirely true, since one of Bowlby's abiding projects was to challenge what he saw to be the defects in psychoanalytic thinking, especially the Kleinian *weltanschauung*. He had four main objections to the attitudes that he encountered in the British society in the 1930s and 1940s. First, he was troubled by the dogmatism and cultism of the psychoanalytic world, and argued strongly for open scientific debate and inquiry. Second, he felt that psychoanalysis had sequestered itself from contemporary science, clinging needlessly to an ossified metapsychology and arcane vocabulary. Third, he was suspicious of theories of childhood that were essentially extrapolations from the couch to the crib and not based on observations of normal development.

Above all, as mentioned in Chapter 1, he felt that psychoanalysis neglected the role of real environmental trauma in the genesis of neurosis, emphasizing instead the part played by infantile fantasy. A paper by Bowlby's analyst Riviere (1936) contains the following passage:

> Psychoanalysis is Freud's discovery of what goes on in the imagination. . . . It has no concern with anything else, it is not concerned with the real world. . . . It is concerned simply and solely with the imaginings of the childish mind. [p. 89]

Bowlby penciled in the margin: "role of the environment = zero" (Rayner 1992, p. 5).

Bowlby's Darwinism, his leftish sympathies and friendships, together with his direct experiences in the London Child Guidance Clinic in the 1930s, combined to make him a firm believer in the central importance of environmental influence in psychological development. With hindsight it seems curious that the psychoanalysts, especially the Kleinians, took such an extreme anti-environmentalist position. This was in part due to the needs of a new discipline struggling to define itself, to mark out a territory of discourse. Perhaps too the idea that an inner world could be separated from external reality was a necessary defense for a generation of displaced European intellectuals, whose world had been shattered by the rise of fascism. Bettelheim (1960) and Levi (1958) have recorded how those with firm belief systems, who were able to detach themselves from what was going on around them, were the most likely to survive in the concentration camps. Whatever the reason, it meant that a certain detachment from external reality existed within psychoanalysis in the 1930s through 1960s, especially in its Kleinian form—an issue with which Bowlby was to struggle over the ensuing decades.

Bowlby's Englishness—his reticence, formal manner, upper-class voice, and Gentile origins—meant that the analysts were somewhat suspicious of him. But his energy, efficiency, and intellectual originality could hardly be ignored and by the mid-1950s he was prominent in the British Psychoanalytic Society, becoming deputy to Winnicott's presidency in 1956.

Meanwhile he had made his reputation with his World Health Organization (WHO) report *Maternal Care and Mental Health* (1951). The views expressed in that report on the impact of environmental failure on child development had gained wide acceptance even within the highly conservative British medical establishment, where, in contrast to the psychoanalytic society, Bowlby's conventional background and mannerisms helped to give his ideas credibility. The completion of the WHO book had left something of a vacuum and Bowlby was searching for a new project when, while on holiday on Scotland, his friend and neighbor Julian Huxley, the biologist and grandson of Darwin's "bulldog," T. H. Huxley, lent him a prepublication copy of Lorenz's (1953) *King Solomon's Ring*. Bowlby suddenly saw in the new science of ethology the framework he had been looking for in which to recast psychoanalysis in a contemporary scientific idiom. Attachment theory was born.

Attachment theory was launched on the psychoanalytic community in three key papers, all published in the *International Journal of Psycho-Analysis*, each of which prefigures a volume of his famous trilogy: "The Nature of the Child's Tie to His Mother" (1958), "Separation Anxiety" (1960), and "Processes of Mourning" (1961). Each of these papers was later expanded into an entire volume: *Attachment* (1969), *Separation* (1973), and *Loss* (1980). Each paper, although typically scholarly and rigorous in its presentation, makes a simple but, in the face of the prevailing Kleinian orthodoxy, revolutionary point. To begin with, there is a primary attachment bond between mother and child, "wired in" (Mitchell 1988) from birth, that does not depend on oral drive or reward by feeding, and whose evolutionary function was protection from predation. Although this view met with violent opposition it was in fact no more than an extension of ideas that were already prevalent among the object relations analysts in the 1950s—Balint's "primary clinging," Winnicott's concept of an "environment mother" as well as an "object mother," and Fairbairn's view that drives are "signposts to the object" rather than vice versa. Similarly, Bowlby's ideas on separation anxiety were little more than a return to Freud's mature view of anxiety, which he saw as an affective response to threat, conceived mainly as the threat of castration, but also as the threat of separation from a loved one (Freud 1926). Bowlby's recognition that separated or bereaved infants and small children could experience grief and mourning no less intensely than adults, strongly supported by the evidence of his film made with the Robertson's, *A Two Year Old Goes to Hospital*, was rejected by a psychoanalytic community wedded to the idea that mental pain had its origins in the internal rather than the external world. When the film was shown at the British Psychoanalytic Society Bion is said to have insisted that the little girl's misery was a manifestation of her envy of her mother's pregnancy, rather than a response to the separation itself.

As well as fulfilling Bowlby's criteria for a scientific developmental psychology—observability, testability, using the ideas of contemporary science, and being based on observations of normal rather than disturbed development—attachment theory differed from prevailing psychoanalytic ideas at a deep level, which was, I believe, why it met with such profound resistance among psychoanalysts. First, it is an *interpersonal* rather than an intrapersonal theory. Second, it implies an essentially harmonious rather than conflictual model of mother–infant interaction, unless the interaction is disturbed by external difficulty, the implication being that therapy will concentrate not so much on conflict as on *deficiency*. The Freudian view of civilization as a thin and fragile veneer superimposed on an untamed and self-seeking monad is implictly challenged. Third, and in keeping with the previous point, the role of sexuality in infant life is downplayed; pleasure is related to proximity, play, and nurturance rather than to orgasmic discharge. Fourth, the key issue in infantile experience becomes not so much power (the power of the phallus, the breast, the logos), but *space*; attachment theory is a spatial theory, in which distance, actual and emotional—where I *am* in relation to my loved one—becomes the key issue, rather than what I can do or have done to me.

Bowlby hoped that his new ideas would reconcile the warring factions with the British Psychoanalytic Society and bring about a new openness and wide-ranging debate. By bringing together psychoanalysis and ethology, I believe, he was also at an unconscious level hoping to reconcile his "town mother"—remote and self-centered, and now projected onto his Kleinian analyst and supervisor—with his "country mother"—warm and child-centered and now represented by the Darwinian discipline of ethology. (As an aside it is interesting to find Klein's famous "Richard" also trying to instill in her the basic principles of ethology, telling her that he is Mom's "chick" and that "chicks do run after their Moms" [Klein 1967, p. 45]). By going back to Freud he was also perhaps appealing to his absent father, away at the battlefront, over the heads of the mother and her nannies in the "patriarchal but father-absent" (Leupnitz 1988, p. 15) world in which, like so many children of his generation, he had found himself growing up.

Whatever the truth of these speculations, the outcome was not as Bowlby had hoped. He *did* succeed in unifying the analytic world; they closed ranks against him in what Grotstein (1990) has described as "one of the most dreadful, shameful and regrettable chapters in the history of psychoanalysis" (p. 116). Bowlby became for nearly two decades almost a nonperson in analytic circles, a fate he accepted with dignity and, apart from the occasional venerable jibe, without retaliation, until his rehabilitation in the 1980s began with his appointment as Freud Memorial Professor of Psychoanalysis at University College, London. A system of mutual projection had perhaps been set up in which each side expelled into the other a feared aspect of their own experience. For Bowlby, perhaps, it was the inner world of fantasy; for the British psychoanalysts, common sense, outer reality, and the need to reconsider their basic beliefs in the "madness" of infancy and the universality of the Oedipus complex in the light of contemporary science.

BOWLBY AND THE INNER WORLD

But, as we saw in the previous chapter, psychoanalysis's loss was developmental psychology's gain. The explosion in mother–infant research that took place from the 1970s can be traced in large part to the inspiration of Bowlby and his collaborators and co-workers, especially Mary Ainsworth. Together, they were determined to establish an account of infancy and childhood that was based on experimental evidence, was interpersonal rather than intrapsychic, and in which the unconscious was seen not so much as the seething cauldron of fantasy, but as containing a representation of the interpersonal world.

Bowlby has been accused of neglecting the inner world, and therefore of missing the heart of the psychoanalytic project. The psychoanalytic reader will find little in the trilogy about free association, dreams, fantasies, the Oedipus complex, or other staple psychoanalytic fare. Toward the end of *Attachment* Bowlby introduces a disclaimer:

> To follow this theme further would be to broach the large, difficult and profound questions of how a child gradually builds up his own "internal world." . . . [These] are matters, however, that raise too many giant problems (and giant controversies) for it to be sensible to deal with them here. In any case systematic research has only just begun and little that is firm is yet known. [Bowlby 1969, p. 418]

In his repeated use of the word *giant* (and he was not a tall man) Bowlby was perhaps reacting against the omnipotent strivings of the psychoanalytic project. He certainly knew his own limitations as well as his strengths.

We can at this point usefully contrast the differing perspectives of attachment theory and Kleinian psychoanalysis, against which it was, to some extent, reacting. Each is in a sense a mirror image of the other—albeit separated for many years by an ideological iron curtain. First, attachment theory focuses primarily on how the inner world is influenced by the environment; how, in Freud's famous phrase (Bollas 1987), "the shadow of the object" falls on the subject, rejecting or inconsistent handling leading to anxious patterns of attachment. Kleinian psychoanalysis is concerned with the converse—how external reality is perceived, and, by projective identification, shaped by the inner world of the subject. From a Kleinian perspective, anxious attachment originates *within* the infant—a manifestation of overwhelming feelings of envy and rage. Second, and following from this, attachment theory sees infant and parent as psychologically separate and interacting from birth, while Kleinian theory remains a derivative of Freud's "egg" model (Hamilton 1982), in which the space between subject and object is both obliterated and populated by projected innate "internal objects" (Hinshelwood 1989). Third, the two viewpoints approach the distinction between normal and abnormal development quite differently. To oversimplify, Klein, like Freud, tries to derive the normal from the abnormal—"normality" is finally achieved when the paranoid-schizoid position is transcended by the depressive position. Bowlby, perhaps more logically, tries to understand abnormality in the context of normal development, postulating primary nurturance at the heart of sanity (Gallwey 1993). In this model, awareness of the object (in Kleinian theory a depressive-position function) *precedes* projective identification and omnipotence, which are seen as responses to loss and environmental failure. Finally, following from the latter, Klein places aggression and destructiveness much more centrally in her map of the human heart than does Bowlby, and so can perhaps more easily account for the intractability, resistance, and masochism that psychoanalysis so often reveals.

It is, I believe, in the space between these two positions that, both theoretically and clinically, the future of psychoanalytic psychotherapy is to be found. Klein, Bowlby, and Freud are not necessarily in conflict; they can be thought of as addressing different *levels* of psychological functioning. Kleinian theory focuses on the intrapsychic world of a single individual; attachment theory is primarily directed at the level of two-person interactions; and oedipal theory is about how the introduction of a "third term" affects the two previous levels. Inspired by the strange bedfellows of Klein and Bowlby, and based on the work of Bion, Winnicott, Kohut, and more recently, among others, Alvarez (1992), Benjamin (1989), and Mitchell (1988), a truly interpersonal/ intersubjective psychoanalytic psychotherapy that takes account of the interactions of these various levels is beginning to evolve. The remainder of this chapter is devoted to discussing some of the social, theoretical, and clinical implications of this emerging paradigm.

ATTACHMENT THEORY AND PRIMARY INTERSUBJECTIVITY: THE CULTURAL CONTEXT OF A PARADIGM SHIFT

One way of approaching the emergence of intersubjective psychoanalytic theories, which occupy the middle ground between Bowlby and Klein, is to see them as emerging from social concerns, especially around femininity and the inner space of solitude, that have been central themes of modernism in the postwar world. I shall begin by examining the fate of Bowlby's most famous concept, *maternal deprivation*, to which he remained faithful to the end of his life. In 1988 he wrote:

> Man and woman power devoted to the production of material goods counts a plus in all our economic indices. Man and woman power devoted to the production of happy healthy self-reliant children in their own homes does not count at all. We have created a topsy turvy world. . . . Just as a society in which there is a chronic insufficiency of food takes a deplorably inadequate level of nutrition as the norm, so may a society in which parents of young children are left on their own with a chronic insufficiency of help take this state of affairs as its norm. [Bowlby 1988, p. 4]

When Bowlby first introduced the concept of maternal deprivation he was championing the rights to love and care for children who were innocent victims of the horrors of war, social disruption, and emotional poverty. He was also advocating the rights of mothers to *be* mothers to their children, to devote themselves to their care and protection, rather than themselves be victims of an economic system that forced them into long hours of debilitating factory work, while subjecting their children to the draconian regimes of institutional care. He was similarly reproaching a State whose hygienist drive led it to separate children from parents it deemed "inadequate."

New and David (1985) comment that in the aftermath of the Second World War Bowlby

> got an audience: women who had been working in munitions factories obliged to send their children for nine or ten hours daily into indifferent nurseries, men who had for years been equating peace with the haven of the family, governments who saw the social and financial potential of idealizing motherhood and family life. [p. 55]

The collective sense of guilt and loss and the desire for reparation both found an answer in the idea of maternal deprivation. Children had suffered terribly as a result of the war, as had the repressed childlike aspects of the adults who had witnessed and perpetrated the horrors of war. This valuation and at times sentimentalizing of the mother–child relationship in postwar Europe can be compared with a similar sentiment that emerged in the nineteenth century in the face of the brutality of the industrial revolution. Bowlby's tenderness toward little children carries echoes of Blake and Wordsworth; his outrage is a continuation of the tradition of Dickens and Kingsley. There had to be a safe place, which could be protected from the violent intrusion of the modern world, and the Christian imagery of mother and child reappears in Bowlby's work as an icon for a secular society.

But, as the historical and social context has changed, so the concept of maternal deprivation has come to be seen as a shackle rather than a liberation. Terrified that even brief separations from their children would produce irreparable emotional damage, mothers began to feel oppressed by the influence of Bowlby, turning with relief to Winnicott, who reassured them that it was good enough to be "good enough." Misreading Bowlby's concept of *monotropism* to mean that *only* mother would do, and ignoring the evidence that what is anthropologically normal is for child care to be shared by a stable *group* of adults of whom the mother is only one, maternal deprivation became, as Margaret Mead (1962, p. 32) put it, a "reification into a set of universals of a set of ethnocentric observations of our own society."

The problem facing the modern family is not so much maternal as *paternal* deprivation due to weak, absent, or abusive fathers and the "implosion" of children onto unsupported mothers. Ironically, the dangers that Bowlby in later work identified as among the most damaging for the growing child—role reversal between mother and child, threats of sending the child away or of parental suicide (often later denied), and physical abuse (like the rest of the psychological world Bowlby came late to appreciating the extent of sexual abuse of children)—may well be made more rather than less likely for mothers thrown into 24-hour constant proximity with their children than for those for whom regular respite is available.

As the quotation above indicates, Bowlby was highly sensitive to the lineaments of patriarchy, of which he was in some ways such a typical example. Many of the revolutionary changes in child care of the postwar period—the transformation of pediatric practice by allowing parents into hospitals with their sick children, the emphasis on foster rather than institutional care for children at risk, political acceptance of the need for universal child benefit paid to the mother (now under threat in Britain for the first time in forty years)—can all be traced in part at least to Bowlby's efforts to counter the patriarchal assumptions of a society that undervalues the "female" principles of nurturance and care.

BOWLBY AND PATRIARCHY

Bowlby's difficulties with psychoanalysis can also be seen in terms of an intuitive antipatriarchal perspective. For Freud the phallus reigned supreme; every growing child has to accommodate to its law. The little boy has to master his castration anxiety in order to identify with the paternal standard-bearer, the little girl to over-come her disappointment at its lack and to await her consolation prize—the baby. This world of male omnipotence was, with Freud's death, transformed in the Kleinian vision into its mirror image—a world of female omnipotence based on the supremacy of the breast (Benjamin 1988).

Confronted by the all-powerful patriarchal principle of con-ventional society, and the equally intimidating prospect of an inner world dominated by ferocious drives and an all-powerful mother, Bowlby escaped into a space between, the hitherto undiscovered country of mother–infant *interaction*. Here he could observe and stalk his intellectual prey without anxiety, just as he could hunt and fish and walk with his country mother as a child. Attachment theory is about the spatial relations of mother and child. The se-curely attached child seeks proximity when threatened, explores when safe; the avoidantly insecure child hovers near the parent in a compromise between proximity-seeking and fear of getting close; the ambivalent child clings and tries to bury herself in the unpre-dictable parent. Bowlby's own patriarchal inhibitions (based per-haps on his never having really had the chance to get close to his father and so be released from the fantasy of his omnipotence) meant that he held back from transposing attachment from the outer to the inner world of *inner space*—the female principle that can balance the phallus, transforming its omnipotent strivings into real potency (Erikson 1968). For it is in inner space that Freud's "dark continents"—the mysteries of female desire and creativity—are to be found. Bowlby's "internal working models," although a useful bridge between psychodynamics and cognitive science, are perhaps too mechanical to capture adequately the world of affec-tive experience.

But by opening out the space between parent and child for scrutiny Bowlby paved the way for a fully interpersonal psycho-therapy. Freud and Klein showed how the apparently coherent self of adulthood, if traced back ontogenetically, can be unpacked into an assembly of intrapsychic components—drives, part-objects,

repressive forces, critical agencies, and so on. Bowlby saw, to para-
phrase Winnicott, that "there is no such thing as an individual."
What is found if the adult self is traced back is not an individual
assemblage, but a *society* of parent and child whose interactions
are gradually internalized to form the intrapsychic structures that
psychoanalysis has delineated.

BOWLBY, WINNICOTT, AND BION

While Bowlby boldly abandoned Kleinian metapsychology, his
fellow Darwinian (Phillips 1987) and, in a sense, alter ego, Donald
Winnicott, much more cautiously and ambivalently, attempted
through the invocation of paradox to remain loyal to the Kleinian
tradition while at the same time undermining it. His concepts are
paradoxical in that they attempt to create an interpersonal perspective out of an intrapsychic model. His paper, "The Capacity to be
Alone" (1965), already mentioned in the previous chapter in relation to the work of Meares, is based on the paradox that successful solitude in adult life (including, in another paradox, the sense
of completeness and unconflictual solitude that accompanies the
merging of sexual union) requires an experience of having been
watched over in childhood by an unobtrusive parent. There is a
direct parallel between the notion of an external secure base that
facilitates the capacity to explore and this Winnicottian paradigm
of inner exploration. As mentioned in the previous chapter, in "The
Use of an Object" and "Hate in the Counter-transference" (Winnicott
1971), he argues that the mutual *recognition* of infant and parent
depends on an active interaction in which the infant repeatedly
negates or "destroys" the parent in fantasy, the parent's task being
to survive in reality (Winnicott 1971). As Bateson (1973) put it
more abstractly, "information is difference" (Hamilton 1985). For
Bowlby, loss, especially in the early years of life, is potentially catastrophic and can at best be coped with by appropriate mourning;
for Winnicott, dealing with the inevitable discontinuities of nurturance is a spur to creativity and an essential part of growing up.

In "The Location of Cultural Experience" (1971), Winnicott quotes a line from Tagore: "On the seashore of endless worlds children play." Here, too, as Benjamin (1989) points out, there is the paradoxical tension between limit and infinite possibility, *endless* worlds on a sea *shore*. Only if one can contain oneself, one's feelings and desires, is one truly able to let go. Autonomy arises out of intimacy; only if one has had the experience of secure attachment can one allow oneself to undergo the rhythm of loss and rediscovery that is at the heart of creativity.

In a similar vein, in Bion's notion of maternal reverie and containment the mother "invites" the child into her own inner space, and on the basis of this the child's inner world begins to open up. But, as Hamilton (1982) has argued, compared with the mutual Einsteinian "holy curiosity" of Bowlby's model of mother and baby, Bion's mother is a more passive, a gnomic bearer of the painful truth that one is forever separated from prelinguistic pure experience.

Both Winnicott and Bion, and to a lesser extent Bowlby, were in their models of infant development also reaching toward an understanding of their position as psychoanalysts. Psychoanalysis itself was also adjusting to the postwar world of modernism, searching for a role and definition for itself. Broadly speaking, there are two polar views of the nature of the psychoanalytic process. In what might be called the *esoteric vision*, the analytic task is the uncovering of a hidden reality to which the analyst, through her training and initiation, is privy, and of which, with analytic help, the patient may begin to get a glimpse. The transference here is a vehicle for elucidating and eliminating the distortions of this reality that neurosis throws up, the analyst a priestly guide into the mysterious underworld. In the exoteric or *co-constructivist vision* (Gergen 1985) to which, had he conceived it in these terms, Bowlby would, I believe, have subscribed, the task of therapy is that of understanding a jointly created psychic reality, rather than replacing it with some secret truth. Transference here is, in Levenson's (1985) words, "A slice of life, intensified yet made manageable by the constraints of the analytic frame" (p. 92), the analyst a coexplorer of a shared psychic space.

ATTACHMENT THEORY AND CONTEMPORARY PSYCHOANALYTIC PSYCHOTHERAPY

Thus far we have considered attachment theory and psychoanalysis in their social and historical context. But psychoanalysis is an autonomous discipline, with its own internal logic and preoccupations, detached—perhaps, I have argued, too detached—from such wider concerns. And there are patients in need of help and understanding. Continuing the thread of the previous chapter, I shall therefore turn now, somewhat schematically at this stage, to the implications of attachment theory for the practice of psychotherapy, considering four main themes: the secure-base phenomenon, narrative, affect and defense, and sexuality. I will conclude with a case example that illustrates some of these theoretical points.

The Secure-Base Phenomenon

As I have described, attachment research has shown that a school-age child's sense of security is greatly influenced by the consistency, responsiveness, and attunement he or she experienced with his or her parents in infancy. Similar behaviors—many of them non-verbal—may influence the establishment of a secure therapeutic bond and thereby affect subsequent outcome in psychotherapy. Research is needed to identify the therapeutic homologues of successful maternal behaviors. For example, responsive mothers with securely attached offspring pick up their babies more rapidly and frequently than mothers of insecure children; similarly the effective therapist "picks up" the cues of his patient and responds appropriately. In Stern's (1985) picture of affective attunement the mother acts as a modulator to the minute-by-minute line of her child's moods, stimulating when activity drops, calming when the child becomes overexcited. The rhythms of psychotherapy sessions can be analyzed in a similar way, with effective therapists intervening enough to keep the patient's thought-bubbles airborn, but not puncturing them with premature or intrusive comments. Just as the secure infant scans his environment until he finds the familiar face to which he responds with smiling and the beginnings of play-ful interaction, so the good therapist creates conditions in which the patient can find an interpretation for himself, and respond with a comparable "ah-ha" of excitement and relief.

Narrative

Psychoanalysis is based on narrative. As suggested in the previous chapter, the patient tells her story, and the therapist listens, tries to make sense of it, to find meaning in its inchoate swirls, to fill in its gaps and lacunae, to shape its eruptions and collapses. Attach-ment theory provides the link between the hermeneutic slant of the consulting room and the empirical world of developmental psychology. Vygotsky (1962) shows how the mother, working at the "zone of proximal development," gives meaning to the infant's innate physiology; the grasp reflex becomes, under her tutelage, a *gesture* of pointing, babble the beginnings of meaningful speech.

Meaning is what enables separation to occur without irreme-diable loss. The secure base is never entirely safe. Breaks, gaps, and losses are as intrinsic to the rhythm of life as are attachment and connectedness. Narrative bridges these inevitable discontinuities in experience, the capacity to survive major losses in later life being built on the overcoming of the minor fissures that appear in the course of normal development. An obsessional avoidance of cracks in the pavement is a poor preparation for the abysses of adulthood. The patient's narrative is the raw material of therapy and provides clues to the interactional matrix out of which it emerged. Discon-tinuities in the way a person tells his or her story reflect breaks in the holding environment in childhood. The therapeutic process leads to a more fluent yet emotionally charged coherent self-narrative. Just as literary narrative can be "deconstructed" into a dialogue between writer and reader, so, as therapy unfolds, a shared narrative is forged to which both patient and therapist contribute, the former mainly through his words and affects, the latter by his responsiveness and attunement.

Affect and Defense

Bowlby, perhaps in a rather simplistic way, saw the suppression of negative affect, as opposed to its being expressed or worked through, as a central cause of neurotic difficulty. Infant research suggests that the modulation of infant affect by an attuned and responsive mother is the essential precursor of secure attachment. The patterns of insecure attachment represent compromises in which an infant is forced to trade off the pain of unmodulated affect against the discomfort of incompetent modulation, defenses designed to maintain contact with the object at all costs. The "avoidant" infant, who attends to the parent's comings or goings but conceals its distress in favor of maintaining a distal minimized relationship, treads a thin line between the loneliness of abandonment and the pain of rebuff. The "ambivalent" infant, whose parent inconsistently neglects or overwhelms, and whose pain on parting is matched by its conflicted response to reunion, cannot risk "destroying" (in a Winnicottian sense) the mother with anger for fear she will either actually disappear or invade its inner space.

Hamilton (1985) has pointed out that the notion of "defense" implicit in this interpersonal account is radically different from the classical Freudian view of defense mechanisms designed to reduce potentially overwhelming levels of psychic excitation arising from *within* the organism. As described in Chapter 1, this view goes some way, for example, to explain the extraordinary loyalty of the abused child to her abuser. Similar patterns can easily be observed in the transference when working therapeutically with abused patients. As Fairbairn (1952) stated, better to cling to a bad object than to have none at all.

Sex and Sexualization in Therapy

Bowlby conceived of attachment as a primary behavioral system in its own right, distinct from feeding and sexuality. Just as this enabled him to dispense with explanations of mother–infant bonding that depended on feeding, so attachment theory presents a challenge to explanations of the emotional life of toddlers and young children that are based on oedipal theory. The triangular rivalries of family life do not necessarily need to be understood in classical oedipal terms, since family members can equally be seen as vying with one another for attachment as for sexual possession. The oedipal triangle is transformed into the triangle of attachment. Here it is not so much the father who *comes between* mother and infant, but the development of a "third term," perspective, or vantage point, which enables the child to begin to separate herself, and which contains within it the seeds of nonattachment (cf. p. 31).

This discarding of Oedipus played its part in putting Bowlby beyond the psychoanalytic pale in the 1950s and 1960s when a belief in the Oedipus complex was an unchallengeable part of the psychoanalytic credo. (Klein was obliged to insist that oedipal conflicts occurred in early infancy in order to retain her psychoanalytic credibility.) However, recent views tend to support the Bowlbian position (Erickson 1993, Slavin and Kriegman 1992). Many psychoanalytic writers (e.g., Hamilton 1982) have pointed out that Oedipus was an abused child, physically attacked (oedipus = swollen feet) and banished by his parents, a victim of Laius's fear of the oracle's prediction that he would be killed by his son, and that his infantile sexuality was a consequence of this rejection.

Both anthropological and ethological evidence suggests that premature sexual behavior and incest are much more likely to occur when there has been some weakening of the attachment bonds between adults and children, for example, if reared apart or if they are reared by non-kin, for example, stepparents. Observations of kin and reciprocal altruism in contemporary evolutionary theory suggest a much less conflictual model of the human psyche than Freud and Klein imagined. Rather than an inherent opposition between primitive instinctual forces of sexuality and aggression and the guilt-inducing civilizing forces of socialization, selective pressure toward group bonding in order to enhance inclusive fitness means (a) that the interests of the parental and infant "selfish genes" coincide in the early months of life and (b) that where they begin to diverge in the oedipal phase, guilt arises out of threats to this affiliation. The overwhelming guilt of neurosis is in this perspective an interpersonal phenomenon, an insistent cry for empathy and attachment, not a manifestation of uncontrollable drives.

Sexualization in therapy is most likely to arise when the secure base of attachment is at its weakest, for example at times of breaks or when there have been countertransferential "frame-violations" (Langs 1978), by the therapist such as lateness, forgetting appointments, and so on. This needs to be differentiated from more mature erotic feelings that may arise in therapy. This more complex and multileveled approach to sexuality and sexualization in therapy is especially important if one component of desire—especially female desire—is conceived in terms of the erotics of inner space. As Benjamin (1989) puts it,

> Psychoanalytic valorization of genital sexuality has obscured the equal importance of erotic pleasure of the early attunement and mutual play of infancy. When the sexual self is represented by the sensual capacities of the whole body, when the totality of space, between, outside, and within our bodies becomes the site of pleasure, then desire escapes the borders of the imperial phallus and resides on the shore of endless worlds. [p 152]

I will try now to bring some of these theoretical points together by further exploration of the case of Katherine, already introduced to the reader in the previous chapter.

CASE EXAMPLE: "BREATHING THE SAME AIR"

Katherine was in her late forties when she sought help for feelings of depression, panic, and futility, focused around her inability to decide whether to settle in England, where her elderly mother lived, or to return to Australia, where she had lived for several years. She had had an unusual childhood, growing up in her parent's progressive private children's home where the regime was much given to nudity and cold showers and where, from the age of 3, she was expelled from her parents' domain into the dormitory with the other children. Her father, who was something of a Laius, ran the home in a tyrannical fashion, resented his children's relationship with their mother, and subjected Katherine to physical, verbal, and sexual abuse. As mentioned, her mother was herself depressed and failed to respond adequately to Katherine's attempts to alert her to her distress—deliberately falling down stairs, and swallowing poison berries and, on one occasion, a nail—by vaguely telling her to go and swallow some bread or "go and see matron."

Pathological Organization and Omnipotence as Defenses Against Insecure Attachment

Katherine dealt with the intense miseries and insecurities of her childhood by developing an elaborate fantasy, akin to Steiner's (1985) "pathological organization," in which she would, each night, with erotic excitement and then relief, systematically inflict pain on herself by pinching or sometimes sticking in pins, while she "turned" herself into a horse. She saw horses as free, group creatures with no personal pain or anxiety, liberated from the intense fear and discomfort she felt when threatened with intimacy with one other person.

The intimacy of therapy was utterly terrifying to her. She dealt with her terror by an instant and intensely sexualized attachment to therapy. Breaks were particularily difficult for her and she would desperately ask for reassurance around the time of separation: "Tell me that you like me," "Tell me it is not surprising I am like I am with a father like that," "Give me something to have from this room while you are away." For the most part I resisted these entreaties and interpreted her separation anxiety. During a break she contacted a former lover and rushed rapidly into a marriage that was in difficulty within a few weeks. She had begged to be advised whether or not to marry. I should perhaps have said, "If I advise you not to marry then, like your father, I will be giving a message that I want you for myself; if I advise you to marry I shall be like your mother, fobbing you off with someone else." But, afraid that any such comment would have been taken as a seduction (and in any case at the time unable to think of anything better) I said nothing.

Separation Protest as the First Stirrings of a Secure Base

In the early months of therapy she was compliant and submissive—in one dream she pictured herself as a servant to me and my wife—but early in the third year began to be much more assertive. She demanded more frequent sessions, a request that, while I acknowledged it would be desirable, I was logistically—and possibly as a countertransferential response to the intensity of her ambivalent attachment—unable to grant. She arrived at a session one day and read out a furious letter in which she accused me of being cruel and punitive like her father, neglectful and indifferent like her mother. By reading rather than directly expressing anger, and by preempting my response through the parental comparison, she was still pulling her punches—but this assertiveness was a definite advance from enmeshed to secure attachment. In the next few sessions she became increasingly anxious, trembling and shaking and experiencing difficulty in breathing. She described for the first time the horse fantasy and spoke of how naked and helpless she felt on the couch, and wondered if the horse "magic" that had saved her as a child from complete madness and disintegration, but which now entrapped her, could be put somehow into reverse so that she could be released.

Intense Separation Anxiety as Insecure Attachments are Given Up and Before Secure Ones have been Formed

As the defensive structures of insecure attachments are relinquished it becomes possible for the first time to form a secure base. For Katherine this meant giving up the horse fantasy—that is, to see herself as a separate individual—and deciding to separate from her unhappy second marriage. At this point a patient's vulnerability—like a free radical in search of a bond or an animal that has just shed its skin—is often also at its height. In one session around this time Katherine developed a full-blown panic attack, and I felt under great pressure to provide some modulatory response—to reassure her and perhaps even take her hand, but held back, feeling that to do so would be to reproduce, albeit in benign form, the abuse she had suffered at her father's hands. Her demand that something be done was intense. Eventually, searching for a metaphor that would be powerful enough to hold her, I said: "You want me to hold you so that you feel connected and safe—but we *are* attached: we are breathing the same air, the air you breathe out I take in, the air I breathe out comes into you." She calmed a little and revealed that she had composed a poem recently that was on her mind all the time, an invocation to her therapist. She felt, she said, that her mouth and genitals had been irreparably dirtied by the abuse, and wanted him to

Make them clean of nastiness and shame
Neither top nor bottom
But somewhere in between
With my breath, through my skin, come in
Knowing me, naming me.

The Necessity and Dangers of Reassurance

The "breathing the same air" comment could be criticized as being essentially a reassurance, failing to get in touch with her intense anxiety about being held, although some such supportive intervention seemed to be necessary at the time if she were to survive the gaps between sessions (cf. Chapter

5). It could perhaps be understood as a transference reassurance, and served the function of protecting the therapeutic alliance at a critical moment, when, as with so many borderline patients, the therapeutic bond was under threat. When, later, she arrived at a session feeling she had got something in her eye, she was able to describe her simultaneous longing for me to examine her and so touch her, and her enormous fear of my actually doing so.

The Emergence of Narrative, as Separation can Increasingly be Tolerated in the Context of a Secure Base

The importance of seeing the secure base as a psychosomatic phenomenon—involving body and mind—was further reinforced some months later, when, now making good progress in therapy, and in a playful way much more able to differentiate reality and fantasy in her narrative style, Katherine described a waking dream or self-guided fantasy in which she had imagined herself lying on a bed with the therapist looking into her eyes, lifting each of her limbs in a calm and gentle manner, touching her stomach, and, in a completely non-sexual way, parting her legs, "Looking," she said, "at the whole of me." In this fantasy she realized to her surprise that her body was preadolescent.

Attachment as a Bodily Experience

I responded by saying that as she described this fantasy I had pictured the careful and almost mystic examination of newborn babies by their mothers. This made immediate sense to Katherine who spoke of her genitals and how she was normally unable to think of them other than with disgust or sexuality, but that in this fantasy she was "perfect" and "complete." I pointed to the double meaning of "the (w)hole of me," and contrasted the loving bond of a parent to a newborn baby with the hollow attachment that resulted from penetrative abuse. Here we can see the contrast between an insecure base characterized by the omnipotent sexualized narcissism of her attempts to get the therapist to admire or even fall in love with her, and the healthy adoration of a parent for a newborn child—true intimacy requiring the positive narcissism that arises out of secure attachment. I suggested that what had pushed her father to intrude and smash up his children's relationship with their mother (mirrored by Katherine's fantasies of doing the same to my family and so have me all to herself) was intense envy of this first all-important bond.

EPILOGUE

Katherine's turning point occurred when she disengaged from her defensive attachments and survived the extreme vulnerability of her new state. In this chapter I have tried to show how Bowlby's capacity to survive the disruption of his ambivalent relationship with psychoanalysis led to the development of attachment theory, and to point to the possibility of a renewal of that relationship through the emerging psychoanalytic paradigm of primary intersubjectivity.

We started with John Bunyan. I will end with another poet. Robert Frost, like Bowlby, was vigorous, long lived, and much feted, a man of action in a world of contemplation, who turned his back on the obscurities of modernism and sought instead the poetry of the everyday, the commonplace, the observable:

> Two roads diverged in a wood, and I—
> I took the one less traveled by,
> And that has made all the difference.

Bowlby's less-traveled road—an initial tentativeness followed by the decisive stride of the repeated "I"—has become a broad highway, with many fellow travelers. The roads of attachment theory and psychoanalysis are increasingly and excitingly convergent. In Frost's "Mending Wall" he says:

> Something there is that doesn't love a wall,
> That sends the frozen-ground-swell under it,
> And spills the upper boulders in the sun . . .
> I let my neighbour know beyond the hill;
> And on a day we meet to walk the line
> And set the wall between us once again . . .
> There where it is we do not need the wall:
> He is all pine and I am apple orchard.
> My apple trees will never get across
> To eat the cones under his pines, I tell him.
> He only says, "Good fences make good neighbors."

Frost's tantalizing juxtaposition—"Good fences make good neighbors" but "Something there is that doesn't love a wall"—evokes many opposing echoes: the security of attachment poised against the call of the wild, boundary and space, defense and exploration, liminal shores and infinite worlds. I turn now to further clinical examples aiming to show how attachment theory can help patients achieve this balancing of opposites implicit in Bowlbian project.

3

Attachment, Detachment, and Nonattachment

This chapter develops the notion of the *triangle of attachment* described in Chapter 1 and explores the nature of the attachment between patient and therapist, and how this may be used for good or ill. This is usually discussed in terms of one of three positions: first, therapist as "mother"—the containing, "being with," empathic, intimacy-promoting function; second, therapist as "father"—the educative, "doing to," limit-setting, autonomy-enhancing role; third, and perhaps more contentiously and less openly discussed, but no less important, the therapist as moral or spiritual mentor—the value-transmitting, "going toward" function. In this chapter I shall suggest that the "compleat therapist," in order to be effective, needs to be able to integrate attachment and detachment into a stance of nonattachment. But first let us consider some of the clinical manifestations of the attachment dynamic.

ATTACHMENT AND DETACHMENT:
PHILOSOPHICAL ROOTS

Secure attachment is vital to survival and to freedom from anxiety, thus providing a platform for creativity and exploration, and to psychological well-being generally (Bowlby 1988). Rather than being a childish requirement, outgrown in those who have achieved autonomy and maturity, attachment needs continue throughout life, even up to the moment of death. The form that attachment takes, and the extent to which it is internalized, alters throughout the life cycle, but the need remains. As it is often put, we need someone to be "there" for us—and if not a person then an animal, a place, an image, an idea, an ideal, a God—to whom (or which) we can reach out for support, succor, comfort, meaning and purpose.

These self-evident truths took a long time to be accepted in psychoanalysis, whose starting point was attachment's counter-part—detachment. For Freud the neonate is an isolate, a self-sufficient psychological "egg," who, bit by bit, slowly finds the object through the experience of frustration and loss, loving at first only himself and only on the basis of that self-love beginning to attach himself at first to part-objects and then whole objects (Freud 1914, Hamilton 1982). Freud saw attachment as a coming in from the cold, the struggle of a split-off self that only gradually and pain-fully learns to love.

Lasch (1979) suggests that Freud's emphasis on separation, especially of the boy from the mother, needs to be seen in the con-text of nineteenth century tightly-knit extended middle-class family structures. Against that claustrophobic background what Freud saw was the struggle for autonomy and differentiation and the oedipal prohibition on intimacy with a mother who is both elusive and all-pervasive. The weakened ties of the contemporary family mean that we can no longer take attachment for granted. What we now see is a mother and baby struggling to bond, and all the problems that arise when that process goes wrong. From a feminist perspec-tive Freud's is very much a father's perspective (Benjamin 1989). From the moment of conception the baby is in intimate contact with the mother, whereas finding the father is a much more prob-lematic process for both parties, a gradual reaching out of amoeba-like pseudopodia (Freud's famous image of how relationships hap-pen) rather than a built-in attachment. Chodorow (1978) brings a gendered perspective to the discussion: for girls the problem is one of separation from the mother and the development of autonomy; boys must of necessity detach from the mother and, as I have suggested, the male problem is typically that of intimacy.

I have described how attachment and detachment are inseparable, as integral to the interpersonal world as the rhythms of breathing or the heartbeat are to our physiological universe. As we breathe in we attach ourselves to the world; breathing out we detach ourselves again. The basis of conversation is "taking turns," a process that starts between infant and caregiver long before words arrive on the scene. In a verbal conversation we speak and then fall silent. Striving to connect, our words reach out, then we withdraw momentarily, readying ourselves to receive the words of the other. The heart fills, contracts, and then lets go: systole and diastole. In Skynner's (1976) apt phrase—one flesh, separate persons. Just as we have to be able to attach ourselves if we are to survive—"There is no such thing as an infant, meaning of course that wherever one finds an infant one finds maternal care, and without maternal care there would be no infant" (Winnicott 1958, p. xxxvii)—so we have also to be able to detach ourselves or die. "We die alone," but we also die if we cannot be alone. The baby who will not relinquish the breast will be rudely pushed off, the teat smeared with dung as in African village practice. In *Great Expectations* Miss Haversham's life remained frozen at the moment of her jilting, her wedding veil yellowed with age, the wedding cake festooned with cobwebs. Over and over again research has shown that the basis of successful analysis is a positive therapeutic alliance (Orlinsky et al. 1994), but at some point we have to detach ourselves from our analysis and start living. The patient has a right to absolute and rapt attention during the therapeutic hour, but, as Winnicott (1958) pointed out, the analyst must be able to "hate" the patient enough to say after 50 minutes that time is up. To repeat the theme of Chapter 1, the overall aim of psychotherapy is to help the patient find a balance between attachment and detachment. Each has its positive and negative forms. Erikson (1968) contrasted intimacy with isolation. Attachment is the basis for intimacy, but runs the risk of engulfment; detachment is needed for autonomy, but can also lead to schizoid avoidance.

Analysts like to take one or another side in the attachment-detachment debate. The Kleinians tend to say hate comes first, gradually detoxified by the love of the "thinking-breast" (Harris and Waddell 1991). They point to the ubiquity of man's destructiveness—not just clinically in borderline and depressed patients, but socially and politically as well. Kohut (1977) and the interpersonal school (Stolorow et al. 1987) argue that bonding and empathy are primary, violence, addiction, promiscuity, and self-hatred being "breakdown products" of parental misattunement and abuse. One side sees how babies fuss and cry and get colic and won't feed or go to sleep, and it postulates a "basic misery" (Bradley 1991) that is gradually overcome as dependence lessens; the other stresses the universality of Erikson's (1968) "basic trust"—the power of "primary maternal preoccupation," the falling in love of mother and baby, and the blissful contentment of successful feeding—with which we are born.

For one group the task of analysis is to root out the hatred and envy that the analytic situation inevitably arouses. From this can emerge the respect for the other that is the basis of true intimacy. The omnipotence of projective identification attempts to deny the reality of hatred and detachment, and eventually has to be faced in the depressive position. On the other side the therapist sees a patient who has been deprived of the experience of secure attachment. The analyst's job is to repair that deficit, to restore the sufferer's faith in the power of the bonds of love, and to accept, for the time being, the patient's need to idealize, demand admiration, to imagine lifelong companionship with her helper, and only gradually, under conditions of optimal disillusionment, to proffer the reality of detachment, and so become more autonomous.

Greenberg and Mitchell (1983) have pointed to the philosophical roots of these two apparently opposing psychoanalytic visions of our earliest years. They link the emphasis in the detachment-based position of Klein and Freud (their drive/structural model) with

Hobbes's and Locke's emphasis on individual fulfillment as the goal of a good life, and with Isaiah Berlin's notion of "negative liberty"— freedom from interference by other men's selfish desires. Psychoanalytically this would mean freedom from interference by one's own envy, hatred, and destructiveness. In the depressive position one learns to tolerate these feelings while remaining attached to the loved object that survives in reality one's fantastical attacks.

In contrast, the relational model of Kohut and the object relations school can be traced back to Hegel and Marx who emphasize "positive liberty," or freedom to join the community of one's fellow men and women. Here, in the community of analyst and patient, faith in the capacity to love (and presumably to work for the good of mankind) is restored. Through attachment to the analyst, through her love, one learns to love oneself, which in turn enables one to love others. Even when one is apparently detached and alone, there is an internal (m)other looking after one—"alone in the presence of the (m)other" (Winnicott 1965). Secure attachment enables one to explore not just the physical world but the interpersonal world of feelings, one's own and those of the other.

Note that psychoanalysis quite unselfconsciously uses language that under other circumstances might be considered religious—we speak of faith, trust, love, hate, community, remorse, guilt, and reparation. The ultimate Christian image of detachment is the foresakenness of the agony in the garden; of attachment perhaps the reminder that "no man is an island, [but] a part of the main" (Donne 1624). We shall return to this point when we consider nonattachment, but first let us, for the sake of clarity, discuss attachment and detachment in more detail and look at how they appear in clinical practice.

CLINICAL ASPECTS OF ATTACHMENT

To recapitulate, attachment theory sees normal development as the result of secure attachment based on "good-enough" parenting (Holmes 1993, Parkes et al. 1991). The securely attached individual has had attuned and responsive care, providing emotional object constancy, an emergent sense of self, creativity in the mutual interplay of the transitional zone, and the capacity to express and tolerate protest about the inevitable separations and failures that are an integral part of being alive. The secure individual is thus poised between attachment and separation; she can enjoy intimacy, and has the capacity to be alone.

As described in Chapter 1, insecure attachment is the basis of psychopathology, and takes one of two main forms, depending on which aspect of the attachment/detachment dyad is suppressed. The insecure-ambivalent individuals cling to the object, terrified of separation; insecure-avoidant individuals shy away from their objects, fearful or dismissing of closeness. From the relational perspective the world appears to the ambivalent person as inherently unreliable; clinging is the best way of maintaining proximity to an object that she expects will let her down (Hamilton 1982). The avoidant person has suffered repeated rebuffs or intrusions; she gets just close enough to her object to remain in touch, not so close as to be hurt or obliterated yet again (Bartholomew 1990). In both cases no stable differentiation of self and object has occurred; the world is seen solipsistically, through a glass darkly, so colored by projective identification that the object conforms to an inner expectation of intrusiveness, aggression, rejection, or neglect. Neither true intimacy nor true autonomy is possible.

The aim of therapy is to transform insecure into secure attachment (Holmes 1993, 1994a), to move from clinging to intimacy, from avoidance to autonomy. In working for this the therapist tries to behave like a responsive, attuned parent-figure who is neither intrusive nor rejecting, rebuffing nor controlling, castrating nor seductive, overwhelming nor neglectful. Of course, transference and countertransference ensure that he constantly fails, both in her own eyes and in those of the patient. Therapy progresses through examining and understanding these failures, moving always toward the goal of balanced intimacy and autonomy, based on a differentiated self and other. The ambivalent individual is so closely fused with her object that the only way she can find it is to separate from it. The avoidant person evades intimacy because whenever she does begin to get close she feels the fear and pain of potential rejection and loss. In therapy she can begin to build fragile bridges that she will eventually cross to join the other. I shall now try to illustrate these paradigmatic positions with two contrasting clinical examples.

Raymond (Continued): The Man Who Couldn't Let Go

Raymond, a large shambling man in his mid-fifties, was referred by his family doctor for psychotherapy because of unexplained severe chest pains for which, despite extensive investigations including cardiac catheterization, no medical cause could be found. He had fought a losing battle for two years to prevent his firm from going into receivership. His difficulties had begun when a new firm had taken over, run, as he said, by 29-year-old upstarts who knew everything about balance sheets but nothing about running a business, especially the personnel management side. His chest pains had started as he was driving home from yet another uncomfortable board meeting at which he had had to swallow his fury at the incompetence of what he called "the clones," their lack of interest in his point of view and that of his workers, and his humiliation at his powerlessness to do anything but submit to their rule.

Another precipitant was his mother's impending death from Alzheimer's disease. The younger of two children, Raymond had no memories of his father, who had been lost at sea during the war. However, he had an idealized picture of an almost perfect man, generous to a fault ("he would have given away his ass and shat through his ribs if he could" was his mother's description), who, after Raymond's birth, had slept on the floor so that the baby could share his mother's bed. His last letter to Raymond's mother in 1940 said that he feared his ship would founder, but "I shan't feel so bad if I do die now that you have Raymond." Raymond was convinced that his father was waiting for him "up there," and he looked forward to their being reunited. He often spoke to his father saying, "I didn't do so bad, Dad, did I?" After his father's death his mother herself joined the Navy and had left her small children with her mother for several months, but when she discovered them neglected in an upstairs room had returned to look after them. As we shall see, fear of abandonment continued to be a guiding theme for Raymond from then on. Later, they lived in their grandparent's pub, where his mother worked until she remarried when Raymond was 8. His stepfather was a good man, but a martinet: "I hated him until I was 18, loved and respected him ever since." He had died from Parkinson's disease some four years previously.

Raymond was a bright, "good" boy, ever helpful and hardworking. He suffered agonies of loneliness when he was sent to a boarding grammar school for servicemen's children. He longed to run away, and on one occasion refused to go back, but his mother and stepfather insisted and he submitted. Attachment and detachment, if they are to lead to autonomy and the capacity for intimacy, form a dynamic. Raymond could neither attack his object with anger and see that it could survive, nor let go of it and feel the pain, later to discover that it was still there for him to reattach. Raymond was frozen with a dead and idealized internal father, and the constant fear that his mother might abandon him again.

The family was poor, and he left school at 17 and became an apprentice fitter. Gradually he worked his way up from the shop floor to become a manager, well known for his intense hard work, probity, and father-like devotion to his workforce. He married out of gratitude and a sense of duty; he had been in the hospital following a motorbike accident and his girlfriend had visited him daily for several months and so he felt he "ought" to marry her. When the marriage broke up he felt deeply guilty and, much to his second wife's irritation, continued to support his former wife overgenerously, visiting her almost daily to see if she needed any help or repairs done. Here again he could neither let go of nor face his own aggression.

There was, by the time he presented, little conversation or expression of affection between him and his second wife, who seemed to revere and tiptoe around him just like the servile employee she had been in the factory where they had both worked and where they had met. "You could drive a double-decker bus between us in the bed, we're that far apart" was his description of their physical relationship.

As well as suffering from chest pains, it was clear that Raymond was deeply depressed, agoraphobic, and in a state of constant suppressed rage and mourning for the factory to which he had been "married" for the past eleven years. He brooded constantly about the past, and how he could prove that he was right and the new management wrong. He felt actively suicidal, could not sleep, go out of the house, or drive a car, and claimed that he spoke more in his weekly 50-minute psychotherapy session than he did in the entire week between sessions.

He made a rapid, but modest, initial improvement, feeling that at last someone "understood" and was taking his chest pains seriously. It was clear that he was going to need to take medical retirement from his job, which had been in a state of limbo while his medical condition was being investigated. Reluctantly he came to see that as inevitable, although he feared that it might mean losing everything that he had built up over the years—his house and the modestly comfortable lifestyle—and returning to the penury of his childhood. But when this and similar issues were interpreted along developmental lines, suggesting that he had psychologically returned to a childhood in which, in the face of loss (his father, the recession), he had struggled to maintain things (the good boy looking after his widowed mother, the 70-hour days leading up to the receivership) but then had to concede (the arrival of his fierce stepfather, the new management), he was unimpressed. Despite his apparent imperviousness to interpretation, things seemed to improve a bit between him and his wife, and they began a joint project in their garden, which had been neglected for many years. He "allowed" her to take over some of the running of the house and to pay the bills; he discovered that she was a person rather than merely a vague undifferentiated presence in his life. His chest pains receded. He began to think ahead toward retirement and started drawing and painting, which he had enjoyed in the past, working meticulously in pen and ink, taking hours over a small picture.

An interesting instance of this improvement, and his ability to integrate or sublimate previously split-off aggression was a sudden longing to paint, not with his usual tiny fantail brush, but straight on to the canvas with a knife, "really smearing it on" (here making violently expressive gestures in the air). This can be contrasted with an earlier episode in which, despite being totally exhausted by work, he had spent all his spare time decorating the house; his wife had come in to ask him "some damn fool question" about paint colors; his response had been to snap, "Please your bloody self," upending the entire five-gallon can on the floor and walking out, leaving her to clean it up as best she could.

After that early improvement things became static. He claimed that he had become "very attached" to therapy, but there was little give, either in the sessions or in his outside life. He seemed to be reproaching me with his lack of progress and I began mildly to dread the sessions and their claustrophic intensity. He felt that he needed to "break down," and wondered if he needed to sign himself in to the hospital (a suggestion that filled me with inexplicable dread; I was feeling, countertransferentially, the claustrophobia of the fused-with object), saying that he longed to cry, but just couldn't "let go," implying that if only I could find the key to his difficulties all would be well.

Exasperatedly I began to enact the aggression that Raymond feared so much in himself, consciously trying to inject some life and movement into the sessions. I said I thought he was so full of hatred and envy of the new management and so convinced of his own rightness that he would never let go, even if it led to his own death. He seemed shocked and commented with some anger and vitality (in contrast to his usual lugubrious manner) that he was surprised to discover that I was not the eternally patient and compassionate therapist he had taken me for. He revealed his secret relationship with his dead father, who he "spoke to" almost every day. I asked him if he had ever imagined as a child that his father was not dead, and if he pictured a joyful reunion. He told me how his mother had gone to the dockyard gates for years after his death looking at the men, often "seeing" her husband from behind only to be disappointed when the man turned around. I began to appreciate the omnipotence of a boy who had missed out on the benign oedipal struggle with a father whom he could both love and hate, and from whom he could eventually separate and so learn the rudiments of autonomony. Instead he had split his father-representation into a "good" dead father who belonged exclusively to him, and of whom his mother had confessed, "I love John [his stepfather] but if your Dad walked up that path today I would go off with him at once," and the "bad" living stepfather to whom he had to submit.

I compared the image of his father with a piece of timber (he was in the wood business) that a shipwrecked sailor might cling to in order to save himself from drowning. Now that he had reached the shore, holding on so tightly was preventing him from landing safely on the beach, but he just could not prize his fingers open, and the harder his rescuer (i.e., I) tried to release him, the tighter his grip became. There was a battle between the real live but potentially unpredictable therapist and his dead idealized father. He could not let go of the factory because in doing so he was letting go of everything he had clung to for all his life. To do so would be to admit defeat, and to feel his helplessness and vulnerability. His wish to break down and to go to the hospital reflected his wish for absolute security, which, in his claustrophobic way, he provided for his workers, and which was so conspicuously absent in his early childhood.

This was in fact an attempt—à la Strachey (1934)—to bring together past, present, and transference in a single image: his clinging to his father's memory and refusal to mourn his death and so lead his own life rather than be a substitute "little man"; his inability to let go of his job and the workers to whom he was so devoted in a fatherly way; and his ancient mariner–like clinging to me in a way that inhibited my therapeutic freedom, drawing me into his problems rather than allowing me to become part of the solution to them.

Eventually his mother died, and in a moving session he finally cried as he described sitting with her body in the chapel of rest, and how he had tied the white silk scarf belonging to his father that he had kept for fifty years around her wrist, so that it was cremated with her.

Raymond's ambivalent attachment meant fusing with his object, fearful of letting go for an instant in case he might be overwhelmed with unbearable anxiety. He had to be in total control to ward off any possibility of abandonment. He was overwhelmed with feelings of shame and failure. His depression not only had exposed his neediness and dependency, but also had revealed him as unable, in his own eyes, to be able to hold onto his object. He was forced to see himself as the helpless weakling that he had spent his whole life trying to shield. He was unable to leave the house for fear of meeting one of his workers whom he would have to tell that he was not coming back. To do so would have been to tell them that they had lost their "father." He clung to his dead job rather than face the possibility that his rage and disappointment had destroyed it, which in a sense it had. He could not visit his dying mother, to whose service he had unconsciously devoted his life—at the expense of his own. Paralyzed by his attachments, he deprived himself of the liberation that accompanies detachment and letting go.

Once in therapy the pattern repeated itself; attachment to therapy became an anchor around which he organized his time and his psychic life, but the anchor was too heavy to be weighed. He was unable to sail free or trust the buoyancy (Quinodoz 1993) of his own being. His struggle was to make the move from clinging to intimacy, which meant being able to face his fears of detachment and to see his object survive angry attacks.

In avoidant attachment by contrast, the sufferer is imprisoned by her freedom, floating, weightless, eternally searching for intimacy, which once it becomes a real possibility threatens to overwhelm her delicately wrought mode of survival. We return now to the case of Katherine, described in the previous two chapters.

Katherine (Continued): The Trauma of Finding the Rejecting Object

The war had also played a significant part in Katherine's development. She knew nothing of her father until, when she was 3, he suddenly appeared in her life. A crucial memory was of being in the bedroom soon after his return while he was playing some sort of game with her two older siblings. She tried to attract his attention but was ignored, and so bit his leg. He responded by flinging her bodily across the room—a prototype of her later relationship with a father who terrorized her childhood with his violence, demandingness, and sexual intrusions, until eventually her parents separated when Katherine was 11, leaving a mother who seemed never to emerge from the depression and devastation of her failed marriage.

Like Raymond, Katherine clung to therapy as a lifeline, always fearful that I would announce without warning that she had had enough, flinging her into outer darkness as her father had done. She never missed a session and was meticulously punctual, gazing imploringly at me with wounded eyes when I opened the door. As mentioned, the weekly therapy witnessed many major events in her life, including a remarriage and a further separation, a change of job, buying and selling two houses, and the death of her mother. It was with the greatest difficulty that I got her to talk about these events since she would have been happy to focus almost exclusively on her feelings toward me. But, curiously, despite this, it was extraordinarily difficult to experience real contact with her during the sessions. We were like two mute ghosts groping toward one another in the dark. Her story was sad, she had been horribly misused as a child, yet much of the time I felt unmoved. Perhaps this was a manifestation of my hardheartedness, which was her own explanation when she felt brave enough to say so. Certainly I felt at times like her violent father, exasperated by his daughter's demands, yet unable to meet them, and at other times like her depressed mother, incapable of responding to her daughter's evident distress.

Nevertheless progress was made. Her life became less chaotic. She settled down and could tolerate her solitude more easily. She became more assertive, able not to submit to the sexual flattery of any man who wished to go to bed with her. She gave up the menial job she had been doing and found work more suitable to her age and abilities. She was less consumed with self-hatred and anxiety. Autonomy had replaced avoidance, but she still had great problems with intimacy. There was more liveliness and mutuality in the sessions, but her difficulties with me continued. One of her preoccupations was with whether or not I liked her. As already described, she longed for me to say so, especially around the times of breaks when she felt unbearably abandoned and rejected and second best. She also frequently asked me to hold her hand or touch her. In one session in which real emotional contact had been made she became very tearful when thinking about her mother and how sad it was that they had only begun to communicate in a more straightforward way in the weeks before her death. I felt with some relief that we were actually beginning to work on a symbolic level. But she returned the following week saying once more that on her way home in the car she had decided that what she really wanted was for me to hold her physically.

This demand gave me a heart-sinking feeling. I found myself saying brusquely that she must know me well enough by now to know that I would not comply, and that if that was the sort of therapy she wanted, why had she come to me, rather than psychodrama or some similar humanistic approach? Slightly stunned at this aggressive outburst and trying to retrieve the situation, I also reminded her that she had in fact been "touched" and tearful in the previous session, and interpreted her need for physical contact in terms of a part of her, identified with her father, that envied and wanted to break up any real contact between mother and daughter by a physical intrusion. I also acknowledged how difficult it was for her to bear the week-long gaps between sessions. She then reminded me of a moment, several years previously, when, before a break, she had tried to embrace me. I had stood there, she said, unresponsive, cold, and lifeless. I suggested that this must have been very traumatic for her; she agreed, and contrasted this real experience of me with a frequent dream in which I put my arm around her in a nonsexual way, giving her a feeling of absolute peace and calm.

In the next session we discussed how her attempted embrace had a biting quality and how my rejection of her wish to be touched uncannily repeated her father's throwing her across the room, and how terrifying it had been to find me physically dead to her, as though her need for closeness, and her anger about not finding it, could only end in complete abandonment. This discussion seemed to be helpful, perhaps because having actually perpetrated a traumatic rejection, she felt at last that I really understood what it felt like to be so

treated. In this circuitous route of countertransferential enactment via projective identification she had finally gotten
through to me. She felt that her mind was in my mind. Our
attachment had become reciprocal and mutual. We had,
momentarily, moved from attachment to intimacy.

Attachment is often characterized as behavioral as opposed to the focus on the inner world of psychoanalysis. This
case illustrates how inseparable are the inner and outer manifestations of attachment. Katherine was in a constant state of
avoidance of her object. When she did find me what she found
was, via projective identification, her own traumatic object:
a "dead" mother and a traumatizing father. Her working model,
or basic assumption, was that when you finally do become
attached, what you find is something unbearably frightening.

To the extent that psychotherapy was effective it enabled her
to reexperience this traumatic attachment, but in a bearable way.
As discussed in Chapter 1, therapy enabled her to bring the trauma
within the "area of omnipotence" (Winnicott 1971), into the transitional zone in which therapist and patient replay the trauma, but
at the end there is no real blood on the stage, or if there is the
wounds are only skin deep. In Fonagy's (1991) terms, the traumatizing parent denies that the child has a mind; the therapeutic
replay of the trauma, followed by acknowledgment of the impact
of my rejection, restored Katherine's sense of having a mind and
of being emotionally alive.

Both Raymond and Katherine were in search of mutuality, an
interplay between attachment and detachment that could enable
"spontaneous living"—another Winnicottian phrase—to take place.
Raymond was fused with his objects, both good and bad; he could
not disentangle himself from his loved father or his hated job. He
had to learn to let go, to allow some space to open up between
himself and his object. Paradoxically, when he did so, and relaxed
his controllingness, the object, whose death he struggled so hard
to deny, came alive; he and his wife could collaborate and begin
to enjoy each other's company. For him the trauma was of sepa-
rateness. For Katherine the very intimacy she longed for contained

the trauma; relationships failed because if she did get close she found the traumatizing object (as was the case with her first abusive marriage), or if she shied away she was bored and dissatisfied (which is what happened with her second marriage).

My role with Raymond was to "be there," but also to push him away, to prize open those clutching fingers, to go with my irritation at his stubborn determination to destroy himself rather than admit he had failed in his job. With Katherine I had to resist the temptation to reach out to her, to create a short-circuit of support that may have temporarily relieved her anxiety but in the long run would have inhibited her search for authenticity. I had to be guided by my intuitive response to each of them, to trust that my anger with Raymond and my unmovedness with Katherine were valid responses, reasonably uncontaminated by my therapist-based countertransference (Steiner 1993). Against that fairly neutral background, patient-driven countertransference could arise in a way that, however mistake-driven, learning could take place.

I have suggested that attachment is played out in the inner world in spatial terms. In both these examples the therapeutic focus was on the spatial relationship to the other—Raymond clinging, Katherine avoiding—as it was played out in the transference, searching for an easy distance from an intrusive, absent, or elusive object. Equally important is the relationship to the self. The patient needs to detach from a false self; to find, know, and be her true self; to accept her self as it really is, warts and all, and distance herself from an idealized or denigrated self. Violent attacks on the self, such as are commonly seen in deliberate self-harm, can also be understood in terms of the attachment dynamic, as the following case illustrates.

Tom: The Attachment Dynamic and the Adolescent Self

Tom was a depressed 20-year-old. As a nervous little boy he had been very close to his mother and had to be dragged to school for several years; he had never felt close to his father and was extremely rivalrous with his two-years-older brother.

At 10 he had discovered how to be a joker, and from then on had made friends, infuriated the teachers, and was eventually expelled at 15. He started working in his father's panel beating business, drank heavily and, in his spare time, began work on his pride and joy—a souped-up off-roader that he used on weekends for illicit offroad expeditions and onroad flouting of traffic regulations. He left home and moved into an apartment with his brother, longing for a girlfriend but too busy drinking and fighting to find one. He pictured himself as a successful criminal, living for the danger and excitement of the moment.

Eventually he did find a willing girl, but when they went to bed he found himself impotent. He was amazed and deeply ashamed: "Me impotent, when I have a hard-on ninety percent of the time!" The next day he got drunk, drove his Land-rover to a remote place, and ceremoniously stoned it until it was a unrecognizable wreck. He then went to his parents and told them what he had done, and they arranged psychological help. I asked him if the Landrover had been a person who it would be; he replied with some insight that it was a part of himself. This symbolic attack on his "impotent," childlike self, the father with whom he could not identify, the brother by whom he felt constantly bettered, and the mother whom he longed to return to, somehow helped. In therapy he began to feel better, and found a new girlfriend with whom he had successful sex, and who was very understanding if he was not quite the stud he wished he could be. He began to look ahead and to imagine a noncriminal existence. Only through this violent and potentially dangerous form of separation from himself and all his destructive identifications could he begin to make some sense of who he really was.

PARADOX AND THE ATTACHMENT DYNAMIC

Freud was fascinated by the compatibility of opposites in the primary process thinking of the unconscious. He cited words like the

Latin *altus*, which means both high and deep (Freud 1911). Like love and hate or light and dark, attachment and detachment are inseparable. To be securely attached we need to learn to be alone. Only in secure solitude do we discover who we truly are, and thereby value the uniqueness of our bond with the other. The specificity, the such-ness, the now-ness of the encounter with the other arises out of this sense of self in isolation. When Katherine was calm enough to attend to her feelings, to know what she really wanted, she was able to make sensible choices; overwhelmed with anxiety she would latch desperately onto anyone, only to be disappointed. Raymond was so fused with his object he did not know who he was, merely that he was his father's son, or his boss's employee.

Psychotherapy provides an opportunity not just for secure attachment—to overcome clinging or avoidance—but also for detachment to take place. Here, too, Winnicott's (1971) ideas are seminal. In psychotherapy the patient is "alone in the presence of the (m)other." By remaining detached, by my refusal to touch Katherine, she was enabled to find the truth, however terrifying, of her inner world—the lifeless object that had traumatized her, which needed to be examined and laid to rest rather than eternally avoided. Gradually the spontaneous encounter of two solitudes—the patient's and the therapist's—could arise. The therapist has to maintain a constant vigilant presence, without being intrusive. Equally, the therapist has to be sufficiently unafraid of the inevitable hatred that such patients arouse to be able to end the sessions when the time is up however distressed the patient, to take vacations, and, in brief therapies, to terminate even when much remains undone.

Attachment theory grew in part out of Bowlby's dissatisfaction with the prevalent Kleinian paradigm of projective identification, which he felt failed to take account of the impact of real environmental failure in creating psychopathology. As we have described, Bion's interpersonal account of Kleinian theory (Symington and Symington 1996) was developed in parallel with attachment theory, but sadly there was at the time little cross-fertilization between them. But projective identification can be seen as an inner version of observable attachment and detachment behaviors. While Bowlby writes of healthy protest, Bion speaks of the capacity of the breast to contain negative projections, and to hand them back at a phase-appropriate moment. The paradox of projective identification is that without emotional investment in the other, without falling in love, without projecting one's own fantasies onto and into the other, intimacy cannot occur; yet it is this very projection that leads to the distortions of relationships from which we and our patients suffer. As I stated earlier, the aim of therapy is to move from static defenses to a dynamic movement between attachment and detachment, an interplay of illusion and disillusionment that leads eventually to what I call nonattachment.

NONATTACHMENT

So far I have suggested that in the course of therapy a number of paradoxical movements occur in relation to attachment and detachment. The patient has to be able to find her object but not to become fused with it; to let go of the object so as to get close to it; to detach herself from her object in order to realize its true nature; to attack her object in order to find her authentic self. Attachment and detachment are two sides of the same coin: thesis and antithesis in search of a synthesis or resolution. I have intoduced the term *nonattachment* to try to capture the essence of this superordinate position, which is not so much a philosophical category as a moral stance. On first hearing, the term *nonattachment* might appear to imply absolute detachment from the object. What I intend to convey, however, is the opposite—a nonpossessive, nonambivalent, autonomous, freely entered into attachment, in which the object is held and cherished but not controlled. Conversely, nonattachment transcends detachment in that it implies a separation from the object based on respect rather than anger or avoidance. The essential quality of nonattachment is illustrated by the following well-known, if somewhat sexist, Zen story (Reps 1971).

The Two Monks and the Beautiful Woman

> Two monks were traveling through the country when they came to a broad river. Beside its bank stood a beautiful woman, looking longingly at the far shore. "Please can you help me," she said, "I need to get across the river but it is too deep for me and I'm afraid I shall drown if I try on my own." Immediately the older monk picked her up on his back, carried her across the river, chatting amicably as he did so, and set her gently down on the farther side. They parted and the two monks continued on their way. After about an hour the younger monk could no longer contain himself: "Do you realize what you have done! It is absolutely forbidden for monks even to look at the opposite sex, let alone to pick them up and talk to them like that." "Ah, my friend," said the older one, "You are still carrying that woman. You must be tired. I put her down at the river bank an hour ago."

The older man's relation with the woman was one of non-attachment. He was able equally to pick her up and set her down, to attach and detach himself from her as the need—her need—arose, neither swayed by sexual desire, nor hidebound by scrupulosity.

Bion (1978), in his famous echo of T. S. Eliot's (1959) words on attachment and detachment, suggests that the analyst approach her patient in a state "beyond memory and desire"—that is, attached to neither the past nor the future. Truax and Carkhuff (1967) speak of empathy, honesty, and nonpossessive warmth, Stern (1985) and Stolorow and colleagues (1987) of attunement and empathic resonance, and Colthart (1993) of "Attention!" The essence of these phrases are that we have in some way emotionally to enter the here and now, the present moment (another Buddhist notion), which contains both the patient and ourselves, to immerse ourselves in it by following our own free associations, our emotional reactions to the patient. In short, in nonattachment, we have to become fully attached to the patient and her material, and then to be able with equal ease to detach ourselves, to reflect on what is being said, felt, or enacted by both parties.

Initially, especially with disturbed patients, this capacity for detached reflection (cf. the concept of reflexive self function [RSF] of Fonagy and colleagues [1994]), will be carried almost exclusively by the therapist. Acting as a selfobject the therapist is a symbiotic extension of the patient's mind. As therapy progresses, if all goes well, this function is gradually reclaimed by the patient, so that at termination two separate people face one another, each aware of the other as a person who has a mind of her own that contains the other.

A significant moment in my own development as a psychotherapist occurred when I realized that my wish to make my patients better was actually interfering with my ability to do so. I was overattached to the idea of cure and frightened of the aggressive implications of detachment. I was unable to synthesize attachment and detachment into a position of nonattachment, one in which I could see my narcissistic need to be a successful therapist for what it was, to balance therapeutic zeal with realism, and realize that ultimately what helps patients to get better is an impersonal force that I needed to recognize and align myself with but could not control.

What does this position of nonattachment mean in practice? Again, there have been various attempts to describe what the therapist should do with her mind in relation to the patient: "listening with the third ear" (Reik 1948); active receptiveness (Winnicott 1971); "evenly suspended attention" (Freud 1912). The therapist must be both active and passive, penetrative and containing, motherly and fatherly, in control but not controlling. I find the idea of focus helpful; one has to focus on the patient, while at the same time being aware of oneself focusing. An appropriate therapeutic mantra for nonattachment might be, "Focusing on the totality of the patient, and the totality of my response to the patient, I am aware that I am focusing on the patient and my response to her."

THE POETICS OF THE PRESENT MOMENT

Gallwey (1991) has coined the word *psychopoesis* to describe the transformation of raw experience into selfhood that is the essence of creative living. This is another version of Bion's (1978) alpha function, in which in the loving interplay between infant and caregiver a preconception becomes transformed into a conception. The idea of entering the present moment; the celebration of the everyday; the capacity to contemplate reality without desire; facing pain without masochistically being attached to it, or manically trying to deny it; and, by the use of words to make a narrative out of it that simultaneously creates a permanent attachment and enables one to become detached—these link psychotherapy and the poetic impulse. Wordsworth is perhaps the outstanding example of a poet who celebrated a relationship to nature and the everyday based on the synthesis of identification and detachment that I am calling nonattachment. Here is the motherless (but not sisterless—Dorothy Wordsworth was the unacknowledged silent presence who watched over much of his solitude [Davies 1980]) Wordsworth's idea of perfect happiness, in "Personal Talk":

> To sit *without emotion, hope or aim,*
> In the loved presence of my cottage-fire.
> And listen to the flapping of the flame
> Or kettle whispering its faint undersong. [my italics]

Psychotherapists must be able, at least in the session, to free themselves from envy, resentment or overidentification with their patients. Here, in "Two April Mornings" is Wordsworth's description of the release from envy in which a parent, bereaved in the month of April, can at last, ten years later, look on another little girl of the same age as his dead child and say:

> There came from me a sigh of pain
> Which I could ill confine
> I looked at her and looked again
> *And did not wish her mine.* [my italics]

A third well-known example from Wordsworth—his "renovating spots of time"—shows his appreciation of the present moment, and suggests how psychotherapy can provide necessary moments of retreat that later illuminate everyday living:

There are in our existence spots of time
That with distinct preeminence retain
A renovating virtue, whence our minds
Are nourished and invisibly repaired.

We shall now move from this picture of domestic quietude and contentment to the opposite pole, a discussion of how attachment ideas can inform our understanding of destructiveness and splitting.

Part II

Clinical Applications

4

Splitting and Attachment: The Scottish Connection in Psychotherapy

The scene: the canteen at the Tavistock Clinic; the time: the late 1980s; the characters: John Bowlby and Jock Sutherland, close friends for half a century, now in their late seventies and early eighties, respectively; silver-haired, vigorous, one on the small side, the other very tall; distinguished, successful, balanced, clever men; sitting face to face, deep in conversation. John, the more serious, meets Jock's eye with its eternal twinkle, wags his finger, and says, "Jock, you know that is a post-Freudian statement!" [Haldane 1993]

One of the aims of this book is to explore what a post-Freudian statement might mean, and to look at the contribution of attachment theory to a post-Freudian state of affairs. I shall approach the subject via the theme of splitting, which can be either creative or pathological. I suggested in Chapter 1 that the patterns of anxious attachment, although restricting in some ways, were also adaptive in that they help the individual to survive in a suboptimal environment. Similarly, in the search for new paradigms, innovative thought often requires a degree of splitting and isolation as necessary precursors of creativity and discovery. By contrast, during the phase of Kuhn's (1962) "normal science," isolation becomes stultifying and retards progress. The contrasting and complementary personalities of John Bowlby and his colleague Jock Sutherland epitomize these two aspects of innovation and consolidation.

I start with a well-known literary account of splitting; mention briefly Freud's break with the conventional neurology of his day; and then, through looking at work of Klein, Bowlby, Fairbairn, and Sutherland, discuss how splitting has emerged as a central issue in contemporary psychoanalytic thought.

The beginnings of psychoanalysis can be dated to a professional split that occurred in 1886 (Ellenberger 1970). Freud, just 30, newly married, returned from Paris full of Charcot's ideas, and presented a paper on male hysteria to the Viennese Society of Physicians. Freud's reception was less than enthusiastic. Austrian medical chauvinism was offended by his espousal of French ideas that, the medical elders claimed, contained nothing they did not know already. Freud, eager for fame and in need of money to settle down, was discouraged by this rejection; turning away from the medical establishment, he began, with the help of first Fliess and then Breuer, to invent the theory and practice of psychoanalysis.

STEVENSON

Meanwhile, also in 1886, another young man, a writer—this one Scottish rather than Jewish—also newly married and short of money, was living in Bournemouth in England (Holmes 1985). Like Freud, he was in the habit of attending closely to his dreams, which he used to furnish him with plots for stories, a mysterious process he attributed to his "Brownies" (Harman 1992a). One night he dreamed of a respectable doctor sitting unhappily at the window of his house, approached by two friends who ask him to come for a walk. At first he readily agrees, but suddenly he slams down the window "with an expression of such abject terror and despair as froze the very blood of the two gentlemen below" (Harman 1992b, p. ix). The dreamer cried out so much in his sleep that, much to his annoyance, his wife woke him up so that the rest of the story was lost. But the fragment, with two others that he could recall, was enough. He started writing furiously, and within three days the first draft of *Dr. Jekyll and Mr. Hyde*—the author was of course Robert Louis Stevenson—was completed.

Dr. Jekyll and Mr. Hyde (Harman 1992b) is the classic literary account of splitting, or, as Stevenson put it, of "man's double being"—multiple personality, somnambulism, and hypnotism being topics much in vogue in the 1880s, in literary as well as medical circles.

Looking at the story from a psychodynamic perspective, several themes immediately stand out. The episode at the window epitomizes the schizoid dilemma: Jekyll, lonely and troubled, longs for closeness, to tell someone what is happening to him; yet, when the possibility of doing so arises, he is smitten with terror and slams down the shutters of communication. The whole work, like a psychotherapeutic treatment, can be seen as a movement from secrecy and silence to open communication. The vehicle of this transformation is the quiet and receptive solicitor Utterson, whose name, like most in the story is highly significant (*Hyde*—*hide* is self-explanatory; *Jekyll* has *jackal* and *kill* hidden within its apparent innocuous respectability). It is Utterson's consistent concern that enables Jekyll eventually to utter his terrible tale of utmost ("utter") horror. Stevenson, too, was an "utter son"—a *puer eternus*, always a son, never a father—whose fateful break with his father's Calvinism was one of the turning points in his life, but whose genius for utterance, in words and on paper, were his salvation. Utterson's silent psychotherapeutic unobtrusiveness has the effect on his friends of "sobering their minds in the man's rich silence" (Stevenson 1886, p. 34), eventually enabling Jekyll to deliver his narrative in the form of a letter.

Hyde's crimes are usually thought of as murder, addiction, and lasciviousness, but the story opens with a horrific act in which, curiously, no one is seriously hurt. Running down a street, Hyde collides at the corner with a little girl coming in the opposite direction, and tramples on her. Her piteous screams and Hyde's indifference to them are what first alert Utterson to the man's evil nature.

Trampling on a child's feelings, an adult's indifference—this is the territory in which splitting arises. Jekyll, one might speculate, was somehow trampled on as a child and has split himself into two parts: a respectable, compliant, law-abiding part, and a hidden, vengeful part that compulsively now does to others what was done to himself. These unintegrated parts are symbolized in the story by the many different rooms that Jekyll inhabits, interconnecting in ways that emerge as the story unfolds, with the locked door or the ghastly operating theater turned laboratory finally smashed open by Utterson at the denouement. The avoidant individual similarly inhabits a divided house in which dependency needs, and his rage at their not being met are kept separate, as in the case of Bob in Chapter 1.

A striking feature of the story is the almost complete absence of female characters, and the same is true of *Treasure Island* and *Kidnapped*. The characters all appear to be bachelors, inhabiting a fog-bound Dickensian London world, a Gothicized version of the Edinburgh middle classes among whom Stevenson grew up: no wives, mothers, or other children (Stevenson, like Fairbairn, was an only child). The dynamic of Jekyll and Hyde is that of father and son. When Stevenson announced his atheism to his parents, his father responded by saying, "You have rendered my whole life a failure" (Holmes 1985). Hyde is consistently described as smaller than Jekyll, a child-man, who, at the end when he is unable to find the ingredients for the potion that will turn him once more into his creator, dresses up in Jekyll's clothes, which were

> enormously too large for him in every measurement—the trousers hanging on his legs and rolled up to keep them from the ground, the waist of the coat below his haunches, and the collar sprawling wide upon his shoulders. [Stevenson 1886, p. 32]

Here, unmistakably, is a little boy dressing up in father's clothes. The struggle between Jekyll and Hyde as each tries to claim supremacy at the end is the struggle between son and father: "Jekyll had more than a father's interest; Hyde had more than a son's indifference" (Stevenson 1886, p. 36). When Jekyll first takes the potion he feels a surge of liberation.

> Younger, lighter, happier in body . . . a heady recklessness, a current of disordered sensual images running like a mill-race in my fancy, a solution of the bonds of obligation, a leap of nature . . . this too was myself. . . . Strip off the lendings and spring headlong into a sea of liberty. [Stevenson 1886, p. 53]

This is in contrast to his bonded, dutiful, fettered self,

> I saw my life as a whole; I followed it up from the days of childhood, when I had walked with my father's hand, and through the self-denying toils of my professional life. [Stevenson 1886, p. 54]

Here we see Stevenson struggling with the irreconcilable split in his nature between ambition and pleasure, security and danger, between the wish for closeness but the fear of being trampled, the longing for freedom but the risk of being disinherited. Stevenson, a lifelong TB sufferer, ever conscious of the proximity of death, and the guilty possibility of punishment for his wish to escape from the coils of Calvinism, writes of "a creature eaten up and emptied by fever, solely occupied with one thought: the horror of my other self."

Reconciliation requires a female principle. For Stevenson his love of Fanny Osbourne, ten years his senior, a woman, as described in his *Chapter on Dreams* (Harman 1992a), married to another man, yet who loved him, but for whom he had to endure torture. A classical psychoanalytic interpretation of *Dr. Jekyll and Mr. Hyde* might focus on the oedipal struggle between father and son, the fear of castration, the masturbatory guilt (Jekyll seeing his hand, already betrayed to Utterson's clerk Guest by it, and realizing that for the first time he has not been able to expunge Hyde entirely)—"If I am the chief of sinners, I am the chief of sufferers also" (Stevenson 1886, p. 56). A contemporary perspective would emphasize how the schizoid split emerges from the lack of a container for Jekyll's rage and desire, which is therefore split off and projected into his alter ego.

The innovator, the creative schizoid, creates his own new forms. For Stevenson his dreaming, his creativity, the work itself, become the container that held together the discordant elements in his nature. Jekyll illustrates the dangers of the Frankensteinian project—the attempt to break the laws of nature by giving birth to oneself is doomed to failure. Only in death can the two split halves be united: "co-heir with him to death" (Stevenson 1886, p. 61). A world without women—and for Stevenson, the lighthouse builder's son, science was quintessentially a masculine enterprise—was doomed to perversity and horror:

> That insurgent horror was knit to him closer than a wife, closer than an eye; lay caged in his flesh, where he heard it mutter and felt it struggle to be born. . . . In the agonised womb of consciousness these polar twins should be continuously struggling. (Stevenson 1886, p. 63)

We see in Utterson, in Jim in *Treasure Island*, and in David in *Kidnapped* Stevenson's central ego, frail but determined, likable, loyal, ever-youthful and—with his Scottish father and English mother—stuggling to hold the divergent elements of his nature together. Like Jekyll:

> No more myself when I laid aside restraint and plunged in shame, than when I laboured, in the light of day, at the furtherance of knowledge or the relief of sorrow and suffering. (Stevenson 1886, p. 12)

In Stevenson's adventure stories the reader's sympathies are aroused more by the outlaws and blackguards—Silver and Breck and the highland clansmen—than with the forces of convention—Trelawny and the doctor, the Lowlanders, and the King's men. Innocents abroad, Jim and David are attracted first toward rebellion, and then reigned in by the need to survive and so conform. A similar polarity is played out between Jekyll and Hyde, which is no simplistic struggle between good and evil. Jekyll is portrayed, albeit sympathetically, as rather stuffy and a hypocrite: "I concealed my pleasures . . . committed to a profound duplicity of life" (Stevenson 1886, p. 66). Utterson, though good, is weak—an observer rather than an actor. Jekyll is attracted—and the reader is fascinated—by his alter ego, as an addict might be by his drug. As Hyde, he is free from conflict and doubt and can pursue his ruthless selfishness and hedonism, untroubled by conscience or guilt.

Stevenson was not alone in his concern with man's dual nature; the theme of the doppelgänger was part of the zeitgeist (Ellenberger 1970, Miller 1985). While the splitting in *Dr. Jekyll and Mr. Hyde* is entirely psychological, the adventure books represent splitting at a social level. In *Kidnapped* the division is between the Highlanders and the Lowlanders, between Jacobites and Loyalists, the gulf between them symbolized by the Firth of Forth. It is only with the help of a pretty peasant girl—the only "love interest" to appear in either book—that David and Breck manage to reach safety. The pirates in *Treasure Island* tear each other apart in their struggle to the death for the buried gold—the mother's love, the breast, which these men deprived of women want above all— outwitted in the end by Ben Gunn, the holy fool, another projection of Stevenson's, who as a sickly child had access to his mother's "treasure" without having to win it by fighting.

FREUD

Implicit in Stevenson then is the idea that man's dual nature is related in some way to the suppression of the female principle— his men are all in one way or another avoidant. They are out of touch with the feminine in themselves, just as avoidant children keep their distance from the nurturing object. Freud's project was to reconcile his clinical experience of splitting as manifest in the hysterics he had encountered at the Salpetriere clinics and in his consulting rooms at Berggasstrasse, with the Helmholtzian ideal of a scientific psychology. His early theorizing moved away from people and their interactions to the idea of psychic energy and its repression or expression. As Grotstein (1992) puts it:

> Due to the constraints of his cartesian logical positivism, [Freud] travelled down the biological road and not exclusively the psychological one. In brief, Freud took the vertical splits of the hysteric's double consciousness and, in effect, rotated them to the horizontal plane, thereby imposing the System Consciousness atop the System Unconsciousness. [Grotstein 1990, p. vi]

The Freudian model was thus predicated on dominance and submission. The two sides of Freud's nature—Freud the innovator and Freud the consolidator—can be seen in the shift in his thinking from his early topographical model of the mind with its emphasis on the liberation of repressed psychic energy, to his later tripartite model with its emphasis on the control of instinctual forces. For Freud the subversive, energy resided in the unconscious, kept at bay by the powers of repression. The aim of therapy was the gradual releasing of repression, or at least finding a compromise between the pleasure-seeking unconscious and the castrating reality principle. With the tripartite model of the mind, Freud moved away from a purely energetic conception of the mind to one that contained at least one prototypical person-like internal object—the superego, a residue of parental prohibitions and restrictions as imagined by the self. Now the therapeutic task is not so much lifting of repression as reducing the unrealistic demands of this superego and reclamation of the vast areas of submerged self expropriated by the unconscious: "Where id is there ego shall be" (Freud 1933, p. 80).

The therapeutic movement in Freud's metapsychology is mainly in the vertical plane, uncovering deeper and deeper layers of the psyche. But already in 1921, the year Freud was writing *The Ego and the Id*, Yeats had seen in the horizontal plane how in the face of increasing splitting the "center cannot hold." The beginnings of a significant shift in the metaphors and ambiance of psychoanalysis was under way: from the subjugation of unruly impulses to the holding together of a fragmenting and incoherent system. Let us look at how three psychoanalytic inheritors—Bowlby, Fairbairn, and Sutherland—carried forward the story of splitting into the contemporary era.

BOWLBY

John Bowlby's father came from exactly the class described by Stevenson. He was a successful London surgeon, a bachelor until he was 40, hard working, God-fearing, practical, and down to earth. Like Stevenson, Bowlby was rebellious and independent, but with an ambitious and conformist streak. During the war years Bowlby joined the War Officer Selection Boards, that "invisible college" of psychoanalysts and psychodynamic psychiatrists, headed by Jock Sutherland, that laid the foundations for psychodynamic psychiatry and psychotherapy after the war. Here the atmosphere was of openness and collaboration, in contrast to the esotericism of the psychoanalytic society at that time. Sutherland insisted that the selection boards be chaired by soldiers rather than psychiatrists; with his intuitive feel for group processes he saw that this would avoid the tendency to split off and marginalize psychological advice, and would, paradoxically, give the psychiatrists greater rather than less influence (Sutherland and Fitzpatrick 1944).

Sutherland and Bowlby emerged from the war as director and deputy director, respectively, of the Tavistock Clinic. They were a formidable pair: outstanding men in their different ways, close friends, at that time sharing a house together with their families in Hampstead. These were heady times of reparation and new vision. Sutherland soon set about building up the "Tavi" as an internationally known center for training in psychodynamic psychotherapy.

While repression, as originally conceptualized by Freud, is essentially intrapsychic, the concept of splitting is necessarily interpersonal since split-off emotions are projected on or into the subject's significant others. The theme of splitting emerges strongly from experimental studies of insecure attachment described in the previous chapters. We can begin to see links between intrapsychic splitting and its interpersonal context—between the Klein-Bion model, which focuses on the inner world, and the Bowlby-Ainsworth one, whose target is the interpersonal environment. Thus, to maintain some contact with his attachment figure the avoidant child has split off his wish for intimacy and anger about separation— the beginnings, in extreme cases perhaps, of a Jekyll and Hyde divide that may erupt in later life when the trampled turns the tables and becomes the trampler. A related splitting occurs in ambivalently attached infants. On separation these children cling unhappily to their parent for fear of losing them again, splitting off competence and autonomy that the child may feel need to be suppressed for fear of further rejection.

Main (1995) suggests that in peer groups, avoidant and ambivalent children can form a system of mutual projection: avoidants tending to be bullies, while ambivalents are their victims. A similar pattern can be found in sadomasochistic marriages. Each person projects into the other the disowned part of oneself, which he or she both envy and cannot relinquish. This aspect of interpersonal theory of splitting is illustrated by the following two examples.

Andrew: A Present-Day Hyde

> Andrew, a bricklayer, now 40, spent eleven years in prison after he followed an unknown woman back to her house from a bus stop and brutally attacked her with a knife, leaving her for dead. She dragged herself to a neighbor and eventually recovered. Andrew gave himself up to the police the next day. Subsequently he had little recollection of the event—"I just can't believe it was me that did that"—but did admit that he had been drinking heavily. His childhood was deeply unhappy. There were eight children, four boys and four girls. His parents fought incessantly, and the children were recruited as allies, with the boys on their father's side, the girls on their mother's; neither side was permitted to speak to the other for days on end. When Andrew was 16 his mother developed lung

cancer, and over the next two years he watched her die a horrible death. Soon after her death he wandered away from home and lost all contact with his family. He married and had a child, but was unhappy. As the rows with his wife escalated he started to drink and it was then that the offense occurred. After a few years in prison he was transferred to Grendon Underwood, an unique experimental prison unit run on psychotherapeutic lines. There he learned that it was possible to talk about emotions. He discovered that he existed as a person, he said, and that other people also had feelings: "I went into Grendon Underwood an animal and came out a man." While he was there he fell in love with his prison visitor and after his release they married and had a daughter. He remained on indefinite parole. The marriage broke up, but they remained on good terms and he was devoted to his daughter. He asked for further help when he began to detect in himself the beginnings of the feelings of depression and violence, which he said had preceded the attack.

Andrew's attack contained the naked rage of a split-off infantile part of his personality when separated from his loved object—a typical avoidant/unresolved pattern. The separation started with the parental fights in childhood, and was tragically reinforced by his mother's death. As his first marriage began to fail the same feeling of schizoid isolation reemerged. The attack was also an enactment of the experience of violent rejection in childhood that often underlies avoidant attachment—like Hyde, the trampled turning trampler.

Vivienne: The Lady and The Tramp

Vivienne was in her mid-fifties, a highly respectable solicitor's wife who had grown up in a large working-class family whose lives revolved around a fundamentalist religious sect. She was close to her mother, but had terrible fights with her father in her teens when she had wanted to wear makeup and go to discos. When at 16 he caught her kissing a boy good-night on the doorstep she was beaten mercilessly. The next day she left home, not to return until his death some ten years later. Meanwhile she found a job in a solicitor's office and gradually a new personality emerged in which, Galatea-like, she acquired the airs and graces of a lady. She married a junior partner in the firm and, despite his many inexplicable absences on business, was devoted to him. They got on well as companions, but their sexual relationship never worked: he seemed to hold back and she was unable to let him know how strongly she desired him. Gradually she began to feel discontented and depressed. Feelings were never discussed between them; they continued to have dinner parties, play golf, and were stalwarts of the rotary club. Then she became convinced that her husband was having an affair with one of the secretaries at work. She challenged him about this but, as always, he remained silent. Word got back to her confirming her suspicions. She became wild with jealousy and fury, and tried to leave the marriage but could not bring herself to do so. Then, one evening, without really realizing what she was doing she put on a scruffy duffle coat of her son's, pulled a woolen cap over her head, put on some muddy boots, and left the house. She found herself drawn to her rival's home. There, outside her door was a shining white car. She picked up a rock and scratched the car all the way around, ending by smashing the windshield. She was not found out and, emboldened, she continued to enact her alter ego from time to time, especially when upset, often going to supermarkets and shoplifting, sometimes going into rough pubs and picking up men.

Finally, with the marriage in tatters, her husband insisted that they talk and seek help. The whole story came out, with much guilt and many tears, but also a note of triumph and glee in Vivienne's demeanor. Her husband had also split himself—ever kind and considerate on the surface, but full of misery and rage inside.

In her ambivalent attachment Vivienne had clung to her avoidant husband, while the rebellious side of her, which had erupted briefly in her adolescence when she left home, was split off into the tramp.

In both cases it was only when a suitable container had been found that these patients could begin to tell their story—for Andrew it was a benign institution, Grendon Underwood; for Vivienne it was the setting of psychotherapy. The process of therapy, the healing of splits, requires the finding of a center that *can* hold—in Bowlbian terms finding a secure base in which split-off affects can be first felt, and then put into words.

FAIRBAIRN

If Bowlby challenged the Kleinian view through observation and experiment, it was Ronald Fairbairn who questioned and extended Kleinian theory.

Bowlby and Fairbairn were both struggling with the constricting atmosphere of religion and middle-class mores in which they had been brought up. They found in psychoanalysis a system of thought powerful enough to rival these values, which at the same time provided both an account of their rebellion and a therapy to help resolve it. Both men had powerful, rigid, and successful fathers; their mothers showed features of "affectionless control" (Parker 1983), which can be precursor of avoidant (or, in Fairbairn's terms, schizoid) attachment (Sutherland 1991).

Bowlby was essentially a man of action and was always more at home with observable behavior than with hypothesized feelings. Fairbairn, by contrast, was a man of contemplation, who, because of his difficulty in micturition in public—a symptom he shared with his father and which neither managed to overcome—found it difficult to travel far away from home. But Fairbairn was a fearless inner traveler, and, in his relative isolation from the psychoanalytic mainstream, had no hesitation in discarding Freud's ideas where he thought them wrong, producing the most radical statement of object relations theory available (Greenberg and Mitchell 1983).

Fairbairn discarded drive theory altogether. Anticipating the findings of developmental psychology (Stern 1985), he saw the mother and infant interacting with one another as people from the moment of birth. Pleasure was a "signpost to the object," rather than the other way about, as Freud originally conceived it. (It is perhaps significant that both Bowlby and Fairbairn were not particularly sensual men, and both tended to downplay the importance of pleasure and sexuality in their theorizing). Fairbairn saw splitting as a fundamental defense, not as Klein imagined due to innate destructiveness, but as a response to environmental failure. The child represses not just his own impulses (which was Freud's view) but also internalized bad objects such as the mother who frustrates and rejects.

Andrew's attack could be seen not just as a desperate attempt to find a container for his unprocessed feelings of rage, but also as an eruption into consciousness of the painful feelings about the rejecting and later dying mother, projected into the unknown woman. Similarly, women who have been sexually abused as children will often choose as partners abusive men, and may evoke a psychologically abusive transference with their caregivers. It is as though there is a compusion to find an object with whom the drama of attachment—however painful—may be reenacted.

For Fairbairn, what is repressed is not just an impulse, but a whole dynamic structure comprising the affect, the ego that feels and responds to it, the relationship to the object to which it is directed, and the resulting behaviors. Split-off dynamic structures cannot be modified by the impact of external reality, especially the soothing and modulating influence of the mother; they become sequestered, and when released they emerge in a primitive and often destructive form. This viewpoint links Fairbairn with contemporary integrative models of psychotherapy like those of Ryle (1995) and Weston (1992), which combine psychoanalytic and cognitive perspectives. They postulate a reciprocal relationship between affects and cognitions, the latter having a soothing and shaping effect on the former. For Fairbairn the split is within the ego itself, not between conscious and unconscious, or between ego and id. This splitting of the ego may be more or less organized, ranging from a vague sense of separate selves or parts of the self, through subpersonalities, to the Jekyll-and-Hyde–like phenomenon of multiple personality.

Fairbairn's position led him to a radically different view of dreams from that of Freud, much more akin to Jung's, and one that I believe most analytic psychotherapists use in practice, whatever their theoretical allegiance. As Fairbairn (1952) puts it,

> Dreams, and for that matter waking phantasies . . . [are] essentially *dramatizations* of endospychic situations involving both (a) relationships between ego-structures and internalized objects and (b) interrelationships between ego-structures themselves. [p. 170, my italics]

Stevenson's window dream dramatizes his longing for closeness and companionship, and his dread of it—his wish to be close to his internalized mother, but his fear that to get close would unleash all the rage and fury he felt in response to her rejection. The pulled-down window represents the typical schizoid or avoidant defense. Fairbairn had been thoroughly thrashed by his mother as punishment for an episode of sexual curiosity with his cousin, and on another occasion for asking questions about a blood-stained sanitary towel. Had he dreamed Stevenson's dream—as he well might—it would have encapsulated the schizoid conflict based on the feeling that his love is inherently destructive.

Fairbairn was also ahead of his time in seeing beyond the Oedipus complex to a more basic internal conflict between the exciting and rejecting mother, projected in the older child onto the actual mother and father, respectively, without needing to postulate, as Klein did, a precocious neonatal knowledge of adult relationships and genitalia.

Fairbairn disliked the term *analysis*, and thought *synthesis* would have been a better term for the integration of split selves that he saw as the essential therapeutic aim. For Fairbairn the neurotic is trapped within a closed system, and the task of the therapy is to transform this into an open interpersonal system. He emphasized the real contribution of the therapist—her empathic understanding, reliability, beneficence, and acceptance, leading to a reduction in hatred and therefore a diminished need for splitting. Patient and therapist are seen as an attachment system, and the need for sensitive attunement is inherent in his view of the successful therapeutic process.

Behind his closed window, Jekyll is a caricature of the evil genius of modern science. Fairbairn and Bowlby are good examples of "positive splitting." By remaining geographically and intellectually at a distance from psychoanalytic hurly-burly, Fairbairn was able to develop his own conceptual framework open-mindedly, with no pressure to adopt any particular line or dogma. Similarly, Bowlby continued to use psychoanalytic ideas creatively throughout his working life, integrating them with those of systems theory and developmental psychology without being too concerned about whose vested interests he would be threatening. The British Psychoanalytic Society of the 1950s and 1960s was, by contrast, a closed system that split off its dissidents, viewing them as "internal saboteurs" (to use Fairbairn's phrase) that were at best ignored, or at worst expelled.

SUTHERLAND

Bowlby was an experimentalist using psychoanalytic ideas to understand human development; Fairbairn was a theoretician determined to improve and extend the psychoanalytically based model of the mind. Jock Sutherland saw the potential of psychoanalysis to help understand group dynamics and influence social policy.

Sutherland seems to have been a natural group leader. Tall, good looking, cultured, immensely hardworking, liked by almost everyone, very amusing with a capacity to use humor to defuse difficult situations, his energy is testified by a career that spanned sixty years. No sooner did he complete one phase than he was on to the next: graduate psychology student, medical student, psychoanalytic candidate, chairman of the War Office Selection Boards, director of the Tavistock Clinic, founder of the Scottish Institute for Human Relations, visiting professor at the Menninger Clinic, and, in his eighties, producing his first full-length book, the biography of Fairbairn. Sutherland brought a remarkable consistency and coherence to whatever problem he was considering, whether it was the selection of officers for the army, the relationship of a patient to his analyst, the role of a psychotherapeutic clinic in the National Health Service, or the position of the central self vis-à-vis its subselves.

Fairbairn and Klein were interested in the way in which outer reality was influenced by the inner world, Bowlby with the impact of that outer world on the developing personality. Sutherland, who possessed "outsight" (Holmes 1992) as well as insight was concerned with the interplay and interdependence of outer and inner, especially within organizations.

Sutherland starts from a basic faith in the supportive and healing power of social groups: "Man as a person is sustained by his social relatedness" (Sutherland 1966, p. 343). Like Bowlby, he thought systemically as well as psychoanalytically, and had been influenced by Kurt Lewin's ideas on the social field (King 1989). He visualized a system as having central "organizing principles" (Sutherland 1980), as needing a well-organized hierarchy if these are to be realized, and he saw above all the need for open communication between different parts of the system. He thought in terms of selves rather than egos and emphasized the "powerful urge of the self to possess its autonomy" (Sutherland 1991, p. 166). His psychoanalytic perspective led him to see early environmental failure resulting in internal bad objects, but his systemic view enabled him to see that these failures can be counteracted by a healthily functioning family and social group system—another point that has subsequently been confirmed experimentally (Rutter 1985):

> Outer objects tend to be perceived in terms of inner ones.
> Normally, however, the outer objects do not behave as badly

as the inner ones. When the former are introjected again
they are therefore less presecutory: social learning occurs.
[Sutherland 1971, p. 111]

But when affect is too disturbing, either because of its intensity or because of the failure of the social group to contain it, "inner
objects are split off and are unmodified by external reality" (Sutherland 1971, p. 72). This leads to impoverishment of the central ego,
and to the Hyde-like possibility of enactment of these unmodulated
roles and affects.

In psychotherapy this hidden aspect of the self is evoked by
the relationship with the analyst, who has to create sufficient intensity for the split-off affect to be reexperienced but not to be
overwhelming. If the therapist can then respond in an accepting,
but not indulgent way, bad affects and roles no longer need to be
split off but can be integrated into the personality. The therapist
acts like an effective parent, neither intruding upon nor neglecting the patient's feelings, and by his modulatory response enabling
affect to be contained within the envelope of the patient's autonomous self. Once again we will return to the case of Katherine to
illustrate this point.

Katherine (Continued): The Gendered Self

Katherine was all too aware of the futility to which Fairbairn
was so sensitive. After splitting up with her husband in Australia she had returned to look after her octogenarian mother,
with whom she found it impossible to communicate in any
meaningful way, but to whom she still felt deeply tied. To
recapitulate: She had had an unusual and very unhappy childhood. Her parents had owned a small school in the 1930s, in
theory idyllic, but the reality, at least for Katherine, was very
different. In the course of therapy she began to recover some
positive memories of her mother's stroking her, but then she
had been removed from her parent's part of the house at the

age of 3 and placed in the dormitory with other pupils: "I was cast into outer darkness." Typically for ambivalent children, no protest was permissible. Her mother, who had been crippled with polio, became remote and unavailable; she refused to kiss or cuddle her own children, as she said this would make the other children jealous. Her father beat and sexually abused her, as he did several of the other pupils. The transference soon reproduced her family situation. The therapist was seen either as a cruel and heartless father who intruded on her and caused her unbearable pain with his interpretations, or as a benign version of the all-powerful father who could, if only he would, set everything to rights with his perfect understanding, love, and admiration. At other times he was the crippled mother who was indifferent to her daughter's cries for help. On one occasion when she was again insisting that the therapist should help her more, she said that there was a "big part" of her missing. He commented that perhaps what she was out of touch with was her womanliness; she had been unable to identify with her mother's femininity because of her rejection, and also because her mother had not felt confident with this aspect of herself. Perhaps what terrified her was the thought that she might have some aspect of her abusive father alive inside her. Could "big part" represent the genital that had abused her? She was amused by this, immediately having an image of herself wearing a codpiece; at the next session she said she had felt much more herself for a few days after this episode.

Katherine exemplifies the clinical reality of splitting of the ego—the horse self, the crippled mother self, the persecuting and persecuted self in relation to her father—and the way in which these were evoked in therapy. It illustrates the therapist's attempt to help the patient get in touch with a central integrative self, which is almost invariably a *gendered* self. With the interpretation of her womanliness she moved from seeing herself *as* a woman to the thought "I *am* a woman." Here, momentarily, was a true meeting of therapist and patient—it was the coming together of tone, timing, content, and receptiveness that made this interpretation helpful. Similar things had been said before with little impact.

Jekyll's monstrous creation of Hyde from within himself is an aberration, a schizoid defense against unattuned desires. When, too late, he finally finds his voice in his last letter to Utterson, his two halves come together in death. At this therapeutic nodal point Katherine could see her split selves as springing from a secure unitary biological core; she could see the possibility of integrating the many false selves which she had created and to which, temporarily at least, she was no longer in thrall.

Sutherland had a subtle appreciation of psychotherapy's role in society. Just as the task of the central self is to integrate subselves into a network of intercommunicating parts of the personality, so the job of the psychotherapy clinic is that of a secure base that can provide training, teaching, and monitoring in relation to other agencies such as psychiatry and social work:

> The psychotherapeutic clinic has a unique role as a control mechanism picking up critical data on damage done within the current social processes. Use cannot be made of the role, however, unless the clinic is integrated with a wider group of institutions in the community. . . . The location of the clinic within its social space therefore assumes a new importance. . . . It has to become one component within a constellation of units— an institute or school of human relations . . . which together share the task of advising on the means to a better society. [Sutherland 1966, p. 345]

In Sutherland's organizational model there are three essential principles, each of which is democratic rather than hegemonic; psychoanalysis is emphatically not seen in some imperial role extending its powers of domination thoughout its kingdom. First, the deliverers of care—family doctors, psychiatrists, social workers —are seen as central, just as in War Office Selection Boards the army remained in control, with the psychoanalysts in an advisory role. This model is vitally different from the view not uncommonly held in psychoanalytic circles of "psychoanalysis unlimited." As Sutherland (1971) put it,

> The attitude sometimes conveyed by psychoanalysts that this kind of work [i.e., social work] is a poor substitute for what more thorough-going analysis might achieve is more a professional fantasy than an established fact. [p. 75]

Second, his model is pluralistic; psychoanalysis works alongside marital therapy (Sutherland set up and continued to be closely involved with the Tavistock Institute for Marital Studies throughout his career), family therapy, group therapy, and social therapies as part of a therapeutic team in which each member has its own unique contribution. Third, his model is open; there has to be open and continuous communication between the center and the periphery.

With his open-minded attitude, working predominantly within the National Health Service—whose dynamics as an organization was another area where Sutherland made an important contribution—rather than the private sector, and through his appreciation of sociological and systemic approaches as well as psychoanalytic, Sutherland succeeded in throwing open the window of the stuffy intrigue-filled rooms of psychoanalysis. His aim of creating a relationship of mutual respect between psychoanalysis and psychotherapy, psychiatry, social work, and the other helping professions is a continuing source of inspiration and struggle. Without explicitly espousing it, his attitudes embodied the principles of secure attachment: responsiveness and the calm exploration of protest and difference.

CONCLUSION

Running through this chapter there have been two interrelated themes that I will now summarize.

Post-Freudian Theory

We can imagine that the post-Freudian remark for which Bowlby was accusing—or perhaps complimenting—Sutherland represented his wish to integrate the psychoanalytic perspective with the emerging attachment paradigm. I suggested in Part I that regulation of affect in the parent–child relationship is a crucial determinant of secure or insecure attachment. Mothers who can modulate their infant's primitive emotions of excitement, rage, disappointment, satiation, boredom, and resistiveness enable the infant to integrate emotion into the developing self—Sutherland's "organizing principle."

The classical "triangle of defense" (Malan 1979), in which the aim of therapy is the uncovering of a hidden impulse, whose surface manifestation is anxiety, needs to be replaced with a "triangle of affect." Underlying neurotic disorders is not so much a repressed sexual or aggressive impulse as a split-off feeling and its relational context. In infancy and childhood modulation leads to integration, while failure of maternal responsiveness results in defensive avoidance of feelings in order to maintain some sort of contact with the object. These feelings are thus not subject to the modifying influence of reality. This can result in later life in Hyde-like explosions of primitive affect; disowning of exploratory competence; or projection of parts of the self, resulting in a hostile worldview and feelings of inner impoverishment or futility.

This leads to a model of psychotherapy in which regulation of affect becomes the central theme. "Where id is, there ego shall be" is interpreted as bringing the impersonal "it" (i.e., unmodulated, unprocessed affect) within the orbit of the autonomous active experiencing self (cf. Eagle 1984) via relational experience. The main function of transference is to evoke and reexperience split-off affect, which is then available to the modulatory influence of the therapeutic process. The timing and tone of interpretations is as important as their content since their therapeutic effect depends on their capacity to promote the modulation and maturation of primitive affective states. The modulatory influence comprises the impact of the setting, the soothing and accepting response of the therapist, and the efforts of the patient to comprehend painful feelings.

The aim of therapy is, through the discovery of meanings, the integration of experience into a shared narrative between patient and therapist. The therapy oscillates between the formation of an attachment bond and the developing story of that attachment. Painful losses are neither denied nor overwhelming. The importance of a shared narrative is underpinned by the observation that autobiographical competence is a mark of secure attachment. Narrative capacity requires a containing boundary and a sense of continuity across time—a movement from the past, however painful, through the present toward the future. Splitting arises where no common boundary between attached and attachment figure can be found, or where the rupture between the generations is so great that no continuity in time can be established.

Splitting and Pluralism

Contemporary societies face increasing fragmentation and splitting along lines of class, race, wealth, religion, and geography. A "confusion of tongues" (Ferenczi 1932) is similarly to be found within psychotherapy as different forms of therapy proliferate and compete. Psychological splitting is a commonplace of current psychotherapeutic practice. The attempt to resolve splitting by a vertical model, in which a dominant authority brings recalcitrant fragments under its sway, is no longer to be relied upon. Whether it is the dominance of one nation by another, of the psychotherapy movement by psychoanalysis, or of the self by a harsh superego, integration will not be achieved that way. A pluralistic politics and a pluralistic psychology are urgently needed, embodying the systemic principles of firm boundaries combined with open communication based on mutual recognition and respect. The Bowlbian categories of avoidance and ambivalence capture the two catastrophic ends of these dilemmas. Avoidance leads to isolation, lack of communication, mutual suspicion, and unprovoked aggression;

ambivalence, based on intrusive contempt for boundaries leads to helplessness and fear of assertiveness, which is experienced as biting of the helping/feeding hand.

Bowlby's drive toward the post-Freudian thought exemplifies benign splitting in which new ideas are forged in situations of relative isolation. Sutherland was the great reconciler, seeing the need for a collaborative relationship between different approaches, each retaining its identity but allowing for cross-fertilization.

Sutherland and Bowlby combined their pluralistic nonsectarian message with strong tribal loyalties. Bowlby was equally at home in the sophistication of Hampstead as in the wilds of Skye; he would have been lost without either. Each Hogmanay (New Year's Eve) the Sutherlands would give a huge party with vast supplies of food and whiskey and lots of reel-dancing. Sutherland had a great respect for tradition but was never hidebound by it.

Sutherland saw that psychoanalysis had most to offer the psychotherapy community when it develops an interactive relationship with other institutions. The attempt to dominate the helping professions is based on an omnipotent fantasy and leads to unrealistic wish-fulfilling dreams; the avoidance of the rest of the psychological community leads to sequestration and a closed society. Like a good parent, psychotherapeutic institutions need to offer attunement, modulation, regulation, communication, instruction, and example, not domination or avoidance.

CODA

Both Bowlby and Sutherland were "utter sons," returning at the end of their lives, near their journey's end, to tell the stories of the explorers who had influenced them as young men (Haldane and Trist 1992): for Bowlby, Darwin; for Sutherland, Fairbairn. Each brought to their subject some reverence, but also an empathic understanding of their specific sufferings, limitations, and weaknesses. The pluralistic spirit that Bowlby and Sutherland represent requires a respect for the tradition and often painful experience of each unique strand in a common society. If Jekyll had been able to face and accept his Hyde-self there would have been no need for them to split apart. Bowlby and Sutherland were seeking a wider or even universal message, but never lost a sense of rootedness— in the body, in a locality, in history. Like good psychoanalysts, by celebrating the patterns and particularity of the past, their work points us to the future. They saw how, in Rilke's (1964) words,

> As a traveler
> On the last hill, for the last time seeing
> All their home valley, turns, and stands, and lingers,
> So we live, forever taking leave.

5

Attachment Theory and Supportive Psychotherapy

Supportive psychotherapy has long been the poor relation of the psychotherapies, a Cinderella (Sullivan 1953) stuck at home doing the routine psychiatric chores while her more glamorous psychotherapeutic sisters are away at the ball. In this chapter I shall suggest that attachment theory may be the much-needed fairy godmother for supportive psychotherapy. Other analogies suggest themselves. The friendly but rather dim giant, Atlas, was tricked into supporting the world indefinitely when his sly companion asked him to take over for a few minutes; he remained there for eternity! The very word *support* has music-hall overtones, evoking the image of a truss, a cumbersome and noncurative holding operation, much inferior to a definitive hernia repair.

This downgrading has come from two very different directions. Freud was keen to differentiate his new discipline of psychoanalysis from the prevailing psychotherapies of his day, hypnotherapy and mesmerism. He contrasted the curative factors of interpretation and insight with hypnotic suggestion—that is, benign advice made effective by the power of the hypnotherapist over his subject—and *rapport*, a term used by Mesmer to describe the supposed curative current passing from therapist to patient

(Ellenberger 1970). As a result "widespread disdain" (Winston et al. 1986) has been the prevalent psychoanalytic attitude toward supportive psychotherapy. On the other side, biological psychiatry has been keen to emphasize the power and specificity of its treatments, and to relegate the implicit support that is needed if pharmacological therapies are to be delivered effectively to the vague realms of "placebology" (Shepherd 1979) and the doctor–patient relationship. Faced with these powerful opponents, and lacking a secure theoretical base of its own, supportive therapy has been content with its subservient role, despite being arguably the most widely practiced form of psychotherapy. Here attachment theory has a significant contribution to make since it can offer a theoretical perspective on support, which both traditional psychoanalysis and psychiatry have eschewed.

Recently there has been a distinct, if modest, change of attitude (Pine 1986, Rockland 1989, 1992, Werman 1984, Winston et al. 1986). Psychotherapists have begun to acknowledge the limitations of "pure" psychoanalysis for treating difficult and disturbed patients and the comparative efficacy of supportive psychotherapy with these patients (Wallerstein 1986). General psychiatrists have begun to examine and value the informal psychotherapeutic content of their contact with patients (Andrews 1993). The need for psychiatrists to be trained in forms of psychotherapy appropriate to their role in the multidisciplinary mental health team has been highlighted (Grant et al. 1993).

The robust research finding that a positive therapeutic alliance, which can be understood as secure attachment, is probably the best overall predictor of good outcome in psychotherapy (Orlinsky and Howard 1986) has helped to rehabilitate both rapport and suggestion. As the economic climate demands that psychotherapists define more clearly the precise nature of their treatments, so supportive psychotherapy (ST) has moved from its previously backstage role to being a full (albeit minor and often understudying) member of the psychotherapeutic cast. ST can be seen as occupying an important middle ground between formal psychotherapies such as analytic or cognitive-behavioral on the one hand, and the routine clinical management of mainstream psychiatry on the other.

THE SPECTRUM OF
PSYCHOTHERAPEUTIC INTERVENTIONS

Supportive psychotherapy is notoriously difficult to define. A fundamental distinction is between the supportive component of all psychotherapies, and supportive psychotherapy as a specific mode of treatment for a particular group of patients. This may be compared with invisible foundations upon which all buildings rest, and the external buttresses that some, especially those in poor condition, require.

Purity of technique in psychotherapy is usually honored more often in the breach than the observance. Although psychoanalysis may characterize itself as a therapy that relies exclusively on transference and interpretation, in practice what goes on is much more complex, theorists often projecting the more eclectic aspects of their own practice into denigrated therapies such as supportive or behavioral therapies, perhaps to reinforce the precarious self-esteem and threatened status of their own discipline.

Greenson (1967) defined a spectrum of psychotherapeutic interventions including empathy, acknowledgment, clarification, challenge, interpretation, transference, and nontransference. Building on this Luborsky (1984) saw the psychotherapies as comprising a number of types ranging from supportive to expressive, with intermediate forms such as supportive-expressive or expressive-supportive, depending on the overall atmosphere of the therapy. Similarly, Shapiro and Firth (1987) describe an expressive-prescriptive spectrum to characterize the differences between dynamic and cognitive-behavioral interventions.

In short, the three components of *support*, *directiveness*, and *expressiveness* are to be found in all psychotherapies. The proportion of them varies, but few therapies exist in pure culture. Freud, for example, was certainly not above giving advice, especially in his more intractable cases of obsessional neurosis or impotence (Roazen 1973). As they take on longer and more complex cases, cognitive-behavioral therapists are beginning to take account of transference (Beck and Freeman 1990). Also, psychoanalysts, in a way that cognitive therapists would feel quite at home with, correct their patient's misperceptions (Segal 1991), as well as interpret the transference. All are, in differing ways, supportive.

SUPPORTIVE PSYCHOTHERAPY AS A SPECIFIC MODE OF THERAPY

Supportive psychotherapy then is an implicit component of all psychotherapies and comprises the regularity, reliability, and attentiveness of the therapist toward the patient, and the working alliance between them. It is also a specific mode of therapy in which these features occupy the foreground, and in which interpretation and behavioral direction play secondary roles. Supportive psychotherapy as a specific mode of therapy usually describes two rather different clinical interventions (Bloch 1995). The first is the brief support that can be offered to basically healthy individuals or families who are suffering from an acute trauma or crisis such as bereavement. Here there is a great overlap between Rogerian counseling and supportive psychotherapy. The second is as a long-term treatment offered to a group of quite disturbed individuals for whom ST, as opposed to other forms of therapy, is the treatment of choice. One of the problems in defining ST, which accounts for its rather blurred identity, is that it tends to be defined negatively, more easily described by what it is *not* than what it is—ultimately, a treatment for patients who are unsuitable for any other type of therapy. To redress this prejudice, Rockland (1987) has described psychodynamically oriented supportive psychotherapy (POST), and Holmes (1992) supportive analytic therapy (SAT).

A distinct divergence between the American and the British literature should be noted. For Rockwell (1989) and Werman (1982) supportive psychotherapy is defined against a backdrop of a predominantly psychoanalytic psychotherapeutic culture. Anything less than "full," that is, four or five times per week, analysis is seen as supportive. Rockwell's benchmark for frequency in supportive psychotherapy is once or even twice weekly 50-minute sessions. What he calls supportive psychotherapy would in Britain probably be characterized as psychoanalytic psychotherapy (Holmes and Crown 1996). In Britain supportive psychotherapy more often implies therapy conducted less than once a week—biweekly, monthly, or even once every two months, lasting from 20 to 50 minutes. But, like any therapy, ST cannot be entirely defined by its frequency. It is the aims, atmosphere, and techniques of the therapy that makes it supportive rather than analytic or directive.

THEORIES OF SUPPORT

Support often makes it presence known by its subsequent absence. Only when our lower limbs or the foundations of our dwellings develop problems do we become grateful for the support they normally provide. Moving concentrically from inner to outer, support derives from psychological defenses, intimate relationships, behavioral routines, and social roles. Psychiatric illness is typically associated with difficulty at each of these levels: defenses inadequate or overcontrolled, relationships absent or unempathic, routines chaotic or overly rigid, and social roles ill-defined or nonexistent.

Fairly general agreement is to be found about the various techniques of ST (see below), most aiming to intervene at one or another of these levels. There is, however, less unanimity about the theoretical basis of ST, which may contribute to its rather fuzzy status and role. Crown (1988), for example, sees ST as inherently eclectic, drawing on a mixture of common sense, Rogerian counseling, cognitive-behavioral strategies, systemic approaches, and psychoanalysis. Similarly Pinsker (1994) sees ST as a "shell program" (a computer metaphor) without a theoretical basis of its own that, shell-like, fits over most psychotherapies. A number of common theoretical strands can however be identified as providing the theoretical basis for support within psychotherapy.

Ego Psychology and ST

Ego psychology is based on Freud's tripartite structural model of the mind (Bateman and Holmes 1995, Freud 1923) in which the ego is a mediator between id impulses, the demands of reality, and the strictures of the superego. It takes as its starting point Freud's definition of neurosis as a "turning away from reality" (Freud 1924). The aim of psychotherapy, whether supportive or otherwise, is to help the patient make a better adjustment to reality. In expressive therapy this is done by strengthening the ego, through a "pupation" model in which primitive and maladaptive defenses are, through regression (Balint 1959), discarded, while more mature, flexible, and better-adapted ones are developed (Valliant 1977). Insight and interpretation help strengthen the ego's "control function" (Horowitz 1988).

Supportive therapy, by contrast, accepts the ego more or less as it is, and aims to improve adaptation by modifying the demands made upon it. The patient is encouraged to expose herself to less stress (external reality), to be less self-critical (superego), and, where possible, to repress instinctual demands (id). Thus a chronically dysthymic patient who feels she *should* work, and who berates herself for not doing so, may be encouraged to see her illness as no less incapacitating than a physical disability and to feel she is entitled to social support. Similarly, a couple whose sex life has dwindled may be urged to consider the positive nonsexual aspects of their relationship and to recall past sexual enjoyment rather than hark endlessly upon what is lacking.

Attachment Theory and the "Real" Relationship with the Therapist

Ego psychology is predominantly an intrapsychic theory. As discussed in Chapter 2, attachment theory (Bowlby 1988, Heard and Lake 1986, Holmes 1993) arose in part as an attempt to provide a more relational or interpersonal basis for psychotherapy. As such it readily offers a theoretical basis for the role of support in psychotherapy. Attachment theory suggests that there is a lifelong psychobiological need for proximity to attachment figures at times of stress, illness, and exhaustion. Attachment behavior is inherently supportive, enabling us to recharge our batteries before returning to the adaptive fray. The regularity, punctuality, reliability, and nonjudgmental acceptance of the therapist and the therapeutic setting provide stability and support that may well be lacking in the rest of the patient's life. The sense of therapeutic space and time that is exclusively "there" for the patient is a central psychotherapeutic theme, and may be contrasted with medical practice at its worst, in which clinics run late, traffic jams make home visits unpredictable, junior staff rotate all too frequently, and senior staff are increasingly tempted to neglect clinical responsibilities in favor of managerial imperatives.

Secure attachment is mediated by effective communication. The attunement and empathy of the caregiver to the infant is based on the ability to "read" the child's affective states and preverbal communicative efforts. As parent and child get to know one another, a store of shared memories, or reciprocal interactions that have been generalized (RIGs) (Stern 1985), is built up. Once speech is established, secure attachment is closely linked first to "event scripts" (Byng-Hall 1995), which are regularly repeated interactive sequences, and then to evolving self-narratives as the child develops a personal, family, and social identity. As I have described in Part I, a similar sequence can be observed in psychotherapy: as treatment progresses, patient and therapist develop a shared narrative, with the therapist acting as a memory store, often to the surprise and delight of the patient. Here at last is someone who "knows" her. The emergence of a structure of meaning from apparently inchoate emotions and events is itself a source of support. The therapist is witness and pattern maker to the patient's distress.

From the perspective of attachment theory psychotherapy is, or should be, inherently supportive. It is hard to imagine much success for a therapy that defined itself as "unsupportive psychotherapy," although some dynamic therapists will warn the patient that they may feel a lot worse before they begin to feel better. Yet Crown (1988), contrasting dynamic (i.e., psychoanalytic) therapy and ST, argues that "if it is supportive it cannot be psychotherapy; if it is psychotherapy it cannot be supportive" (p. 267). How then do we account for the apparent incompatibility between psychoanalytic psychotherapy and support?

This can be answered in a number of ways. First, as already mentioned, there was the historical need for psychoanalysis to differentiate itself from other forms of psychotherapy, a need that continues to fuel current psychoanalytic suspicion of ST. Second, it might be argued that by supporting what *is*, the emergence of something *new* is prevented; if the personality is in need of restructuring, supports need to be removed, and propping up what is there will be countertherapeutic. Third, support implies that the therapist makes a direct contribution to the patient's well-being rather than presenting herself as an imaginary object onto which fantasies can be projected; support and transference seem to be mutually incompatible.

If the two main goals of psychotherapy—autonomy and attachment—are seen as incompatible, there appears to be an irreconcilable gulf between support and other forms of psychotherapy. But from the perspective of attachment theory, secure attachment is a precondition of autonomy. People need to feel safe before they are ready to explore the outer world of people and things or the inner world of emotions. Freud (1912) recognized this in his notion of the "unobjectionable positive transference," which forms the basis of successful psychoanalysis. Among the psychoanalytic pioneers, the Hungarian school of Ferenczi and Balint emphasized the idea that the psychoanalyst contributes more than a setting, an opaque transferential object, and interpretations, "It is the physician's love which cures the patient" (Ferenczi 1955, p. 19). Similarly Strachey's (1934) seminal paper on the "mutative interpretation" emphasized the role of the analyst as an auxiliary ego, temporarily providing support while the patient was in a state of regression. His benign response (becoming here an auxiliary superego) to the patient's projection of a punitive superego, helps disconfirm the vicious circle of neurosis, leading to the internalization of a more accepting view of himself.

The most important shift toward acknowledging the role of support in psychoanalysis has come from the work of the independent group in Britain (Kohon 1986, Rayner 1991) and, in the United States, from Kohut's (Kohut 1977, Stolorow et al. 1987) school of self psychology. As psychoanalysis began to tackle more disturbed borderline patients, the limitations of the classical conflict-defense interpretation model became apparent (Bateman and Holmes 1995, Greenberg and Mitchell 1983). Since the majority of such patients have suffered from environmental trauma and deficit (Gunderson and Sabo 1993), psychoanalytic treatment is called upon to provide the commitment and nonintrusive attention and concern that was lacking in the patient's past—in short, support. How to strike the right balance between sufficient support to enable treatment to proceed but not so much that it interferes with growth and development is a technical problem for any long-term therapy with such patients, and is the subject of extensive, and sometimes acrimonious, psychoanalytic debate (see, for example, Casement 1985, Kernberg 1984, Kohut 1984, Pedder 1986).

Integrative Models of Psychotherapy

Eclecticism in psychotherapy—the coexistence of potentially incompatible models of therapy—must be distinguished from *integration*, in which different approaches are synthesized within a wider theoretical perspective. The reconciling of the apparently incompatible objectives of autonomy and support within attachment theory would be one such example. Two integrative models influenced by attachment theory will be mentioned. Ryle's (1990, 1995) Cognitive Analytic Therapy calls for "active participation in change," and is an explicitly collaborative approach in which therapist and patient work together to formulate the problems and set goals for their resolution. The therapist is explicitly supportive, for example through a written formulation in the early weeks of therapy and, at the end of treatment, a "good-bye letter." These letters tend to emphasize the patient's strengths and courage in the face of pain, communications that are clearly supportive rather than interpretive.

Linehan (1993) has developed an impressive approach to the therapy of borderline and self-harming patients, based on what she calls *dialectical behavior therapy* (DBT). Linehan argues that disturbed patients have two apparently incompatible needs: to accept themselves as they are and to change. Thus therapy needs to be both supportive *and* mutative. Cognitive behavior therapy (CBT) provides good methods for helping patients change, but is not necessarily supportive, in that it undermines the fragile survival-strategies the patient has devised for herself, and can reinforce feelings of incompetence and low self-esteem. Linehan therefore explicitly couples conventional CBT with supportive techniques derived from Zen Buddhism, based on self-acceptance and mind-fulness of the "present moment," or, in the terminology of this book, nonattachment. She argues that these two apparently incompatible strategies will be integrated "dialectically" by the patient into less self-injurious behavior, and the results of controlled studies of DBT seem to bear this out (Linehan et al. 1991).

Social Constructionism and the Search for Positive Meanings

Another influence on a psychotherapeutic theory of support that can be linked with attachment theory is the social-constructionist, life-narrative approach (Gergen 1985), mentioned in Chapter 1. These ideas have had a great impact on family therapists (White and Epston 1990), who argue that the emergence of meaning through finding a positive story of how pain is negotiated and problems dealt with can play a central role in overcoming dysfunctional family patterns. Cognitive therapy and psychoanalysis are also clearly concerned with revising personal meanings in a positive direction and the establishment of a coherent affectively colored self-narrative. If the patient is to feel better, new meanings must ultimately be positive, although this may entail the "negative positive" of the acknowledgment of guilt and the experiencing of previously warded-off pain and grief. In family therapy paradoxical techniques—"prescribing the symptom" and similar "no-change" messages—explicitly undermine the negative spirals of insuperable problems and ineffective solutions by instructing the patients to stay with their symptoms, thereby at least giving them some control over them (Holmes 1992). Thus support frequently depends upon the systematic assignment of positive meaning to what appear to be negative situations.

RESEARCH EVIDENCE AND THE INDICATIONS FOR ST

Specifying the indications for ST is vitiated by the imprecise definition of what constitutes ST, and by the paucity of research data in this area. There have been few studies explicitly designed to look at ST. However, the body of psychotherapy research showing that nonspecific factors make a major contribution to psychotherapy outcome, producing moderate effect sizes, are clearly relevant (Stiles et al. 1986). These results are consistent with Frank's (1986) notion of common factors that contribute to good psychotherapy outcomes: "remoralization" or the installation of hope, a relationship with the therapist, and a set of procedures that the patient can follow between sessions. Only in the relative absence of the latter does ST perhaps offer less than other forms of psychotherapy.

While some authors (Andrews 1993) have used these results to question the relevance of psychotherapy to general psychiatric work, more useful are attempts to identify those patients for whom ST is especially effective. Horowitz and colleagues (1984) looked at the impact of ST and dynamic therapy on a group of bereaved patients, finding that those with weaker ego strength—those more likely to be insecurely attached—tended to do better with ST, while more integrated individuals prospered more with a dynamic approach, a finding consistent with clinical intuition. In a different clinical setting Roberts's (1992) studies of life narrative in chronic psychosis suggest that patients with elaborate delusional systems tend to fare better clinically and socially than those whose thought processes are more fragmented, suggesting that for these patients psychotherapeutic strategies designed to support rather than eliminate delusions may be more effective.

Wallerstein's (1986) magisterial 25-year follow-up study of the Menninger project also showed, in the group of highly disturbed mainly borderline patients under scrutiny, that ST was, on the whole, more effective than psychoanalysis, and that many patients needed to be transferred from pure psychoanalysis to ST in the course of their treatment. Proponents of ST should be cautious in interpreting these findings, however, because, as mentioned earlier, Wallerstein's ST is equivalent to European psychoanalytic psychotherapy, rather than ST as defined here. Further studies of ST, including United States and European comparisons, are urgently needed.

In the absence of firm research evidence, decisions about embarking upon ST will be made on clinical grounds, based on the patient's diagnosis, personality style, and the psychotherapeutic resources available. Rockland (1993) suggests that some patients with chronic physical illness, ambulatory schizophrenia, chronic dysthymia, and borderline personality disorder will be suitable for ST. The assessment of the patient's coping strategies, maturity of defenses, and psychological mindedness is as important in deciding on ST as their diagnosis.

In most psychiatric settings there is a small group of patients who are in urgent need of psychological containment, for whom conventional clinical management and traditional forms of psychotherapy have failed. They have often had multiple admissions to psychiatric and general medical hospital beds, they frequent outpatient departments or GP practices, have been prescribed numerous psychotropic drugs, may fall foul of other agencies such as social work or probation departments, and are a great worry to employers, family, and friends. These patients, often diagnosed as suffering from borderline personality disorder, are perhaps the psychiatric equivalent of the "kitchen sink" or "black hole" patients described in the general practice literature (O'Dowd 1988). Brief therapies have often been tried, sometimes with good but only short-lived results. Long-term psychoanalytic therapy is thought likely to provoke regression and destructive dependency, leading eventually to "malignant alienation" (Watts and Morgan 1994), rejection by staff purporting to help them, and the strong risk of suicide. The patient may lack the metaphorical and verbal capacities needed to engage successfully in analytic therapy, which may indeed have already been tried and failed. For such patients ST is positively indicated (Rockland 1993), and, especially if backed up by a well-communicating network involving the patient's GP and attendance at a day hospital or day center, can dramatically reduce inappropriate usage of services and have a powerful containing effect.

These are the extreme cases. There are others, less dramatically disturbed, who can benefit from a deeper psychotherapeutic approach than is usually offered in clinical management, but who shy away from conventional forms of psychotherapy, because of either unconscious recognition of the fragility of their defenses, or previously unsuccessful attempts at therapy. ST provides a therapeutic space for patients who want and need something more than clinical management, but less than full-blown psychotherapy.

CLINICAL TECHNIQUES IN SUPPORTIVE PSYCHOTHERAPY

Holding and Containment

ST was earlier facetiously described as a "holding operation." Holding is central to the supportive function, in the sense of holding in mind, and acting as a secure container for the fears, madness, and guilt that beset the patient. The patient will openly discuss her abnormal experiences with the therapist, leaving them with him until the next session. The therapeutic space becomes a stabilizing influence, safe deposit, anchor point, or, as one patient described it, a nuclear waste recycling plant, which enables reasonably normal functioning to continue between sessions.

The role of physical holding is controversial, but would certainly be more admissible in ST than in analytic therapy. Pedder (1986) argues that attachment theory's postulate of a need for nonsexual attachment makes touching and holding much less problematic than analytic theory would suggest. The provision of copious tissues and a warm handshake at the start and finish of sessions are a routine part of the author's practice of ST.

Holding and containment can be understood developmentally in terms of a series of concentric circles of attachment. The newborn infant is held by the mother, who in turn is protected by her partner, mother, and extended family, who are themselves cared for by social institutions such as welfare and health services.

Enid Balint (1993) saw "being there" as one of the most important functions of the analyst, especially for disturbed patients. In ST the therapist presents herself as an enduring real object whom the patient can expect to be there as long as is needed, at low intensity but with high reliability.

Case Example: Eating Disorder in ST

> Annabelle, a 37-year-old woman, suffered from anorexia nervosa and borderline personality disorder. In the course of a six-year ST, her weight doubled from the original 56 pounds with which she was originally admitted to the hospital in a near-moribund state, but she continued to have major relationship difficulties. She complained frequently to her therapist: "One day I know you will tell me I have had enough, and that someone else's case is more important than mine." Rather than interpret this anxiety in terms of projected aggression, or sibling rivalry, the therapist simply replied: "Your anxiety is realistic, especially given the number of different doctors you have seen in your time, but, health permitting, I will be available to you for as long as is necessary until I retire,

and after that I shall expect my successor to continue with the work we are doing." (The therapist should perhaps first have consulted with his business manager before making this rash promise.)

"Holding" in ST involves the capacity to do nothing, simply to be with the patient within the confines of the therapeutic frame, providing a still point in a chaotic world of illness and struggle. To achieve this minimalist position with its economy of effort is not easy for the therapist, who has to contain her own anxious striving to *do* something for the patient, however much she knows that this may be ineffectual.

The Active, "Real" Therapist

In ST the therapist will often initiate the session and ask questions about different areas of the patient's life: "What sort of week have you had?" "How are things going at home (or work)?" This is an approach described by Lewis (1979) as "distributive psychotherapy." Leaving the initiative to the patient may provoke overwhelming anxiety and repression.

Lucy: From Analytic to Supportive Therapy

> Lucy was a 35-year-old librarian suffering from chronic depression. She was initially treated with once-weekly analytic therapy. She found the passivity of the therapist and the silence at the start of therapy unbearably threatening, and in one session sat for nearly a whole hour in total silence, eventually leaping up in a highly distressed state and rushing from the room. Soon after this she was readmitted to the hospital. After discharge the therapy was changed to biweekly ST and the therapist made a point of starting the session by asking, "How are things?" Later she described her feelings of total panic and humiliation when she had felt expected to initiate the ses-

sion—a conflict between her compliant self wanting to please the therapist, and her feeling that in therapy she was required to be spontaneous.

Another important characteristic of the supportive therapist is her realness, or transparency. The therapist is more prepared to reveal herself and to answer questions than is conventional in analytic therapy, presenting herself as a real person actively implicated in the patient's life, rather than as an ambiguous or "virtual" object of projection and misperception. This is not a license for unbridled therapist self-revelations, and persistent questions may have to be gently deflected with a reminder that the focus of the therapy is the patient and her difficulties. The purpose of therapeutic transparency is to maintain the positive alliance, to foster a sense of common humanity, and to help see therapy as a joint project in patients who often feel "different" and humiliated by their need for help. Here is an example of therapeutic reticence and revelation in the same patient.

Lucy (Continued)

Lucy was always to be found in the waiting room with her head in a novel. Despite the therapist's intense interest in literature, he never directly asked Lucy about what she was reading since he felt this would distract from the therapeutic task, and make her feel she was required to produce a clever literary analysis. On the other hand, when Lucy was talking in a highly distressed way about her daughter's difficulties in adjusting to a new school, he commented, "Yes, starting school *can* be a terrible ordeal, can't it, especially for sensitive children," thereby implicitly revealing that he too was a parent, and that he knew what it was like to worry about one's children.

Patients' remarks like: "I don't suppose your other patients are as bad as me," or "I'm sure your life runs completely smoothly— you probably can't begin to understand how difficult I find the simplest things in life," can be met with normalizing and reassuring responses with vague references to the therapist's personal life that do not deflect the focus away from the patient and her problems. Similarly, shared humor can be a very important part of the ST relationship, helping the patient to feel validated, and at least a momentary source of enjoyment rather than burden for the therapist.

The patient in ST may need to know where the therapist is during vacations, and instead of playing the conventional analytic guessing game, should be told something like "I shall be away in France for the next three weeks; if you get into difficulties you can contact Dr. X, who looked after you once before when I was away." The therapist in ST is an explicit attachment figure, good object, and safe haven, whom the patient needs to be able to locate physically in the external world, not just as an object in an uncertain inner world.

Positive Reinforcement

Praise ("You've done really well to cope with moving without getting ill again"), mild flattery ("You seem to have a knack for finding beautiful clothes in thrift shops"), and positive comments on the patient's appearance ("You're looking a lot better this week"), which in an analytic context would be seductive or distracting, are an important part of the therapeutic repertoire in ST. The narcissistically damaged patient needs the self-object mirroring of the therapist in order to restore her sense of self-esteem and well-being. The patient needs to make the most of her assets, rather than dwelling continuously on her faults and failings. Patients who appear resourceless and passive may in a supportive context be encouraged to rekindle old skills and achievements.

Working Positively with Defenses

Appelbaum (1989) describes how parents work positively with their children's defenses, always trying to move them in the direction of maturity and greater integration. The very use of words to describe feelings is an example of a positive defense. Pine (1986, p. 528) describes words as a "cool medium," which enables the parent/therapist to "strike while the iron is cold." If a child is obviously upset, the sensitive parent's first priority is to soothe the child, and only later try to explore what was making her so unhappy. Similarly in ST the therapist may help a patient who is visibly disturbed to do a relaxation exercise, or even prescribe an antidepressant or anxiolytic, and perhaps later, when things are calm, say, "You seemed pretty upset before; I wonder what was going on then?"

Alvarez (1992) is critical of the psychoanalytic tendency to assault insensitively necessary defenses in children. She reframes the manic defense positively as a way of imagining a better, less helpless future, a goal toward which the child can strive. Entering a fantasy, say, about what one would do if one won a million dollars, or had a fairy godmother who could grant three wishes, rather than being an avoidance of reality, can be a helpful technique in ST, widening the patient's constricted horizons, instilling hope, and arousing the possibility of a good object, however idealized. Alvarez also defends the abused child's right "not to know," and to be able to forget trauma. ST can similarly help patients to repress traumatic memories and distract themselves from painful feelings or hallucinations.

Rockland (1987, 1989) argues ingeniously that in ST the therapist should ally herself with the patient's defenses, encouraging the obsessional patient to write copious notes on her moods, giving plenty of advice and encouragement to dependent patients, and so on.

Coping

The notion of *coping* (Lazarus and Messer 1988) can also be seen in terms of reinforcing positive defenses. Helping the patient to cope with her illness and its consequences is perhaps the most basic of all ST techniques used in medicine. Many patients suffering from major mental illness feel ashamed and embarrassed by their plight, feeling that they are in some way responsible for it, and fearful of stigma and ridicule of others. Used inappropriately, the analytic focus on the patient's own, albeit unconscious, contribution to their predicament can reinforce this sense of guilt. ST counteracts this tendency by encouraging benign projection: "Through no fault of your own you are suffering from a serious mental illness; unfortunately it is not visible like a broken leg, nor widely understood like diabetes, but it is nonetheless real. You inevitably suffer from anger, sadness, and at times despair at the way illness deprives you of many opportunities that you would otherwise have had in life. This can be compared with the grief you would feel if you lost someone precious to you. But let's also see how you can best live with your illness, minimize its effects on your life, and even find the strengths that can come from adversity overcome." A message such as this, broken up into more manageable bits, would be offered in the course of a supportive treatment.

The illness metaphor is a good example of a half-truth, "inexact interpretation" (Glover 1931) or benign projection (projecting pain into "your illness," "chemicals in the brain," "your genes," or "your very difficult upbringing") that can be helpful in soothing the patients and giving meaning to their distress, rather as a widow, herself agnostic, might reassure her child that "Daddy is happy in heaven," holding the child's pain until maturation allows her to face it more fully.

A Therapeutic Half-Truth

The author was an admiring witness on a home visit in which a violent psychopathic man demanding admission to the hospital was very effectively calmed and deflected by his family doctor who told him: "You are suffering from a psychopathic personality disorder. Unfortunately we have no good treatment for that at the moment, any more than we do for many physical illnesses such as multiple sclerosis, but much research is going on, and we hope that at some point in the future we may be able to cure your condition. For the moment our job is to help you live with it as best you can."

As an advanced technique in ST the method of *positive reframing*, developed by systemic therapies, can be a useful part of a coping message. Here, however apparently distressed the patient, symptoms are seen in a positive light.

A Positive Connotation

A 30-year-old doctor had had to give up her work due to depression, and developed a highly dependent relationship with her consultant, ever hopeful of some new drug that would at last cure her. She lived with her elderly parents, who looked after her devotedly, and who seemed remarkably adjusted to her preoccupation with death and almost daily suicide threats. In her ST sessions her therapist praised her, in a slightly surprised way—implying that he imagined that she would have failed miserably—for managing to get to the session in spite of the severity of her illness, for looking so smart, and for the fact that she had taken the dog for a walk every day that week. Knowing that she was a keen crossword puzzler, he asked her opinion about a particularily difficult clue that had baffled him that morning.

Rockland (1987) suggests that in working supportively with self-mutilating patients the therapist may have to remind herself, and at times the patient that "ultimately self-mutilation, however flamboyant, is preferable to death, and consider the possibility that the patient is really is doing the very best she can" (p. 352). Here the search for positive meaning borders on paradox in a way that may seem manipulative, contradicting the Rogerian emphasis on "genuineness" in effective therapy. Such subtle challenges are designed to mobilize healthy anger in the patient, but like any paradoxical intervention should always contain a kernel of truth, be used sparingly, and be delivered in a warm tone of voice in the context of a continuing committed therapeutic relationship.

Counteracting Negative Cognitions

Cognitive therapy systematically helps the depressed patient to identify and then challenge the negative cognitions and assumptions that dominate and perpetuate their depressive world view. In ST the patient is similarly helped to develop alternative and more positive ways of looking at events that may trigger negative emotions.

The Therapist Nonplussed

> Anna, suffering from borderline personality disorder, had a long history of self-cutting and self-burning, chronic depression, and substance abuse. After long spells in the hospital she was finally back at home looking after her 5-year-old daughter. Her days felt empty and boring, and were often given over to excessive cannabis smoking. She had lost all sense of competence or creativity. When she went to pick up her daughter from school she felt odd and different from the other parents. In a desperate attempt to find some positive way forward her therapist asked if there was anything she was interested in, or liked to do. Her reply was, "Yes, horror!" She loved horror books and videos, the more gory the better. Gritting his supportive teeth, the therapist suggested she write a precis of a Stephen King novel and bring it to the next session!

Transference and Countertransference in ST

Although positive transference is probably the basis of successful ST, making transference interpretations is usually eschewed. However, it is important to take up obvious emotional reactions in the here and now, for example if the patient is clearly distressed or angry because of some failure, such as lateness on the therapist's part. By contrast, self-monitoring of countertransference (preferably with the help of a supervisor) is essential, perhaps even more so than in conventional therapy, since the opportunities for acting out on the part of the therapist are so much greater than in the more rigid framework of more formal therapies. The therapist has to decide when to give an emergency session, and when to ask the patient to wait for the scheduled session; when to offer half-hour sessions, and when 50 minutes are appropriate; when to prescribe, and when to refer the patient to her family doctor; when to reveal herself, and when to be reticent; when to chat, and when to get down to business. These choices cannot easily be legislated, and depend on the therapist's sensitivity and intuition, but should be driven by the needs of the patient rather than those of the therapist.

Involvement of Relatives

Since a central principle of ST is that stress on the ego should be directly reduced, it is important whenever possible to involve and work with the patient's immediate family. Informal couple or family therapy should be a routine part of ST. There is no standard pattern; the patient may be seen for half an hour and then an ever-dutiful spouse brought in for the latter part of the session, or individual and family sessions may be mixed in varying proportions. Here too the therapist should stress the value of positive coping and praise for the couple or family for bearing the burden of illness with such fortitude. Just as the supportive therapist reinforces rather than challenges individual defenses, so in family work group defenses are strengthened, and no overt attempt is made to reframe the illness as a systemic problem. Reframing is done by stealth, for example by asking how family members react when the identified patient becomes ill, and by defining the difficulty as a shared one that, in different ways, will affect all members of the family.

CLINICAL EXAMPLE

It is not easy to convey the impact of a successful ST in a brief vignette; interventions tend to be low key, and the benefits are cumulative, often extending over many years of therapeutic collaboration. I will conclude with an example of one such case that highlights some of the themes discussed.

Lucy (Continued)

Some aspects of Lucy's treatment have already been mentioned. She had suffered with depression since at least her teens when, while at university, she had made a major suicide attempt and been admitted to a psychiatric hospital for 18 months. Lucy is the younger of two sisters, and her mother had had a severe puerperal depression following a stillbirth and had been in the hospital for nine months when Lucy was about 3. She had been looked after by her father, whom she grew to detest, and, in the course of her biweekly ST, began to believe that his care at that time was severely defective or even abusive. Her parents owned a bar. She experienced her mother as intrusively offering the "affectionless control" that is often a feature of depression.

Throughout her twenties and thirties she lived the life of a semi-invalid, restricting her social life, plagued with overwhelming feelings of rage and despair, spending large parts of the day in bed, and working only very intermittently at her job as a librarian. Her first marriage had foundered, but in her second she had married an older man who was immensely tolerant, appearing to be immune to her violent verbal attacks and enormous dependency. She entered therapy, which, as mentioned earlier was soon converted to ST, after the birth of her son, fearful that without help she might not be able to manage motherhood.

The first four years of therapy seemed to produce little benefit other than perhaps stabilizing her life and providing a container for her aggression and dependency. She would at times launch into a vicious attack on the therapist, whom she saw as a superior, heartless treatment machine on whom she had become inextricably dependent, whose sole purpose was to humiliate her. Until a ST model was adopted, the sessions were often silent, repetitive, and static, leaving the therapist feeling trapped and impotent, although in her less furious moments Lucy confessed that she did value the treatment since, apart from her husband, the therapist was the only person in the world to whom she could express her hatred. On two or three occasions she required brief hospitalization when her depresssion became overwhelming, but this too only served to remind her of her hopelessness and inability to cope.

Then, suddenly, her husband became ill, and, after a period of illness in which she nursed him magnificently, died. The two years following his death saw a remarkable transformation. She grieved greatly but at the same time her confidence increased; she began to think of herself as normal rather than an alien creature; she started to enjoy her son and her friends; she began to travel, venturing into territory that in her previously restricted life she would have avoided. She made a partial reconciliation with her parents from whom she had completely cut herself off. She met a new man with whom she developed a much more equal relationship, and with whom she could, when necessary, argue in a productive and mature way, compared with her dependent destructiveness of before.

Pari passu with these external changes, the therapy became far less static, and a warm therapeutic relationship began to develop. Breaks in the therapy, which previously had often led to breakdown, were tolerated without mishap. The therapist began to feel more like a real person in the sessions rather than a vague object that Lucy either attacked or from whom she gained some frail warmth.

The basis of these changes seemed to be Lucy's positive identification with her dead husband. She said that she felt that he was inside her, and that she was drawing strength from his guidance. When faced with difficulty, she would ask herself what he would have done, and it was usually right! He became the good object who, although physically dead, had at a psychological level survived her attacks. He had, in Klein's (1940) word, been "reinstated" within her. Her inner world was, for the first time in her life, secure. In parallel with this she felt more autonomous. A similar process, it could be argued, was hatching within the therapy. ST is perhaps more clearly client-oriented than other forms of therapy, and in responding to Lucy's need *not* to have analytic treatment but to remain attached, while being consistent and committed, the format of ST allowed a gradual identification, enhancement of self-esteem, and capacity for self-soothing to emerge.

CONCLUSION

Eight years seems a long time for any therapy to last, especially in the context of modern publicly funded health services looking to brief therapies for the psychiatric equivalent of keyhole surgery. But Lucy, who had spent at least two years in the hospital prior to coming into therapy, was hospitalized for no more than six weeks in the course of her eight-year ST. The frequency of her sessions was as sparing as seemed possible. The challenge for ST is to justify this kind of approach as cost-effective, and to argue that long-term treatments, often supportive, are needed if a significant group of highly disturbed patients are not to be disadvantaged.

ST remains the Cinderella of the therapies, but not for ST the miraculous transformation scene, or glamor of the ball. There is no Prince Charming waiting to whisk these patients away into eternal happiness. But ST can help the patient to sit more contentedly by the hearth, to enjoy plain pumpkin soup, to have fun playing with the mice, and to value the tatters and rags that so often make up a life. In its celebration of the ordinary, of the heroism of simply coping, its stress on the need to be in touch with reality, ST—informed by attachment ideas—represents an important moral and cultural counterweight to the bright lights of contemporary brain science and dramatic psychotherapies.

6

Suicide And Attachment Theory

Not long ago two young people on the unit where I work killed themselves. Both were suffering from schizophenia, and both had been very ill for many years. As it happened, neither was my patient, but I was deputizing for their consultant who was on vacation on each occasion—a fact that may or may not be significant.

The first patient died at about 7 A.M. When I came into the office around 8:30, the shock and distress was palpable, and the nurse who had found her, a universally liked and respected young man, was being comforted by his colleagues. I found myself compelled to make reassuring remarks to the staff, and to the hospital officials who mysteriously materialized on the ward, to explain that psychiatric illness, like any other illness, carries a significant mortality. Around 10 percent of schizophrenia sufferers kill themselves, rather more in manic-depression, I said. I compared this patient with someone suffering from leukemia or heart failure who had been kept alive for several years by intensive medical intervention, but who had finally succumbed. We should be praising the staff for succeeding in keeping her going for so long, rather than criticizing them for "failing," I insisted to the worried-looking hospital officials.

At the patient and staff groups that followed, and over the next few days, a great deal of sadness and hopelessness was expressed, and not a little anger. Once again I found myself saying reassuring things along the lines that the patient was at peace and no longer in mental torment; that it was inevitable we should feel guilty and blame ourselves, but that it is the illness rather than ourselves that is to blame; and that ultimately however hard one may try to prevent it happening, if patients are determined enough to kill themselves, they will.

The suicide had a huge impact on the ward atmosphere. Everyone seemed to be in that tender and hyperaware state that follows a bereavement, and the nurse who had been assigned to the patient was treated with great gentleness by his colleagues and was encouraged to take a few days off. On his return he was the focus of several staff groups. As a result I felt I understood him better as a person, rather than merely seeing him as a competent nurse.

The second suicide was different in that it took place off the ward. The patient, a young man with a devastating schizophrenic illness, was spending Saturday afternoon at his parents' house, as he often did. As they were watching TV he suddenly got up, saying, "I can't stand this any longer," and went into the back garden. Suddenly his father saw a ball of flame in the garden where the boy had poured gas over himself and set fire to it. It took his father several minutes to extinguish the flames. The patient was conscious when he was admitted to the emergency room but died in intensive care in the burn unit later that night. When I went to the ward the next day, the staff was shocked, but less acutely than in the first case, partly because no one felt directly responsible, partly too because there was a real feeling of relief that someone who had been in torment for many years was finally at peace.

Visiting his parents at home later that morning, it was possible to listen calmly to their deep distress, his mother sitting, crying but in repose, on the sofa, while the father paced up and down, talking about his son's life. I felt overwhelming sadness about the waste of a young life, at parental hopes dashed, the horrific image of the human torch that would stay with them forever, but also at the strength of support that such a tragedy evokes, as the doorbell and telephone rang constantly, neighbors and other members of the family ensuring that the parents need not be alone until they were ready.

I have told these stories partly to emphasize that suicide can sometimes be a release from suffering, but also to show how comparatively easy it is to be helpful when one is not personally involved. Had these two patients been mine, I know my reactions would have been very different. I would have been struggling with that mixture of shock, numbness, guilt, disbelief, anger, and diminution with which I am all too familiar in theory but which is no less painful when it hits one in practice, as it inevitably does when a patient for whom one feels responsible—and attached—dies. I would have wanted to walk out on the hospital, to return home in search of comfort and forgetting. I would have been asking myself why I do this job, why I do not live in the world of normality, why I choose to immerse myself in misery, sadness and failure.

Failure. Failure. Failure. The very word is like a knell. A hollow empty sound that resounds through the mind. I think of my many failures. Suicide represents only the most final, the most unequivocal of these. I think back twenty-five years to the middle-aged man who, while I was a medical student in psychiatry, told me how suicidal he felt, of how I failed to pass this on to the nurses, and how that night he poured lighter fuel over himself and put a match to it, dying of renal failure ten days later. Why did I not give up all ideas of psychiatry then?

I think of the suicides I know of in my patients since then—a rate of approximately one every two years—one of them, as I shall describe, a psychotherapy case. For all the comforting words and rationalizations I have received, each represents for me a failure of vigilance, of communication, or that thin wedge of "malignant alienation" (Watts and Morgan 1994) that can build up between caregivers and patient, so that, at the end, the patient stands alone, can feel legitimately that no one wants him, that it would be better for all concerned if he were dead.

SUICIDE AS A BEREAVEMENT

In some ways we react to suicide as we do to any loss. Among others, Bowlby and Parkes (Parkes et al. 1991) have drawn up the painful map of bereavement. After the first knife-thrust of shock, our first reaction is often denial. When a normally rather jovial GP rings me to tell me that my patient has gassed herself in her garage that night, I assume at first he is joking: "No, tell me *really* why you are ringing," I ask. I cannot believe that she could have done this. Or rather, narcissistically, that she could not have done this *to me*. Then comes anger. In my mind I rail against the patient: How could you be so stupid? You would have gotten better. How do you think your family feels now? That was what you wanted isn't it, to make us suffer as you have been suffering? Was that the only way you could get across how bad things were? We were trying to help—you just wanted to tell us all how useless, what failures, we were, didn't you?

With anger goes blame. It has to be somebody's fault, as the hospital officials were only too aware when they came onto the ward that morning. Blame can go inward or outward. I can blame someone or something else: "the system" for not providing enough staff, the inadequacy of psychotropic drugs, the ward staff for allowing the patient out, the patient's parents for failing to notice his distress (he had repeatedly made threats of this sort over the past five years). Or I can turn blame inward, berating myself for my lack of commitment and capacity to care, my failure to notice the little signs that so often precede a suicide: an indifference signaling a retreat into the inner world, grim hopelessless, that little secret smile of triumph.

Then the searching begins. In my mind I go through the events leading up to the suicide, desperately replaying it with a different outcome. If only I had prescribed a less-lethal antidepressant. If only I hadn't had to cancel that appointment. If only I had realized that she was not suitable for psychotherapy. If only the lottery collector had come around early (an event that saved one of my patients from certain death). If only she hadn't been so damned obstinately determined to prove herself right and all of us wrong. If only I hadn't ignored the warning signs, that, now, are so obvious: my own increasing worry about the patient, her own unexpected recent serenity—the calm before the suicide.

Then comes sadness and a sense of finality. Someone who was *there*, a living, breathing, complex being, someone whom we knew, cared about, and struggled with, has gone. A space has appeared where once there was a person, and the world seems an emptier place. Everything looks slightly different. Time slows down, things no longer rush past but seem more real and significant. I realize what a beautiful place the world is, now that someone has left it. Alternating with this is a contrary feeling of superficiality, in which everything appears painted and artificial, pointless and dried up. All our purposes are futile, self-centered distractions in the face of all-powerful forces of fate over which we have no control.

Gradually the feelings fade; the preoccupations of the moment take over. The suicide remains as a painful scar, a sore spot to be avoided if possible. Perhaps lessons will be learned. There is gain as well as loss. For a few weeks or months I am especially vigilant in thinking and asking about suicide. Patients are kept on a tighter reign. I am more aware of the fragile balance between life and death. I try to penetrate the mystery of suicide. I search for an explanation, a meaning, a theory. Theory can be a defense, a retreat, a form of denial perhaps, but, as understanding leading to nonattachment, is also essential to psychic survival as a caregiver—without it, a part of oneself dies irretrievably with the patient.

SHAME AND HATRED

The urge to deny death is incredibly strong. Even as they were being packed into transport wagons destined for Auschwitz, the victims of the Holocaust believed that a new life awaited them in work camps. Most of us cling to life, however miserable or restricted it may seem. As parents we invest our children with our hopes of eternity, assuming that our genes will survive even when we are gone. As adults we appear in our maturity to understand and accept our limitations, but our self-centeredness is never fully transcended, none of us is free from residual secret pockets of narcissism and omnipotence. We play the lottery, dream of a better life, experience surges of adolescent sexuality, cannot conceive of a world indifferent to our needs or able to manage quite well without us. None of us is free from superstition—even writing about suicide seems to be to tempt fate. A patient's suicide breaches our narcissism. For a moment we catch a glimpse of how frail and powerless we are. We see the soft center to all our concern, the limitations of our professionalism. What is worse, the world can see too. We fail every day in greater or lesser ways, but much of the time these failures are invisible, even to ourselves. A suicide exposes our weakness not just to ourselves but to those around us. Through our colleagues' support and concern we sense tinges of *schadenfreude*. Seen in our naked failure, we are ashamed.

A relationship—between us and the patient—has broken down. To be unattached is the ultimate danger. Alone on the primordial prairie, the wolves and hyenas will soon have us. Because we are unattached, we are exposed, vulnerable to attack. We long to escape—home, into retirement or less stressful forms of work. Here perhaps is a clue to the communication the patients are making through their suicide. Perhaps shame drove them to it, shame at their inability to sustain relationships, the feeling of futility of a life without connections. Attachments protect us as surely as the homeostatic mechanisms of our physiology. Insecurely attached primates' heart rates and temperature regulation react wildly to change, as compared with their securely attached couterparts (Kraemer 1992). The mental pain that drives people to suicide is a signal of such dangerous exposure. A person is never so much in need of attachment as at the moment of suicide. As designated helpers of the human tribe, psychiatrists and psychotherapists have to be able to bear the intensity of our patients' needs, and to share it if it is intolerable for one helper to carry.

For the suicidal the human contract has been broken. Suicide is a sacrifice and a bargain. By killing the "bad" part of the self the hope is that a better future awaits the "post-self" (Schneiderman 1993). At a suicidal moment, in order for life to be endurable, there has to be a death. The artist who one chill November day left her comfortable London house, took the train to Brighton, and walked into the sea until the waves consumed her, was killing herself so that her husband could (as she imagined) live, rather than be dragged down by her depression. At the same time she was seeking the all-enveloping mother whom she had longed for since her death when she was 4 years old.

The Laufers (1984) have argued that suicidal adolescents are engaged in a murderous attack on the sexual body that has in some way failed to pass muster, letting them down in the same way that the parental "body" failed to love, nurture, or protect them as children, often actively attacking their bodies through physical or sexual abuse. When a patient in therapy kills herself, this process is reenacted in the transference-countertransference matrix.

At times we wish that our patients would go away, putting themselves and us out of our misery. This feeling may be entirely unexpressed and out of awareness. Via the "bipersonal field" (Langs 1978) and reverse countertransference, it may lodge in the patient, who, also below consciousness, senses resentment in our tone of voice, body language, and compassionless gaze, or alternatively in our overconcern and our inability to set limits or face up to their deviousness and desperation. As Bowlby (1988) pointed out, this covert psychological murder is highly dangerous if it remains unacknowledged, a death waiting to be enacted. As Winnicott (1947) says of the therapist, "However much he loves his patients he cannot avoid hating them and fearing them, and the better he knows this the less will hate and fear be the motives determining what he does to his patients" (p. 217). When patients kill themselves we feel responsible, as though we have murdered them, because, unconsciously, we have wished them dead many times.

Most psychiatrists encounter suicide as an infrequent but unavoidable part of their work (Brown 1987, Chemtob 1988, Cryan et al. 1995). For psychotherapists suicide is a much rarer and much more devastating experience. One of my supervisors used to boast that he had never had a suicide in any of his patients. For a working psychiatrist like myself to make such a claim would be an extreme form of denial (Kahane 1968). So far, however, only one of my patients has actually committed suicide while in psychotherapy. I shall now describe this case in some detail (cf. Holmes 1992) to draw some more general lessons that may help others to avoid the pitfalls that I blundered into, and, if they cannot be avoided, to survive and learn from an experience that, for me, has continued to nag as one of the nadirs of my working life.

CLINICAL EXAMPLE

Alison was a separated woman in her late forties. Her difficulties started when her husband left her for a much younger woman, whom he had met through an amateur orchestra. For the first year or two she coped well, busying herself with looking after her two teenaged children, finding somewhere to live, and fighting her husband's company, which she felt owed her compensation after all the work she had put in as a manager's wife. She blamed God in much the same way that she felt let down by her husband. As a Christian she felt angry with Him for allowing the divorce to happen, especially as she served Him so faithfully for many years. Then, just before Christmas she began to feel depressed and despairing, and told her family doctor that she intended to kill herself. His referral letter about her ended with the question: "What does one do about someone who appears to have a rational wish to commit suicide; she doesn't appear to be psychiatrically ill and yet she is determined to end her life?"

I saw Alison for assessment a few days before Christmas. I was very worried about her and considered her a serious suicide risk. However, she absolutely refused admission, saying that for her to be away from her children at this time of year would be impossible—actually I think she was determined that they should not go to her ex-husband. As happened so often subsequently in her treatment, I felt that whatever I offered was wrong. Not admitting her was tantamount to dismissing the seriousness of her distress; admitting her compulsorily would have been hard to justify and would have further compromised her already fragile sense of self-esteem and autonomy. I arranged to see her immediately after Christmas, but nevertheless she took a serious overdose and was admitted to the ward. Within a few days she had convinced the staff that her overdose was just an example of "silliness." The staff was angry and outraged that Alison could contemplate killing herself in cold blood, given the dependency of her two children. She exasperated them by her refusal to accept the fact of her husband's desertion, and by her insistence that they were welcome to their superficial modern relationships, but her marriage was made in heaven and was indissoluble. On the ward she alternated between defiance and a kind of mocking compliance, and it was with some relief that the staff allowed her to go home to look after her children. But within a few weeks she had again made a suicide attempt and was readmitted. This time she remained on the ward for several weeks and on discharge entered once-weekly analytic therapy.

Therapy was stormy from the start, and I soon wondered what I had gotten myself into. Alison began to show more and more borderline features as she regressed in the therapeutic situation. She would think longingly about suicide. She alternated between elation and despair. She began to harm herself in minor ways, and take risks with unknown men and alcohol. She accused me of depriving her of the one thing she wanted most—death. She insisted, as the transference developed, that she was staying alive simply for my sake, not for herself, or even for her children, who would be much better off without her, living with her husband and his new woman. She accused me of trying to make her accept the shallow values of a society that she rejected, of trying to make her come to terms with what to her was unacceptable. She complained bitterly about the lack of reciprocity in the therapeutic relationship, and taunted me with the accusation that I was just doing my job, and would be glad to be rid of her.

Alison was the younger of two children. She had always felt second best in her mother's eyes compared with her idolized older brother. She described herself as a difficult child who spent "half my life" sitting on the stairs—the family punishment in which the worse the misdemeanor, the nearer the bedroom she had to sit. She could recall few memories of childhood, and those were factual rather than affectual. She had nothing good to say about her mother at all, seeing her as cold and distant and preoccupied with her brother. She had felt close to her father, who was a traveling salesman and often away from home. She remembers sitting next to him on the sofa with his arm around her, and how good this felt, but how he sprang guiltily away when her mother came unexpectedly into the room. Despite considerable academic and athletic potential (she had played at junior Wimbledon), she defiantly left school at 16 to get a job as a secretary, much to her father's disappointment. Soon after this she became a strongly committed Christian, and the Church then became the focus of her life. She had no real boyfriends until she met her husband in her late twenties, through the church where he was lay preacher.

Alison's therapy continued for the next eighteen months. For most of the time it felt like a battle, an interminable game of tennis in which she knew she would eventually wear her opponent down and so win. I could not find a way to break into her avoidant facade, which so obviously shielded so much unresolved pain. She remained actively suicidal for much of this time. On one occasion, just before a holiday, I was convinced she intended to kill herself, and had to physically wrestle with her in the consulting room until she could be compulsorily detained. Later she confessed that she had found this exciting and reassuring. Once on the ward she again irritated the staff with her emotional withdrawal and her "silly" attempts to "escape." She left the hospital on extended leave, while remaining legally detained on her commitment. Her family doctor had asked for this, since it made it easier for him to readmit her if need be, and the hospital staff found it provided some degree of symbolic containment. By exercising this control the balance of the internal struggle between the conformist and rebellious parts of her was shifted slightly: she insisted that she would never kill herself while the commitment was in effect, but at the same time she complained that she felt utterly humiliated by it.

Gradually, some signs of improvement began to emerge, at least in her external life. She joined a tennis club, slept better, and formed some friendships in the village where she lived. But there was little change in the atmosphere of therapy, in which my task was to try to guess what she was feeling underneath her breezy, compliant manner. She would defiantly challenge the rules of therapy, for example by sitting on the floor rather than the chair. Almost any suggestion or interpretation was dismissed as irrelevant speculation. She made it clear that there were only two things she wanted from therapy: permission either to die, or to marry her therapist! Since both were impossible, she would taunt me with remarks like, "Well, when are you going to get fed up with me and let me have what you know I want?" (i.e., death). Her envy was overwhelming—she envied her husband who had got off scot-free, her brother who went off on expensive vacations while she was penniless, her daughter who had a boyfriend, her son who got on well with his father, and me whom she saw as happily married and with a satisfying job.

Alison meanwhile continued to do battle with the hospital and complained to the Mental Health Act Commission about the way her commitment had been imposed—while at the same time insisting that she stay on it! It was only too easy to use interpretations as verbal weapons, as for example when I suggested that she saw me and the hospital as an uncaring mother into whom she projected all her own envy and disappointment, and whom she was punishing with her difficultness. She was not ready to reintroject any of her "bad-ness" and our task seemed to be to contain and try to me-tabolize it as best we could. Therapy was clearly a lifeline for her, and special arrangements, which she mockingly but accurately called "babysitting," had to be made for her to see someone else when I was away on vacation.

Eventually her commitment came up for renewal, and the decision was to rescind it; it was simply not justifiable to go on with it in view of her apparently normal mental state and continuing improvement. Immediately Alison began to wean herself off her medication. Her behavior in sessions became increasingly mute and peculiar. Such was her shame about needing help, she refused to sit in the waiting area, hiding in the lavatory until the moment came for her session. The possibility of another commitment was considered, but somehow it seemed too depressing to restart that process yet again, and patience was wearing thin. Christmas, always a difficult time for her, when her loneliness and envy were at their height, was approaching. An elderly relative of mine sud-denly became seriously ill, and I had to cancel a session in order to visit him in the hospital. I phoned Alison several times to let her know, but there was no answer. She therefore arrived at the session the next day not knowing that I was away. She walked straight into the consulting room and lay down on the couch, where she was found by the receptionist (whom she knew well through her church connections), who talked to her for a while and made an appointment for her to see me the next day. But she gassed herself with her car exhaust that night, and was found by her 15-year-old son the next morn-ing dead in the garage.

Discussion

It is almost unbearable to recall this whole miserable episode, and especially to think of how I failed Alison's children who will carry the pain of their mother's death with them for the rest of their lives. What are the lessons to be learned from it?

One mistake was undoubtedly my attempt to combine a psychotherapeutic and a psychiatric role with Alison. She correctly sensed that as a psychiatrist I was committed to keeping her alive. This inevitably interfered with what I saw as the psychotherapeutic task of trying to help her understand her feelings and behavior, without any attempt at judgment or control (which would have been enactments of the maternal transference). The knowledge that I was determined to stop her dying, even to the extent of physically wrestling with her at the end of the session, paradoxically gave Alison the lever she needed to win her macabre game of tennis to the death. And yet, I omnipotently argued at the time, who else in the multidisciplinary team would it have been fair to ask to take her on? (Our psychotherapeutic resources have since improved, and it would be easier now.) Or is this an example of how I was shaped by projective identification into playing God, the useless God who died for her when her marriage ended? I was unable to stay nonattached in my desperate attempts to stay connected to someone for whom the first truly autonomous act of her life may have been taking it. She evoked in me the "three most common narcissistic snares: the aspirations to heal all, to know all, and love all" (Maltsberger and Buie 1974, p. 631). The result was confusion: a split developed in which my "hate" was played out in my psychiatric role, while the "love" was all concentrated in the psychotherapy sessions. This in turn reinforced the concentration of unleavened hate needed for her to kill herself. Because my "objective hate" (Winnicott's term denoting, I think, justifiable and non–transference-based hatred) was split off in this way, it was harder for her to feel she could reach out to "objective" (i.e., non-manipulated) love.

For most of the time I was at least aware of these difficulties and as a staff team we discussed them many times. However, I did not receive formal supervision for my psychotherapeutic work, and this too was a great mistake for such a disturbed patient, however experienced one thinks one is. At moments of stress the "thinking breast" stops thinking, and is liable to enact the projections it contains. At the end Alison tried to vanish and to become the non-person she felt she had been for her mother as a child. This projection was momentarily but fatally enacted by me when I gave up after only a few attempts to contact her about the canceled session, leaving it to the receptionist to cope next day. This was, in a sense, grossly negligent. Perhaps my "forgetting" did represent my exhaustion and unconscious wish that she would die. The best psychotherapeutic safeguard against suicide is for the therapist to keep the patient's mental pain in mind, and for the patient to be aware of this. That, psychologically, is what it means to be attached. When Alison felt that she did not exist in anyone's mind it aroused the utmost despair. Her suicide was in part protest, in part recognition of her pervasive psychic loneliness. Suicide was the expression of total detachment, for which I, as her therapist, bear a measure of responsibility.

CONCLUSION

Facing the truth—and absolution—helps one survive the death of one's patient. "Any man's death diminishes me" (Donne), but I can also learn from it, and try to do better next time. "Holding" the bereaved therapist in a staff group has the effect of reducing shame, of absolving him, helping him to feel that he is still part of the human chain, and that he does not, through denial, have to commit psychic suicide by killing the guilty part of him that failed the patient.

Since Alison's death I have had a much clearer idea of the scope and limitations of psychiatric and psychotherapeutic roles, and have tried to keep them separate. I recognize more easily how readily one can get caught up in the omnipotence of suicide. I worry whenever I don't have a sense of the patient's pain inside me in some way. I recognize how suicide represents an attempt at fusion with the perfect mother, a denial of ambivalence, of the inevitability of separation and suffering, an assault on the fact that caregivers cannot devote all their time to one person, and therefore always try to arrange shared care where suicide is a real possibility (Campbell and Hale 1991).

Also, in an objective way—I hope not merely as a denial or self-justification—I recognize that suicide is inevitable in some cases, and that, in our work, failure is where we start from. I continue to struggle with the sense of shame that suicide engenders and wish that our culture could fear death less and accommodate the idea of a "noble suicide," as seems to exist in Japan (Iga 1993). Suicide may represent an escape from an intolerable situation, as Nietzsche (quoted in Alvarez 1971) ironically said: "The thought of suicide is a great comfort: with it a calm passage is to be made across many a bad night" (p. 3). Even Alison's death may have been preferable to the miserable life she was leading and inflicting on her children; her death meant that they could go to live with their father, something she could not tolerate in life. Perhaps suicide can occasionally be an expression of mature nonattachment, rather than purely destructive detachment. In trying at all times to stop suicide we arrogantly assume that the life we offer is always preferable to oblivion. Can we be so sure? I sometimes wish I could find some way to say of a suicidal patient, like Mark Anthony of Brutus who fell on his sword at Philippi: "This was the noblest Roman of them all . . . *this* was a man."

Part III

Wider Implications

7

Attachment Theory as a Mediator Between Psychiatry and Psychotherapy

On New Year's Eve 1992 a man suffering from schizophrenia climbed into a lions' cage at the London Zoo and was badly mauled. This event, and others like it, provoked a full-scale moral panic among the British media and government, the tragedy seeming to violate many of the comfortable myths about progress in psychiatry. Whatever we may wish, in reality the lion does *not* lie down with the lamb. Daniel, the visionary, the interpreter of dreams, the one who asserted that *his* God, the God of angels and saints with power over man and beasts, would eventually endure, while all earthly kings were found wanting, emerged from the lions' den unscathed—but secular, psychiatric, detached, decarcerated, visionless, late twentieth century man does not.

In Daniel the vision and the reality, the soothsayer and the king, are kept separate. The story of the triumph of spiritual powers is perhaps a compensatory fantasy expressing the aspirations of an oppressed and displaced Jewish nation. In our society too there is a split between psychotherapists, who are cast in the role of visionaries, and psychiatrists, who represent power and adaptation. Was the tragedy at the zoo emblematic of this divide? Could these disasters have been avoided if the insights of psychotherapy had been welded to the "outsight" (Holmes 1992) of psychiatry?

161

The idea of a psychotherapeutically informed psychiatry seems such a simple and obvious one and yet the divide between psychotherapy and general psychiatry—between "brainlessness" and "mindlessness" (Eisenberg 1986)—has, until recently, seemed unbridgeable. In this chapter, which is something of a collage, I shall explore this split from different perspectives and suggest how attachment theory can contribute to a reconciliation. The main thrust of the chapter is to try to convey something of the feel of practicing psychotherapeutic psychiatry, using an attachment perspective as a framework.

It should be remembered that the divide between psychotherapy and psychiatry is a reflection of a much more general cultural fissure, and to illustrate this point I start with a familiar literary example.

E. M. FORSTER AND THE "TWO CULTURES"

E. M. Forster's *Howards End*, published in 1910, but still with enormous contemporary relevance and power, is perhaps the classic literary account of the debate between the "two cultures"—science and the arts. The novel centers around the cultural polarities of class, culture, and gender, symbolized in various ways by the two protagonistic families—the Schlegels and the Wilcoxes. The Schlegels are female, Bloomsbury-style liberal intellectuals, concerned about poverty and social justice, perhaps in their clinging together exemplifying ambivalent attachment. The Wilcoxes are male dominated, conservative, business-rich, accepting and exploitative of their class position—typically avoidant in their approach to emotional matters. Like psychiatrists, the Wilcoxes are practical people who make and *do*, while, like psychotherapists, the Schlegels are dreamers who feel and *see*. Forster summarizes the tension—sexual and literary—between the two principles, using images that evoke Drake and Shakespeare's John of Gaunt, projected onto the English landscape:

England was alive, throbbing through all her estuaries, crying
for joy through the mouths of her gulls, and the north wind
with contrary motion blew stronger against her rising seas.
What did it mean? For what end are her fair complexities, her
changes of soil, her sinuous coast? Does she belong to those
who have moulded her and make her feared by other lands,
or to those who have added nothing to her power, but have
somehow *seen* her, *seen* the whole island at once, lying as a jewel
in a silver sea, sailing as a ship of souls . . . ? [my italics, p. 152]

Forster's use of the simple word *seen* reflects the whole Bloomsbury ethos of sensitivity and reflection, or of narration as one might
put it from an attachment perspective. The movement of the novel
is the working out of the interchange between these two principles.
Mrs. Wilcox bequeaths a country house, Howards End, to Margaret Schlegel, who later marries Henry Wilcox. In an ideal world
the Wilcoxes and the Schlegels should complement and enrich each
another, the lion *should* lie down with the lamb. For Margaret:

Only connect! That was the whole of her sermon. Only connect the prose and the passion and both will be exalted and
human love will be seen at its height. Live in fragments no
longer. Only connect, and the beast and the monk, robbed of
the isolation that is life to either, will die. [p. 213]

But reality never quite conforms to our ideals. Henry just could
not connect, "for there was one quality in Henry for which she
was never prepared . . . his obtuseness. He simply did not notice
things." Helen becomes furious with him, his hypocrisy (frequent-
ing prostitutes while refusing to allow Margaret's single-parent
sister into his house), his blindness to feelings: "'Not any more of
this,' she cried. 'You shall see the connection if it kills you, Henry!'"
(p. 241). But it is Leonard Bast, the autodidact, the working-class
scholar and husband of Henry's former call girl who dies, sym-
bolically crushed by a bookcase, not Henry himself.

Despite Margaret's fury, and Henry's failure to respond, the
novel ends optimistically with a partial reconciliation between

them, Margaret living at Howards End. This suggests to us that perhaps the two typical defenses of avoidance and ambivalence if they can be brought together somehow complement one another, leading to a less restricted and more coherent whole. Hope is symbolized by the new baby (despite being fatherless) and the promise of a bumper harvest. It is perhaps only this arcadian optimism that dates the book, since the conflict between liberalism and capital, not to mention the sexual hypocrisy of men in high places, is as relevant today as it was eighty years ago.

Howards End serves to remind us that the debate between idealism and realism, between the romantic vision and practical application, between the poetry and the prose, between mind and brain, antecedes the emergence of psychiatry as a profession, and dates at least to that "dissociation of sensibility" that T. S. Eliot claimed began with the Renaissance. Forster's work also reminds us not just of the essential complementarity of the psychiatric and the psychotherapeutic visions, but also of the need for creative conflict as well as compromise between the two approaches. The debate between psychiatry and psychotherapy is located on one of the great geological fault lines of philosophy. It would be surprising if there were not occasional eruptions!

TWO "TRUTHS" OR ONE?—A STORY OF NARRATIVES

Following Freud's lead, the early psychoanalysts tended to assume an automatic scientific status for their findings, which philosophers such as Popper (1968), and more recently Grunbaum (1984) have questioned. The case history, the cornerstone of psychoanalytic theorizing, suffers from two serious flaws. First, it is not clear what sort of data case histories are, since they are inevitably contaminated by the assumptions and preconceptions of the therapist, who, if one views psychoanalytic relationships from an attachment perspective as a "bipersonal field" (Langs 1978), is himself as much a part of the data as is the patient. Second, the method of "enumerative inductivism" (Fonagy 1993)—"It's like this, isn't it," "When I made such and such an interpretation the patient got better"—is no longer acceptable as a scientific procedure, although clinical observation remains an invaluable precursor to more rigorous scientific investigation. As Jaspers (1963, p. 96) put it: "Freud's mistake was to take meaningful connections (understanding, coherence) and erect them into pseudo-theories (explanation, correspondence) of causal connections."

As discussed in the first chapter of this book, one way that psychoanalysts have dealt with this onslaught is by shifting their ground, arguing that psychoanalysis is not a natural scientific discipline but an interpretive or hermeneutic one. They draw on the distinction in nineteenth century German philosophy between *naturwissenschaft*—natural science—and *geistgewissenschaft*—social or mental science—and on the two philosophical approaches to the establishment of truth: correspondence and coherence. As we have mentioned, Spence (1987), in his now well-known distinction, argues that psychoanalytic theories have narrative rather than historical validity and should be judged by their internal consistency and the ways in which they account satisfactorily for the therapeutic data, rather than by whether they correspond with the actual facts of the patient's past life, which are essentially unknowable.

Another distinguished proponent of the narrative approach is Jerome Bruner (1986), who combines an interest in literary theory with his career as one of the founding fathers of developmental psychology. He speaks unapologetically of "two modes of thought," corresponding with Freud's (1911) "two principles of mental functioning" and Jaspers's (1963) "understanding" and "explanation":

> A good story and a well-formed argument are different natural kinds. Both can be used as a means for convincing another. Yet what they convince of is fundamentally different: arguments convince of their truth, stories of their lifelikeness. The one verifies by eventual appeal to procedures for establishing formal and empirical proof. The other establishes its truth by verisimilitude. [p. 16]

Bruner argues that psychological insights almost always contain narrative as well as "scientific" elements. A favorite example to set alongside the famous nineteenth-century chemist Kekule's dream of snakes-biting-their-tails benzene rings is Bohr's idea of complementarity in quantum theory—the impossibility of thinking simultaneously about the position and velocity of a particle—which came to him just after his son had confessed to shoplifting and he was contemplating the impossibility of seeing his son simultaneously in the light of both love and justice. Zukier and Pepitone (1984) conducted an ingenious experiment in which they presented their subjects with a description of a person—"Shy, bespectacled, helpful, slightly withdrawn, orderly"—and then told them that it was drawn at random from a collection of a hundred such character descriptions, of which seventy were of salespersons and thirty of librarians. Who would not override scientific probabilistic bias and, guided by narrative, decide that this *had* to be one of the librarians?

This narrative stance is essentially postmodern, in the sense that it points to an ungraspable chaos that lies behind apparently solid realities, suggesting a plurality of fictions each of which has its own truth, each attempting to make sense of this chaos. The deconstructing of truth is highly relevant to a psychiatry that is a mixture of established scientific fact and ideology. For example, viewing the current epidemic of suicide in young men purely in terms of psychiatric illness leaves out a psychosocial account that picks up on themes of endemic unemployment, urban decay, racism within society, the relative failure of education to engage boys as compared with girls, the ideology of consumerism, society's ambivalence about aggression, men's changing role within the family, and so on (de Zulueta 1994).

Postmodernism makes a virtue out of what seems to be the flaw in the narrative approach to psychoanalysis—if all we have are stories, why worry about whether they are true or not? Postmodernism may reflect and resonate with the fragmentation of modern life, but does one have to make a virtue out of it in one's epistemology? For the scientifically trained the uncomfortable problem remains of assigning equal value to any narrative that happens to be convincing and coherent. Does anything really go? Are spiritualist, psychoanalytic, and biochemical accounts of, say, schizophrenia equally valid or invalid, and is the notion of schizophrenia itself merely a cultural product of twentieth century capitalism? To be sure, as Wallace (1988), who advocates a "perspectival realism" as opposed to the subjectivism of postmodernism, puts it, "Human reality is constructed, but it is constructed from *something*" (p. 140).

However, from an attachment perspective the narrative approach can at least be partially reconciled within conventional scientific discourse. My argument is based on the idea that narrative is not just an artifact, a product of culture rather than nature, but a biological reality—culture being one of the stories that nature tells. As Phillips (1987) puts it, "Stories are lived before they are told" (p. 39).

Behavior is structured and encoded in memory like a story—narratives with beginnings, middles, and endings, structured in sequences, or "event scripts" (Byng-Hall 1995) such as, "When I did this, she did that," or, in Luborsky's (1984) terminology, (a) wish, (b) response of other, (c) response of self to response of other. Indeed, any process that unfolds over time can be considered as a story, whether this be the story of evolution, or the developmental tale that takes us from embryo to adult. In the light of this I shall now look briefly at psychoanalytic models of the development of the mind, and then go on to question the nature of "biological psychiatry" as a story-free domain.

Let us start with Freud. His gloss on the mind/brain debate was the concept of "formulations on the Two Principles of Mental Functioning" (Freud 1911)—the primary and secondary processes, each with its own modus operandi, the one imaginative and wish-fulfilling, the other adaptive and reality-serving. He pictured their relationship in developmental terms, in which the lion-like primary processes are gradually tamed by the forces of socialization—seen by the neo-Freudian Lacanians as the ascendancy of the masculine principle of logos, the phallus, prohibitive rather than generative: "*le no(m) du pere*" (the name of the father/the no of the father).

Freud's contribution to the debate was original in that he saw the mind/brain problem as a biological reality rather than an unsolved philosophical conundrum, a problem as much for developmental psychology as for philosophy. In his view the idealism of the primary processes is developmentally prior to the realism of the secondary process. Object relations theory (Greenberg and Mitchell 1983), by contrast, sees primary and secondary processes not so much in opposition as complementary, based on the Winnicottian (and Kohutian) notion of an area of overlapping interaction between mother and child in which imagination and reality coincide (Winnicott 1971). Stern (1985) somewhat mischievously suggests that Freud's developmental sequence should be reversed, the secondary adaptive processes being in fact *prior* to the primary processes of imagination and fantasy. In his empirically based model of early infancy, mother and child are highly adapted to the realities of one another, and it is only later, with the advent of language, that imaginative (i.e., primary process) thinking could truly be said to be possible. Thus minds emerge from brains, meaning from mechanism, intimacy from attachment.

According to Rycroft (1985) Freud faced a paradox in his view of secondary processes as superior to and superseding the primary:

> Since psychoanalysis aims at being a scientific psychology, psychoanalytic observation and theorising is involved in the paradoxical activity of using secondary processes to observe, analyse, and conceptualise precisely that form of mental activity, the primary processes, which scientific thinking has been at pains to exclude. [p. 166]

This issue perhaps becomes less problematic if adaptation is seen, as in Stern's model, to precede imaginative alterations of reality. Imagination is not, as in the Kleinian vision, a response to deprivation ("no breast–therefore imagine a breast" [Bion 1962, p. 42]), but, rather, the fruits of satisfaction. The securely attached infant is free to play; the insecure infant clings or avoids in order to survive (Bowlby 1988). Thus if we characterize psychiatry as the domain of adaptation and psychotherapy as that of imagination, there is a sense in which psychiatry takes precedence over psychotherapy, in that the patient needs to be attached and capable of understanding before meaningful psychotherapy can begin. With better awareness between the two disciplines the need for paranoid splitting becomes less and a real relationship can begin to develop.

Bowlby (1988) bemoaned what he called the "kidnapping" of the term biological psychiatry by opponents of psychodynamic psychiatry. The story of evolution is a paradigm that underlies the entire science of biology. Psychodynamic ideas are, or should be, no less biological than biochemical theories. Neo-Darwinism can be applied to psychotherapy in interesting and illuminating ways (Slavin and Kriegman 1992). As suggested in Chapter 2, the notion of kin altruism helps to explain the attunement or "primary maternal preoccupation" of Winnicott's (1971) "ordinary devoted mother," and the primary narcissism of the newborn, for whom, thanks to the overlapping interests of mother and child's "selfish genes," the world really is his or her oyster. But, a year or so later, the oedipal child is in a very different situation. His genetic interests are now no longer identical with those of his parents, who will want to produce other children as well as to maintain him. The reality of this conflict will however be concealed from him, in order, Skynner (1976) argues, to protect him from unbearable envy. The oedipal child is thus entering a world—familiar to biologists—of deceit and camouflage, in which the ability to "read" other's intentions and to experience guilt and pain when one is thwarted are essential to survival. If adult sexuality is imported into this arena of potential conflict between generations, especially via a biologically unrelated adult, the stage is set for childhood sexual abuse, which is present (Herman et al. 1989) in such a high proportion of hospitalized psychiatric patients.

Research in the biology of attachment suggests how social events may have direct structural effects on brain functioning. Kraemer (1992) has studied the effects of maternal and peer separation on the development of rhesus monkeys. Monkeys reared in isolation have consistently lower levels of cerebral amines in their cerebrospinal fluid than those reared normally, and their behavior patterns in later life, especially social and sexual behavior, are grossly disrupted. This work can be related to the emerging new paradigm of neural Darwinism, particularily associated with the ideas of Gerald Edelman (Rose 1993). This suggests that learning and memory proceed by the interplay between random events and the strengthening of cortical neural pathways underlying useful behaviors by value systems or "wired-in" reinforcers in the midbrain. It seems likely that maternal attachment behaviors greatly enhance these reinforcing effects, and that this will be reflected in cerebral amine metabolism. In this way the random, or narrative, aspects of an individual's unique biography become embedded in the structural biology of the brain.

In summary, then, the divide between the narrative and scientific accounts of the world is by no means as radical as Bruner would have us believe. But here we find another paradox, since narratives can be seen as accounts of the world that, by encoding time into some enduring structure, represent an attempt to escape into a world outside time. As Shakespeare put it, "As long as men can breathe, and eyes can see/So long lives this and this gives life to thee."

I shall again change gear, this time telling my own story, and one in which time plays an all-too-prominent part. My purpose is to try to convey some of the tensions in trying to combine a psychiatric and a psychotherapeutic vision in one's daily life as a psychiatrist. There is nothing special about this story—it is a version of one that many working in the field of mental health could tell. It is an attempt to get into the narrative structure of the daily rhythms of psychiatric work: the tightrope one walks between the detachment necessary to get things done, and the attachment necessary for them to be meaningful.

A DAY IN THE LIFE OF . . .

Monday morning. I go into the office, glance nervously at the board to see if there have been any new admissions over the weekend, and check that X. has not harmed herself or absconded. The team assembles. A few remarks about the weather, Monday morning jokes. The pile of notes looms ominously. We drag our feet, chatting, not really wanting to make a start. Oh well . . . better get going, we've a lot to get through. Already there is a feeling of the pressure of time, of difficulties ahead, of having to balance the demands of the task with the need to keep the group satisfied, amused, awake. The temptations toward avoidance, to adopt a strictly medical approach, are great; like all avoidant strategies it is a way of surviving, of getting by.

Avoidance and Ambivalence in the Face of Serious Illness

The first patient, David, is a young man suffering from schizophrenia who has been on the ward for three months, held there against his will. He is a waif-like, Bob Dylanish creature whose main interests are fishing, painting, and smoking cannabis. He leads a solitary existence in his bleak apartment, which under the influence of his voices he has frequently smashed up. With medication the voices have gone, but otherwise in the ward he has made little progress, and his only ambition is to be discharged and to return to his former life. We have reluctantly decided to discharge him, mobilizing community support in the pessimistic knowledge that in the past David has refused to cooperate with such offers of help. His parents come in so that we can discuss all this with them. They are a strangely incongruous couple. Father is an ex-soldier, all military bristle and tight as a drum; mother is good looking, slightly artistic in her dress, smiling to hold back tears. They are clearly desperately worried about their son's impending discharge. Then, without us really wanting it, everything spills out. They have been getting on terribly badly; they fight all the time about David; father thinks mother is far too soft on him, giving him money and food, mollycoddling him, while he was out earning his living at that age; she sees him as cruelly hard in his dealings with David, hates his habitual drinking, and dreads the fights that break out between father and son, one of which precipitated this admission.

Their distress, so different in its manifestations is palpable. Worry about David has activated intense attachment behavior in mother; she wants to be with him all the time, can't relax for a moment while he is alone in his flat, worries about suicide. Father is equally tense and worried, has slept badly for years, feels that what David needs is a good kick in the backside, and is fed up with our inability to do much— all the classic features of avoidance. Gradually we try to help them work more together as a team. I compare David to a wounded buddy on the battlefield, ask father how he would help? Father replies that he would get him to the experts as soon as possible! I try to discourage their sweeping criticisms of one other: "You are *never* kind to David, always hassling him," says mother; "You *always* give in to him," replies father. I compare the words *never* and *always* with landmines in a family that can gradually destroy them. Like E. M. Forster's Wilcoxes and Schlegels, if only they could connect, David would be less drawn into their differences, more likely to find a way forward for himself. Eventually after nearly an hour, arrangements are made for family therapy and they depart, leaving us moved and confronted with the terrible pain of severe mental illness, our inadequacy in the face of it, and yet with some sense of having tried our best and having moved things forward a little.

We clear our minds in readiness for the next patient.

The Meaning of Delusions

Martin, a man in his early thirties suffering from schizophrenia, drifted onto our ward when he was thrown out by the hostel where he was living, and seems to have taken root here, quietly avoiding attempts to engage him in occupational therapy or to strike up much of a relationship with his ward therapist. He spends most of his day lying on his bed and only becomes animated when it is time for him to receive the analgesics that we have agreed to give him if he in turn will take the major tranquilizers we think he needs. Pain is his problem, pain in his mind when "they" attack him with "ESP" ("You know all about that Doc," he says conspiratorially), pain in his back, which means he hasn't been able to work for the past ten years, pain in his groin when "they" attack him there. He is pale, distant, leans away with a frightened look when one tries to talk to him. The nurses feel they can't get through to him. We make a more determined attempt than usual. He speaks of his childhood, of his parents' fights, of his alcoholic mother who terrorized them: "She used to beat me black and blue—the pain of it." He wants his "drugs" reduced. "I can't hear the voices, it feels empty and lonely in there"—indicating his mind. He goes out. We feel something has been achieved, through the link with the traumatizing childhood a *story* has emerged and so his pain has become a little more explicable, although there is little we can do for him. The discussion moves onto practical arrangements. Who will contact the housing department about accommodation? Why is it all taking so long?

The morning continues. A stream of suffering—girls with arms crisscrossed with self-inflicted scars, weeping and hateful of their womanhood; boys, jerky, staccato, inarticulate, full of fury and violence; women crushed by their responsibilities, or, their children and husbands gone, dried up and useless-feeling; men who have lost everything—their skills no longer needed, wives who have decided they will no longer submit to their demands and threats. The devastation and emptiness of madness—and sometimes its wild crazy humor: The patient who—much to the rest of the team's glee—punctures my pomposity with: "Shut up, you cheeky monkey." Patients who wheedle, manipulate, drink when they should not, refuse to eat when they are starving, sleep in the day and stay awake all night, leave when we want them to stay, refuse to go when we have had enough of them. Patients who are pitiful, funny, heartwarming; patients who threaten or seem inaccessibly remote. People who arouse our affection, fear, pity; people we hate or who leave us cold. Old friends, and people we hope never to see again. The flotsam and jetsam of humanity swept in by the morning tide.

In each encounter we try above all to make contact, to connect; to get a picture of the patient's mind into our own minds; to attune ourselves to their pain and suffering; to accept their anger, acknowledge their feelings of rejection and abandonment and abuse. However brief the conversation, that is the aim. At the same time we must not become overinvolved, we must retain a degree of nonattachment. Inevitably, we fall back on our routines of anxious attachment—without them the pain would be overwhelming. We are busy *doing*—planning, arranging, moving on, prescribing, committing, nudging, confronting, encouraging, stimulating, sedating, arousing, and getting to sleep. And always a sense of the pressure of time, never enough time, a job always half done, getting by, doing our best, wrestling with what seem sometimes like insuperable problems with inadequate means. Having to balance that with a much longer perspective on time, with the knowledge that this too will pass, with a sense of the cyclical nature of difficulty and suffering, that people do recover, adapt, find their own solutions, and that what overwhelms us today will by next week have been replaced by a different seemingly impossible situation. Also, escaping from the uncertainty of the work into the certainty of what we do know, sometimes defensively (but often appropriately) into diagnosis, mental state, prescription. Always trying to come back to the present experience: the encounter with the patient right now in the room, with the buoyancy and humor of the team, with a sense of doing what we can do, and not trying to do what we cannot.

It is afternoon now. A family therapy clinic (FTC) where some of the intractable morning problems can be tackled at leisure and in depth. Leisure. A dangerous word. Can we allow ourselves the luxury of leisure in today's climate? Is it justifiable to tie up a whole team for an entire afternoon to work on two families? What about the drug clinic running simultaneously—are they not struggling with the wretched of the earth while we enjoy ourselves? (We were moved by these considerations—and by a team member's husband, who happened to be law professor, who, as a taxpayer, questioned the justification for seeing a family whose presenting complaint was that the wife objected to her husband taking a nap after lunch!—to make a rule that we would only see patients in the FTC who had been ill enough to be inpatients.)

For enjoy ourselves we do. There is enough time. We do our best. We can offer the families a commitment to staying with them until the problem is resolved. Above all we enter into the experience and meaning of the illness, how it affects the reality of patients' lives. In theory the same is true of psychiatric work, and it is certainly the job of the psychiatrist to make sure that through his encounter with the whole team the patient has a sense of being held and of shared meaning, but the personal encounter with the patient is often so brief that it feels fragmentary and ephemeral.

I should not idealize the family clinic. Families cancel, key people (often fathers) refuse to turn up, homework is not done, families feel stuck and we are often baffled by them, and even those with whom we think we are successful reveal that it was really the secret visits to the healer that made the difference!

Next day is my psychotherapy morning. For whatever reasons, good or bad, it is a fact that my portfolio is skewed toward young, attractive, verbal, intelligent, successful patients. Many are long-term patients I have seen for several years. Several are medical colleagues, caught in crises in which the work to which they have devoted themselves seems, with the health service reforms, to have turned to ashes, facing the emptiness of their family lives that overinvestment in work has shielded them from, but that now stares them in the face.

Burnout

Paul, a two-month follow-up brief therapy case, is a nurse who had become profoundly depressed following the breakup of a relationship. He is now much improved, no longer suicidal or drinking, and enjoying and using his solitude. This is an interesting case because Paul had been briefly on the inpatient unit and had been quite shocked when on rounds I had firmly challenged him about his drinking in a way that would have been much more difficult in the psychotherapy sessions. During a subsequent therapy hour he had been able to talk about how furious and humiliated this episode had made him feel—his rather avoidant clinging relieved by this outburst of anger. This enabled him to recall similar feelings aroused in him by his father, a stickler for correct dress and manners, who had abandoned Paul to his demanding and sickly mother when he was 12. The combination of firmness and sticking with him; his ability to challenge me; working through his feelings of intimidation and humiliation to a sense of shared meaning and purpose; feeling that he could do things his way, while remaining in emotional contact with a therapist who was warm but nonpossessive; the sense of comprehensive care so that when he needed admission it was available, and when he needed to talk about the impact of the admission that was possible too—all these seem to have contributed to his rather unexpected temporary recovery.

The satisfying morning is balanced by a clinic afternoon, work guided by necessity, guilt, and the pragmatics of offering supportive therapy to two types of very difficult patients. Some of these are unsuitable for formal therapy, because of violence, muteness, extreme dependency, addiction, unreliability, or a personality that might disintegrate under the pressure of therapy. Providing them with something—a "minimum necessary intervention" (Skynner 1976)—often little more than nothing, perhaps 20 minutes every two months, enables the psychotherapy department to refuse treatment with a clearer conscience. I see it as a challenge and an important part of my role as a consultant to do this work. Others are also difficult patients, but nevertheless are in some form of therapy and also need a medical point of reference to prescribe, assess suicide risk, take an overview of their needs, and, with the primary therapist, to act as a symbolic "combined parent" who they may eventually internalize.

This supportive work is hard; as with doing rounds, one is constantly aware of time, but the work can be rewarding, perhaps like playing simultaneous chess on twelve boards on once. Every minute of each encounter has to tell. One has to focus on the present moment while remaining nonattached. The patient must feel that you are acutely attuned to them with all your attention. What do you offer? Acceptance, continuity, stability. Paradoxically, given the briefness of the encounter, a sense of timelessness. As time goes by there is a sense of shared history. The session becomes perhaps a reference point in the patient's life. Patient and doctor gradually get to know one another. Sometimes one is the necessary bad object, the source of all a person's disappointment and frustration; sometimes one is idealized. Sometimes there is catharsis, with many tears; sometimes very little seems to happen. One patient, for whom my refusal to give her more is a well-gnawed bone of contention, writes to me after each session, to which I reply, usually briefly, so there is a parallel therapy going on by correspondence. No doubt this work has a good deal of avoidance and defensiveness on both sides. Perhaps I am avoiding the real encounter with disturbance and dependency that would be unleashed if the patients were offered proper therapy. Perhaps I cannot face the rage and disappointment that might accompany outright refusal to help the unhelpable. Perhaps I am not even offering half a loaf, just crumbs of comfort, mere smidgens that whet the appetite but fail to nourish. But against this is the implicit facing of reality—the refusal to offer false hope, the determination to achieve something worthwhile, even within the desperately narrow constraints of the emotional impoverishment that so often underlies psychiatric disturbance, and the organizational impoverishment of contemporary publicly funded psychiatry.

CONCLUSION

If integration between psychiatry and psychotherapy is to be achieved each side will have to abandon traditional ways of thinking. Here an attachment perspective can be an invaluable framework for shaping interventions. We shall have to find some way of offering severely disturbed patients a secure base. This can no longer be the cold avoidant corridors of the "stone mother," the traditional mental hospital. Nor should it be the confusion and transience and chaos of inadequately funded community care. Seeing the paramount importance of attachment needs can inform therapeutic strategies, as the following case tries to illustrate.

Example: The Demon Lover

Anna, already mentioned in Chapter 5, was 27, suffering from borderline personality disorder with typical features of alcohol abuse, anorexia/bulimia, violent mood swings, poor impulse control, repeated deliberate self-harm (including a near-fatal burning), intense self-loathing, and unsatisfactory relationships. She spent many months in the hospital in a suicidal state. Antidepressants, electroconvulsive therapy, cognitive therapy, and family therapy had all been tried without lasting benefit. Intelligent and obsessional, she spent much of her time on the ward trying to evade the nurse whose role it was to prevent her from leaving the ward and harming herself, which she nevertheless managed to regularily to do.

Anna was the middle of three children. Her mother had left home when she was 10 to live with another man, but after a year she returned and the marriage was patched up. Anna was privy to her mother's affair and had felt miserably unhappy about it, but had been unable to tell anyone about her feelings. She had entered into an abusive relationship with an older man soon after she reached puberty.

During a family interview Anna's husband and mother had turned on the psychiatrist and accused him of failing to protect Anna from herself, and complaining that she was no better now than she had been when her illness started four years previously. The psychiatrist felt a mixture of barely concealed rage and helplessness in the face of this onslaught, but in response to Anna request to be "put to sleep for a few days to get away from my horrible thoughts" the team decided to try to implement an even more vigilant special policy in an attempt to create a greater sense of holding and secure base for her. At the same time regular psychotherapy was started in which she began to explore for the first time her abusive relationship.

Despite these efforts she continued to harm herself, and the consultant and ward team again felt useless and furious. It was suggested to Anna that, through her actions rather than her conscious intentions, she was putting the team in the position she had been in as a child, faced with her mother's abandonment, and that, through her actions, she was communicating the feelings of rage and powerlessness she had felt then to alter or influence her mother's behavior. She became very angry at this, saying, "So you're telling me there's nothing you can do, no hope." The consultant went on to suggest that she was in love with death; her constant thoughts of dying were like a love affair, exciting, alluring, all-consuming, and that she experienced the ward staff as trying to separate her from this demon lover. Her primary attachment figure had become death and destruction itself. This led to a much more open discussion about her sexual confusion, her shame and guilt about the conviction that she might be gay. She revealed that at the moment when she had "inexplicably" burned herself she was particularly tormented by this confusion.

It was only when Anna was securely and firmly held by the ward environment that anger and rage could be faced—her own and that of the staff—and it was only then that her true *story* emerged, the meaning behind her "inexplicable" acts of self-destruction. Attachment theory emphasizes the importance of separation protest, and its acceptance and metabolism by the attachment figure, but to reproduce such security within the environment of contemporary psychiatry remains an enormous challenge.

A second concluding point, may, in view of what has been said so far, seem paradoxical: the greater the integration between psychiatry and psychotherapy, the more the need for a clearly defined boundary between them. It is all too easy to practice a mishmash of basic psychiatry and half-baked psychotherapy—an antidepressant here, an anxiety management group there—without clearly defined roles, limits, or objectives. Opening up one's practice of psychiatry to psychotherapy can be confusing. Losing the certainties—however artificial—of a narrowly defined medical or psychotherapeutic approach, one can end up feeling neither fish nor fowl. As I have repeatedly suggested, strategies of anxious attachment are, for all their restrictiveness, still strategies; they serve their purpose, and the danger of giving them up is that it opens the way as much for disorganization as for a more secure solution.

Part of the great success of Sutherland's model of a psychoanalytic contribution to the war effort in World War II, described in Chapter 4, was his insistence that the military remain in managerial control, with the psychotherapists merely as advisors and supporters. I have described in a previous chapter the disastrous consequences of trying to combine a psychotherapeutic and a psychiatric management role with the same patient. Hybrid vigor, yes; chimeras, no. Rounds on a psychiatric ward should be a facilitating environment in which feelings can be openly expressed and discussed, but is more like a family meeting than a psychotherapy session, however much we may try to use psychotherapeutic ideas to inform and deepen our understanding of our patients and decisions about them.

This brings us back to our beginning. A chimera is a creature with a lion's head, a goat's body, a serpent's tail—a pluripotential creature representing both the fantasies of early childhood in which all is still possible—when the "double difference" (Chasseguet-Smirgel 1985) between the generations and between the sexes is not yet fixed—but also a nightmare world of confusion and terror. Secure attachment not only arises from connectedness and attunement, but also depends on firm boundaries, on the capacity to protest and say no, and to acknowledge difference.

In this chapter I have tried to relate a very practical problem—the relationship between psychiatry and psychotherapy—to the historical and philosophical forces that shape everyday thought and professional behavior. Philosophical dualism underlies the "two-cultures" split as it does the divide between mindful psychotherapy and brainy psychiatry. Yet our very notion of mind and brain may be in need of revision. Research, much of it inspired by the ideas of attachment theory, can now begin dimly to envisage how the personal narratives of the mind are signposted and etched into the brain by sociobiological reinforcers. In the next chapter I shall explore some of the ethical implications of these emerging paradigms.

8

Nonattachment and
the Role of Values in Psychotherapy

To state that values are important in psychotherapy can be highly provocative or entirely uncontentious. Freud (1940a), an implacable critic of religion, saw himself as a scientist, offering "a method not a doctrine," in search, as Rieff (1979) puts it, of "truth but not 'The Truth'" (p. 7). In this view science and values are separate, mutually incompatible approaches to the world. Science is descriptive and depends on verification, while ethics is prescriptive and is based on justification. But in practice, as I have argued in the previous chapter, this neat distinction is far from the everyday realities of either science or ethics, especially as applied to psychotherapy. Attachment theory, for all its roots in scientific observation, is no less a form of advocacy than other approaches to psychotherapy. In this chapter I shall develop the idea of nonattachment as a positive value in a postmodernist world. To set this in context, let us look first more generally at contemporary ideas about values in psychotherapy.

Whatever their views on the scientific basis of their discipline, most psychotherapists would sharply differentiate their tasks from those of priests or politicians or other overt purveyors of values within society. But recently, however, there has been a call (Bergin

1991), by no means universally accepted (London 1984), to recognize that therapists' personal value systems significantly influence practice, and that it might be better explicitly to acknowledge this rather than to sweep it underground, and also to accept that therapeutic effectiveness depends on a degree of congruence between the patient's values and those of the therapist.

Less contentiously, it is clear that psychotherapists, like other professionals, operate within an ethical framework comprising a set of socially prescribed values such as respect for individuals, avoidance of doing harm, alleviation of suffering, adherence to the law, and so on. It is also apparent that, at times, psychotherapists are called upon to make distinct moral choices, as, for example, when confronted with a potentially violent patient, they have to choose between preserving confidentiality and the need to protect society at large.

In contrast to Freud's view of psychoanalysis as a value-free scientific activity, there are those who argue that psychoanalysis is an *inherently* moral discipline, albeit one of a rather unusual type: "He [Freud] is not only the first completely irreligious moralist, he is a moralist without even a moralising message" (Reiff 1979, p. 13), and "psychoanalysis is a mature natural religion." At a practical level Lomas (1987) and Smail (1988), among others, argue that what matters in psychotherapy is not technique, which they see as the shibboleth of a narrow materialist culture, but the personal qualities of the therapist, her capacity for love and honesty.

This polarization between those who view psychotherapy as a science and those who claim that it is a species of secular religion needs to be qualified by recent developments within the philosophy of science and applied ethics. First, science itself, and in particular human science, is never entirely value-free, in the sense that it is inevitably influenced by the prevailing mores and concerns of society. To take a familiar example, Darwin's theory of evolution emerged in the context of the Luddite unrest of the 1830s and incorporated the Malthusian notion of the the survival of the fittest. Second, moral viewpoints need to be supported by rational discourse to which the scientific methods of observation, classification, experimentation, and refutation can make a vital contribution. Third, a comparable practical discipline such as medicine, which looms over ethical discussion in psychotherapy as both exemplar and point of differentiation, is both science-based *and* permeated with questions of value and ethics, many of which have psychotherapeutic reverberations—over euthanasia, abortion, the just distribution of scarce medical resources, or whether lifestyle should influence eligibility for costly treatments such as transplant surgery, to take familiar examples.

VALUES AND PSYCHOANALYSIS

Psychoanalytic approaches to values and ethics have gone through three distinct stages, starting with Freud's initial espousal of science and disparagement of religion. This was followed by a recognition that not only does psychoanalysis embody a system of values but that it has important things to say about the origins of the sense of good and bad, about reparation, forgiveness, and moral maturation. Recently there have been attempts to link psychoanalysis with more transcendental themes of fate, beauty, chance, and "nothingness." These stages correspond roughly with those of classicism, modernism, and postmodernism, and can likewise be mapped onto Kant's three areas of human understanding: science, ethics, and aesthetics (Rustin 1991).

Psychoanalysis: An Ethical System

Phillip Rieff's (1979) classic, *The Mind of the Moralist,* remains a key text in the rehabilitation of values within psychoanalysis. Rieff attempted to "back-translate" what he saw as Freud's conversion of moral discourse into the language of science: "Psychoanalysis is the triumph in ethical form of the modern scientific idea" (p. 27). Just as nature is deceptive, its trompe-l'oeils requiring the subtlety of the scientist to yield up their secrets, so too is our inner world, requiring the probes of the psychoanalyst to reveal what is latent within our moral (and immoral) nature.

For Rieff, the "scientific" language of psychoanalysis is a metaphor that enabled Freud to put across his moral message in a secular age. The values of truth and honesty, and their verbal expression, are central to Freud's thought. His mission was to find a language with which to describe inner experience. He believed that the power of neurosis could, like Rumplestiltskin's, be broken if only the right words could be found to describe it:

> What for Freud is "repression" psychologically understood, is "secrecy," morally understood . . . sickness may be viewed as an ingrown gesture . . . the way a patient speaks even when he is mute. [Rieff 1979, p. 317]

This passage evokes links between attachment status and narrative style as discussed in Part I and the previous chapter. Rieff sees psychoanalysis as an expression of the enlightenment values of autonomy and democracy as manifest within the individual psyche. Analysis leads to an enfranchisement of the unconscious, limiting the powers of the autocratic superego, and educating the ego in self-government, as embodied in Sutherland's social vision of psychoanalysis (see Chapter 4). However, as Rieff and many others have pointed out, Freud's liberalism was as conservative as it was revolutionary. He aimed to rid us of our illusions about the perfectibility of man: "Men must live with the knowledge that their dreams are by function optimistic and cannot be fulfilled. . . . Every cure must expose him to new illness" (p. 319). Rieff comments wryly on Freud's famous prescription for "transforming . . . hysterical misery into common unhappiness. . . . It is a curious sort of promise to have attracted so many followers" (p. 321).

Rieff links Freud's paradoxical ethical stance of optimistic pessimism, or active passivity (which also have their clinical resonances) with the philosophy of the Stoics and Epictetus, and Eastern religion: "There is something Oriental in the Freudian ethic" (p. 320), the aim of psychoanalytic spiritual guidance being to wean away the ego from both heroic and compliant attitudes toward the surrounding community.

Psychoanalysis as a Profession

Freud was ambivalent about the status of psychoanalysis as a profession. He bracketed it with government and education as "impossible professions . . . because one can be sure beforehand of achieving unsatisfying results" (Freud 1937a). Thus he half-acknowledges that psychoanalysis cannot be understood as a purely technical discipline, but depends on a sound therapeutic alliance and on the will of the analysand if it is to succeed. If we compare psychoanalysis or psychotherapy with other liberal professions such as the law or medicine, three obvious differences stand out. First, moral difficulties in psychotherapy arise from the fact that it is not just a treatment for psychological sickness; it also aims to be a prophylactic, strengthening the character against further illness. This is not just an idle claim: in the National Institute of Mental Health (NIMH) treatment of depression trial, psychotherapeutic treatments were, compared with antidepressants, on the whole *less* effective in relieving symptoms but *more* useful at maintaining patients symptom-free following a period of treatment (Elkin et al. 1989). Second, relief of symptoms—depression, anxiety, obsessionality—is much easier to define than it is to decide what constitutes "good health," especially good psychological health.

Third, the normal contrast betwen moral framework and technical content does not hold fast in psychotherapy in the same way as it does in other professions. Much of the technical content of psychotherapy is directly concerned with moral difficulties: Rieff (1979) again: "All the issues which psychoanalysis treats—health and sickness of the will, the emotions, the responsibilities of private living, the coercions of culture—belong to the moral life" (p. 11). Whereas a patient may similarly present to a doctor or lawyer with a moral dilemma, the main business of their transaction is essentially technical—physiological or legal. Indeed these professionals often recognize this when they recommend to a client that what she "*really* needs is to see a psychiatrist."

Post-Freudian Ethics

Contemporary psychoanalysis is a pluralistic melting pot containing a number of differing perspectives, of which ego psychology, object relations, the interpersonal school, self psychology, and Lacanianism are the most significant (Bateman and Holmes 1995). Each embodies a distinct ethical perspective. Shafer (1992) traces the development of Freud's thought from "guilty man" of the Oedipus complex to "tragic man" of the death instinct. Ego psychology presupposes a relatively benign society to which a healthy individual can adapt, and aims to free the ego from its conflictual constraints, leading to a greater sense of freedom and autonomy.

In object relations theory, as developed by Klein and Bion, the emphasis is on relationships with oneself and others. The movement from the paranoid-schizoid to the depressive position implies a more coherent and integrated self, less dominated by the need to project unwanted feelings into others, the development of concern for the object, and the capacity to experience remorse and reparation. Only in the depressive position is real intimacy possible, both with one's true or authentic self and with the other. Object relations, especially as developed by post-Kleinians, provides a contemporary account of the nature of evil, seen in terms of perverse splitting in which the object is sequestered and terrorized by unmodulated aggression and envy. Throughout this book we have looked at the ways in which attachment theory describes the developmental conditions leading to psychological health, showing how meanings—and secure attachment—arise out of the sensitivity and attunement (or otherwise) of the parental environment.

In the Christian tradition pride is seen as a sinful obstacle to a good life. The psychological equivalent of pride is narcissism, which implies omnipotence and self-centeredness. Self psychology distinguishes between healthy narcissism—good self-esteem, pride in one's real achievements—and pathological narcissism—a defensive retreat in the face of an unempathic nurturing environment. Finally Lacanian psychoanalysis is critical of the conformism implicit in ego psychology and the notion of a conflict-free area of the personality. Lacan insists on a "return to Freud" and to the ineluctable law of the phallus—the "*no(m) du pere*"—the word. However, words also contain the possibility of liberation. In the "symbolic order," through the expression of feelings in language, relief and maturation are possible.

Psychoanalysis, Aesthetics, and Religion

The third phase of psychoanalytic values is the realm of the aesthetic. As a science, psychoanalysis tries to uncover the truth about the nature of the psyche and its development. As an ethical system psychoanalysis is Keatsian: truth is goodness and goodness means an absence of splitting—an acceptance of one's "bad" parts without the need to deny or project them. The aesthetic dimension emphasizes the search for a form or container within which feelings can be truthfully symbolized and so objectified. This container may be the analytic relationship itself (Bion's "thinking breast"), art in all its varied forms, or religion.

If psychoanalysis values above all the symbolic expression and containment of inner feelings, this leads to a perspective on religion very different from Freud's original critique. Symington (1994) distinguishes between primitive religions, whose main function is as a social defense against infantile anxieties, and mature religion as expressions of man's highest spiritual leanings and ethical striving. Black (1993) similarly sees religions as comprising internal objects enabling the believer to "speak more truthfully of, and relate more fully to, the larger matrix within which the human world is situated." Symington's "God-term" (Rieff 1979, p. 188) is not the unconscious, but "the Other." Basing his approach on the Christian philosopher MacMurray (1957), for whom "the religious activity of the self is to enter into communion with the Other" (p. 117), Symington sees psychoanalysis as a secular religion whose aim is to help its patients to find better and more satisfying relationships not with an external deity, but with the Other. His distinction might be compared with that made in Chapter 1 between attachment and intimacy, primitive religions providing attachment to a God as a defense against anxiety, mature religions offering a pathway to intimacy with oneself, one's God, and other people.

Psychoanalysis and Postmodernism

The term *postmodernism* attempts to capture a number of contemporary philosophical, political, and aesthetic perspectives, including multiculturalism, feminism, pluralism, contextualism, narrative, and linguistics. Despite tendencies to pretentiousness and obscurity, postmodernism represents a serious attempt to characterize and theorize aspects of the fragmentation and confusion of modern, especially urban, life.

In his exploration of ethics in an era of postmodernism, Rorty (1991) draws extensively on Freud:

> Beginning in the 17th century we tried to substitute a love of truth for a love of God, treating the world described by science as a quasi divinity. Beginning at the end of the 18th century we tried to substitute a love of ourselves for a love of scientific truth, a worship of our own deep spiritual or poetic nature, treated as one more quasi divinity. . . . Freud . . . suggests that we try to get to the point where we no longer worship *anything*, where we treat *nothing* as a quasi divinity, where we treat *everything*—our language, our conscience, our community—as a product of time and chance. To reach this point would be, in Freud's words, to "treat chance as worthy of determining our fate." [p. 39]

Rorty's heroine, or rather antiheroine, is the "liberal ironist" who questions all the "grand narratives"—liberalism, Marxism, science, even psychoanalysis—of the last two centuries, seeing them in relativistic terms, as languages rather than absolute truths, but who nevertheless carries on without relapsing into nihilism and despair. The typical expression of this position would be E. M. Forster's (1925, echoing Butler) "I disbelieve, Lord, help thou my disbelief" (p. 2). Freud's stoicism, coupled with its constant examination of the unconscious context of conscious thought, might make psychoanalysis a perfect candidate for the Rortyian position. But psychoanalysis as an institution struggles just as much with its transference to Freud and psychoanalysis as any other grand narrative, and certainly falls short of the Whiteheadian criterion: "A science that fails to forget its founders is doomed" (Whitehead 1958, p. 72).

For Rorty, contingency and irony are key concepts for contemporary ethical theory. *Contingency* is the term that expresses the chance-based "de-divinization of the self," which he sees as the essence of postmodernism. Here he is very close to Freud in his sense of the dethroning of man's narcissism. We think we are in control of our destiny, make rational choices, and determine our fate, but in reality we are products of history, not just in the grand-narrative Marxist sense, but in our unique developmental history, in the ghosts that inhabited the particular nursery in which we grew up. In the psychoanalytic view, it is not just Man whose narcissism is dethroned, but each one of us, every man and woman. We have to learn first to love ("divinize") ourselves and our parents, and then to outgrow ("dedivinize") that self-love, a movement described in self psychology as "optimal disillusionment," and which can be seen in terms of attachment theory as a pathway from attachment and intimacy, through detachment and autonomy, to what I have called nonattachment.

For Rorty, the self is a "tissue of contingencies": of the random accidents of history that have made us what we are. This is the destiny that Bollas (1987) sees us continuously exploring and symbolizing in our lived lives. We are constantly creating a story, a narrative, of that destiny. We need these stories in order to live, charts that take us through the vagaries of contingency. Psychoanalysis helps us first to be able to symbolize—to dream our lives as Bollas puts it—and then to create more relevant and more subtle narratives.

What remains if, Ozymandias-like, all grand narratives are found wanting, if our attachment to any idea—even the idea of rational discourse—is questioned? At a philosophical level we are left with Rorty's nothingness. Must we then see Freud as a nihilist? No. Nothingness can be seen as an aspect of what Buddhism calls "impermanence," or Freud "transience," and can be related to the notion of the death instinct. As an explanatory term the death instinct may be questionable and even tautologous (to argue that we envy or destroy because of the death instinct is similar to Molière's doctor who claimed that hypnotic drugs make us fall asleep because of their "dormitive properties"); but as an ethical principle it has much in its favour, if it reminds us to see our passions and to bear our unhappiness from a more detached vantage point.

Psychoanalysis and Activism

Critics of psychoanalysis, of whom Singer (1994) has recently been one of the most articulate, have criticized psychoanalysis for its "inward turn," its concentration on the self, and turning away from attempts to improve the all-too-obvious inequalities and suffering of the world. Singer argues that in order to lead a more ethical life—one that is based on solidarity with the wider community of humanity—it is necessary to overcome self-centeredness and to "take the perspective of the universe" (p. 188). But Singer takes no account of the unconscious. For him, all that appears to be needed if people are to be persuaded to act less selfishly is to present the rational arguments for humane treatment of animals and for more just distribution of resources, and to demonstrate the emptiness of a life based on consumerism. He fails to acknowledge that many consciously noble attempts to improve the world have ended in disaster, and he does not tackle the sense of will-sapping despair inherent in the unhappiness of the borderline character, which is often only temporarily relieved by action; nor does he appear to recognize the need for psychological maturity if selfishness is truly to be overcome, and hate and envy harnessed by beneficence.

How then do we build community and solidarity out of a position that emphasizes emptiness and transience? For Rorty a key quality of the liberal ironist is her "skill at imaginative identification." He sees the ethical themes for the twenty-first century as the personal search for autonomy, and public avoidance of inflicting pain on others. Rorty sees these private and public spheres as essentially unrelated, and is suspicious of attempts to link them through such soft slogans as "the personal is the political." But psychoanalysis provides a link between personal freedom and wider concern for the other, based on scientific investigation of the inner world of childhood and emotional disorder in adults. As discussed in Part I, "emotional autonomy" (Holmes and Lindley 1989)—the discovery of the true self—arises out of a relational context of secure attachment in which the child discovers his spontaneity and begins to build up a picture of the mind of the other. Postmodernism is similarly built around the crucial insight that we inhabit an inescapably *relational* linguistic universe, and that truth "out there" is inseparable from the language we use to describe it. The Wittgensteinian view that private languages are impossible can be turned around to the idea that we inhabit a world of others. Winnicott's (1958) much-quoted aside—"There is no such thing as an infant" (p. xxxvii)—suggests not just a baby feeding from a mother, but also a mother and baby communicating with one another, albeit in the proto-language of "babyspeak."

What is special about psychotherapy as a moral discipline, and what makes it so relevant to the postmodernist world we inhabit, is that, without proselytizing, or purveying any of the varieties of grand narrative, but simply through her skill at imaginative identification the therapist is helping her patient to inhabit the human community more comfortably, more fully, more spontaneously, and so to be able to attach and detach herself more authentically and autonomously. The therapist does this on the basis of her own ethical values. These comprise at one level the standard psychotherapeutic ethical precepts: reliability, attentiveness, confidentiality, nonintrusiveness, and respectfulness of boundaries. At a deeper level they require a texture of moral integrity, the capacity for spontaneous gesture, for love and hate, and for picking up and letting go that I have tried to encapsulate in the term *nonattachment*. I am not saying that psychotherapists must become saints or priests or Zen masters, but it does mean that psychotherapy should be seen as a discipline that requires moral development on the part of·the therapist as well as acquisition of technical skills.

VALUES AND PSYCHOTHERAPY RESEARCH

Psychoanalysis is only one of many forms of psychotherapy. In the less-rarefied atmosphere of psychotherapy a similar movement from a narrowly defined scientific ideology to a concern with values and ethics has also taken place. In 1980 a small bombshell hit the world of empirical psychotherapy research when Bergin (1980) published his paper "Psychotherapy and Religious Values," in which he argued that despite their reticence about admitting it, psychotherapists generally had a set of firmly held values about the constituents of a good life, which could loosely be called religious, and that the existence of such values was positively correlated with mental health. Bergin's "coming out"—religion being the last taboo, after sex and death, in psychotherapy—led, he claimed, to an explosion of welcoming letters and requests for reprints, and initiated intense research activity in the field of values in psychotherapy.

A number of important findings have emerged from this work. Strongly held religious beliefs are indeed protective against mental illness (Bergin et al. 1988). Psychotherapy process researchers have investigated the question of congruence between the values held by patients and those held by therapists, which, it might seem, would be likely to be linked to favorable outcomes. In fact the relationship between congruence and outcome is subtle. Patients do assimilate their therapists' values in the course of therapy, at least as perceived by therapists, but the best outcome arises when the values of the patient and therapist are moderately similar, neither too close nor too divergent. This would be consistent with viewing autonomy as one of the central goals of therapy since to be autonomous is to discover one's own set of values, based neither on slavish adherence to, nor rebellious rejection (Erikson's "negative identity") of, authority.

Therapeutic Neutrality

Perhaps the most contentious aspect of Bergin's broadside is his assault on the hallowed notion of therapeutic neutrality. He argues that this is a myth, that even the most nondirective of therapists have firmly held values and that it is helpful to the patient if their therapists are explicit about, for example, their valuation of freedom, fidelity in intimate relationships, work, the need to be truthful at all times, and espousing a set of higher or spiritual values. Bergin's argument, however, is weakened by his conflation of an ethical *framework* and *technique*, and by his failure to distinguish different levels of value judgment. Psychotherapists operate within an implicit moral framework. In the context of family therapy Boszormenyi-Nagy and his co-workers (1991) bring socially accepted public values such as justice and responsibility to bear on the private inner world of the family—their techniques aim to ensure that justice is done and responsibility taken, as the family confronts its tasks.

However, an essential component of the technique of psychotherapy is the suspension of judgment and the creation of an atmosphere of acceptance. A balance has to be struck between facilitating a trusting relationship by letting the patient know that she and the therapist share certain values, and the need for reticence if unconscious feelings are to surface in the service of fostering the patient's autonomy. In attachment terms there has to be a middle path between responsiveness and intrusion. People might, for different reasons, seek out Christian counseling, feminist psychoanalysis, or a therapist from the same ethnic minority as themselves. Therapist and patient need to inhabit a similar moral universe and thus to share common higher level moral assumptions. But at the level of specific beliefs—that abortion is always wrong, marriage is invariably disadvantageous to women, for example—the therapist's values, if they intrude, may hinder rather than foster progress.

Values and the Triangle of Attachment

It is perhaps best to see psychotherapeutic values as based on higher levels of generality than specific beliefs about, say, fidelity, or the existence of a particular type of deity. For Freud the aims and values of psychoanalysis were summarized as to help the patient to be able to "love and work"—to which Pedder (1995) adds "play." Bergin's goals are freedom, love, identity, truth, universal values, symptom management, and work. The triangle of attachment, described in Part I, comprising autonomy, intimacy, and nonattachment, underlies the technical and ethical principles of the psychotherapies. Each of these is at a sufficiently general level to be uncontroversial and nonprescriptive. Rokeach (1973), who is credited with having devised the most reliable instrument for measuring values, distinguishes between "terminal" and "instrumental" values—*what* we are trying to achieve, and *how* we try to achieve it. Each item in the attachment triad is instrumental and terminal, representing both a goal and a means. As argued in Chapter 1, they are also closely interrelated. A robust sense of autonomy, which includes the notion of taking responsibility for one's feelings and actions, is based on the internalization of intimate relationships—a secure base. True intimacy, as opposed to dependency, requires the sense of a relationship in which the other's autonomy is respected—a state of emotional autonomy. Nonattachment, as opposed to isolation or denial, can be seen as an attempt to synthesize the apparently contrasting ideals of autonomy and intimacy at a higher level, and arises out of the experience of closeness to and respect for and from the other.

Nonattachment is an ethical ideal, a cognitive stance, and technical skill. As an ethical ideal derived from Buddhism it implies an escape from the tyranny of desire that is perhaps akin to Freud's (1933) precept "where id was, there ego shall be" (p. 80). As a stage of intellectual development it evokes the ironic stance of Fonagy and colleagues' "reflexive self function," in which one is able to see oneself from the outside, and to subject even one's most firmly held beliefs to critical scrutiny. At the level of technique it is reminiscent of the Rogerian principle of nonpossessive warmth, guarding against overinvolvement with clients and their difficulties.

VALUES IN PRACTICE

This chapter has distinguished between technique on the one hand, in which neutrality is a central theme, and the therapist's moral framework on the other, in which values are of great importance. In practice this distinction is not so clear-cut. Therapists can be trained to be more honest, open, warm, and nonpossessive, which suggests that moral qualities are also matters of technique. An often-debated question in psychotherapy circles is whether one can be both an effective therapist and morally reprehensible in one's personal life. History (Ellenberger 1970) and common sense suggest that this is not infrequently so, and one of the functions of ethical codes for psychotherapists is to scrutinize the boundary between professional and private life.

Bloch and colleagues (1994) show how the therapist approaching a family is inescapably caught up in moral choices and has to maintain a delicate balance between her personal moral framework and those of the family and the wider society. These choices exist on the fringes of practice, a faint drumbeat that draws the therapy in one direction or another, which arises out of the therapeutic context that has been created, but of which therapist and patient may be only dimly aware. For example, therapies with patients who have been traumatized or abused can assume a flavor of righteous anger and blame, in which the patient is exclusively seen as a passive victim of malevolent perpetrators. Some therapeutic approaches might emphasize the patient's contribution to their own continuing victimhood and stress personal responsibility and the need to leave the past behind. Others might try to help patients move from hatred and blame to understanding and acceptance. Whatever the approach, the ethical themes of suffering, retribution, forgiveness, justice, and responsibility are unavoidable.

For Freud, neurosis was a turning away from reality, although what we call reality is always contestable. Therapists' expertise lies in their familiarity with the idealizations, omnipotence, denigration, and cognitive distortions of reality that are characteristic of the inner world. If the unique feature of analytic psychotherapy as a system of expert knowledge is its emphasis on the workings of the unconscious, then therapists must strive to recognize these out-of-awareness moral influences. Values operate mainly at an unconscious level, and probably arise out of developmental experiences that precede rational thought. Consciously held values may be undermined by, or defensive against, forces of envy, hate, and destructiveness that are the very opposite of what is overtly espoused. Therapists should make deliberate efforts to become aware of how their own values affect their work. Was I too encouraging when that patient announced that she intended to leave her husband? Did I side too openly with that adolescent in his rebellion against his rigid militaristic father? Did I appear morally censorious, enthusiastic, or pruriently curious when this man boasted of his sexual conquests? Was there an edge of aggression in my challenge to this agoraphobic patient's fears? Was I impatient with the suspiciousness and emotional withdrawal of this person suffering from schizophrenia? Was I too enthusiastic in my attempts to rid this person of his obsessional doubts?

These everyday clinical questions may be considered as examining the ethical countertransference. Symington sees the process of self-examination as based on the Socratic principle that one cannot do something vicious and know that one is doing it at the same time, which brings us to what might be the most central psychotherapeutic value of all—the Delphic injunction to "know yourself" (Brown and Pedder 1993).

Moral outcomes in psychotherapy can be quite subtle. For Bergin marital fidelity is an absolute value to which all therapists should aspire. But the moral quality of fidelity is exactly what might be at stake in a therapy. Thus patients might enter therapy with sexual doubts and difficulties that mean they are unable to be unfaithful to their partner, and by the end of therapy might have achieved the sexual confidence to do so, but have decided to opt for fidelity both because their current relationship is now more satisfying, and because they choose not to cause pain and unhappiness, seeing respect for others as a greater good than momentary pleasure. The key issue is not so much fidelity in itself, but autonomy and capacity for intimacy as the bases of mature fidelity.

CONCLUSION

It is difficult, if not impossible, and perhaps even undesirable, to write about values without revealing, implicitly at least, one's own value system, or least some part of it. And yet at the same time one should strive for objectivity, subjecting one's own beliefs to the same critical scrutiny one devotes to others. In this chapter I have argued that beliefs and values are important in psychotherapy. I have suggested that as a profession, or a would-be profession, psychotherapy shares common values with other professions, typical of liberal democracies. There are also crucial differences, first, because the distinction between ethical framework and technical content of the work in psychotherapy is less clear-cut than it is in, say, the law or medicine; and second, because ambiguity—or irony or paradox—is inherent in psychotherapy in that it deals with unconscious as well as conscious ideas and forces. This means that when psychotherapy becomes certain of itself or its values it ceases to be psychotherapy and becomes something akin to a proselytizing religion. On the other hand the zeitgeist seems to have created uncertainty in the heart of religion itself, at least in its mature forms, so perhaps there is room for rapprochement.

To the extent that psychotherapists hold to moral values, and inevitably they do, these should be framed at the highest level of generality so that in practice they will be open to individual interpretation and, where necessary, can be contested. Psychotherapy reflects and transmits the values of the prevailing culture, but also—for example, through its valuation of emotional autonomy, stress on the importance of the inner world, and the self-reflexive posture I have called nonattachment—makes its own unique contribution to the cultural and ethical development of the complex local and global societies in which we find ourselves. These themes form the epilogue to this book.

Epilogue: Attachment Theory and Society

The borderland between culture and politics is exciting but dangerous territory. The work of Arthur Miller, arguably America's greatest playwright, has always been located there, reflecting a life typical perhaps of many left-wing intellectuals that in his case (born in 1915) coincides almost exactly with Hobsbawm's (1992) "short 20th Century." A communist sympathizer in his youth, student reporter at the first US factory occupation in the 1930s, signer of many petitions, later disillusioned by the corruption of the unions and the Soviet system, Miller refused to confess or to betray former comrades when interrogated by McCarthy's House UnAmerican Committee. Personally grateful to his psychoanalyst, he also feared for the effects of analysis on his creativity, and was disappointed by its disconnectedness from social concerns. As president of PEN, he was influential in protecting the rights of writers throughout the world, including securing the release from prison of Wole Soyinka when General Gowan received a personal telegram from Marilyn Monroe's former husband! In his 70s, Miller plants trees in his Connecticut home, builds a cabin, and contemplates the coyotes:

And so the coyotes are out there earnestly trying to arrange their lives to make more coyotes possible, not knowing that it is my forest, of course. And I am in this room from which I can sometimes look out at dusk and see them warily moving through the barren winter trees, and I am, I suppose, doing what they are doing, making myself possible, and those who come after me. At such moments I do not know whose land this is that I own, or whose bed I sleep in. In the darkness out there they see my light and pause, muzzles lifted, wondering who I am and what I am doing here in this cabin under my light. I am a mystery to them until they tire of it and move on, but the truth, the first truth, probably, is that we are all connected, watching one another. Even the trees. [Miller 1987, p. 599]

Connection, watchfulness, and ecological awareness—these could be the starting points for a 21st Century politics. Security rests on recognizing and valuing our connections, locally, nationally, internationally and interspecifically. But coyotes are predatory as well as fellow earth-dwellers. They need watching by us, just as we do by them. So security depends on watchfulness, a gaze that is the essence of curiosity and triumphant scientific and artistic exploration, but also of defensiveness and paranoia. There is a hierarchy of human needs, starting with the needs for food, water, and shelter, which take precedence before the sublimities of freedom, education, and creativity can be counted. As comfortable assumptions about ever-expanding productivity seem less and less tenable, a central issue for contemporary politics has become security itself, which as well as being the precondition for a good society, can, in one of capitalism's cruel ironies, also be a commodity to be bought, sold, hoarded, seized, or expropriated.

Psychotherapy and politics are alike in that, although buttressed by scientific argument, the one from psychological science and the other from the social sciences, both are essentially moral discourses (Bradley 1991). Both put forward a view about what it is to lead a good life, and what conditions are required for this to be possible. The notion of security is a useful meeting point for psychological and political dialogue, and among psychotherapeutic discourses it is attachment theory above all that has emphasized security as a central human need. So in this epilogue I shall try to show how the basic ideas and findings of attachment theory can act as a useful point of entry for psychotherapy into the social debate, as a contribution to a more psychologically informed politics. This enterprise, however, is not without its dangers. There is something faintly absurd about the psychoprofessions straying out of their sphere to comment on social events, a kind of attention-seeking in what is still a marginal profession trying to assert itself, handfuls of gravel thrown against advancing tanks. Conversely, social comment on psychological matters often seems, to the professional, inept or far too general to be of much practical use. But ideas *can* turn back tanks as well as set them rolling. The times demand it, and, as W. H. Auden's "Shorts" mischievously puts it, "Private faces in public places/ are much nicer than/ public faces in private places."

There are some interesting parallels between the positions of liberal/left-of-center politics and psychotherapy today. Both find themselves, after years of marginalization, in positions of potential influence and power. Both are in search of new paradigms upon which to base themselves. Many revisionist psychotherapists feel that the basic tenets of classical psychoanalysis need to be rewritten to take account of contemporary developments in cognitive science, systems theory, and psychobiology, just as socialism and liberalism have had to lose their sentimental attachment to the past. Both have had to overcome factionalism within their ranks—indeed, ecumenism within psychotherapy has driven some psychoanalysts to form their own separate enclave, rather than dilute their principles beyond all recognition. Finally both have had to come to terms with a changing reality. Psychoanalytic psychotherapy, previously highly suspicious of "instrumentalism," has, in response to enforced exposure to the cold wind of the market, had to adapt rather than die, and open itself up to scientific evaluation.

The left and psychoanalysis have both had to learn to sup with the devil—the Beelzebub of behaviorism and its cousin, the market. Psychotherapy, which in its origins in Britain was, through the Bloomsbury movement, quite strongly allied with the Fabian left (Hinshelwood 1995), is beginning once again to take account of the social context. With mass unemployment and the relative retreat of trade unionism, politics of the left can no longer take the workplace as its primary arena, but must focus on the family and the ways in which society permeates personal experience.

INSECURITY AND SOCIETY

The context in which these changes are happening is one of tremendous personal, professional, and social insecurity. Although Thatcherism and Reaganomics are usually held responsible for the climatic change that has come over British and U.S. political life and their social institutions, both were surely a manifestation, albeit a particularly malevolent one, of much wider global changes in economic systems and the shifting balance of global influence. Thatcherism was perhaps an example of "identification with the aggressor," in which global insecurity over which we have little power is embraced and celebrated as the engine of change. In Marx's poignant description of the effects of capitalism upon feudalism, "everything that is solid melts into air" (Marx 1848, p. 109). The confluence of psychotherapy and left politics may be a grasping at thin air, or a straw in the wind that can lead us in new directions.

The notion of insecurity and the search for ideas that will hold fast in the face of uncertainty brings us to the main theme of this epilogue. As described in Chapter 2, John Bowlby had strongly held left-of-center views. His two closest male friends were Evan Durbin, a minister in the postwar Labor administration who was tragically drowned off the coast of Cornwall in 1948 while trying to save his daughter; and his brother-in-law, Sir Henry Phelps Brown, the distinguished Labor economic historian. Attachment theory emerged from the great period of political and social ferment following the Second World War.

A central theme of this book has been John Bowlby's attempt to revitalize psychoanalysis by introducing ideas from evolutionary biology and the scientific study of child development. He also saw relationships as central from the start of life and strongly disagreed with the prevailing psychoanalytic view at the time of the infant as an "autistic" unsocialized, self-absorbed creature, only gradually and with great difficulty learning about and accepting the existence of its fellow creatures.

The search for security is common ground between contemporary politics and psychotherapy. Attachment theory starts from the vulnerability and helplessness of the newborn baby. Adults and infants are programmed to bond to one another for survival's sake. A baby that was not so programmed would have soon died from predation in the environment of evolutionary adaptiveness in which our species emerged. Hence Winnicott's (1958) oft-quoted phrase, "There is no such thing as a baby—only a mother and baby together." We are intensely social animals; without community we could not survive. Margaret Thatcher's even more famous reversal of Winnicott—"There is no such thing as society"—was, to view it charitably, an attempt to emphasize the importance of individual choice and responsibility. But individuality and the capacity to choose are end products of the psychological growth within the family and schools, which market-driven policies have done so much to stunt for so many in the Western world today.

ATTACHMENT THEORY

How do adults and infants become attached to one another? To recapitulate the main themes of this book, infant research has revealed how exquisitely aware of one another mother and baby are; within hours of birth a mother can pick out her own child's cry from those of others' (just as ewes choose their own lamb's mews from others in the flock). A newborn baby turns preferentially toward the smell of its own mother's milk, and will often imitate her mouth, tongue, and facial movements in the first week or two of life. Parent and child are aware of each other from the start—Trevarthen's (1984) "primary intersubjectivity." Mother and baby are no strangers; already in the uterus the child has absorbed the rhythms of the mother's heartbeat and speech patterns. Stern's (1985) word *attunement* describes the emotional alignment of parent and child that lays the foundations for secure attachment.

Attunement implies an intimate knowledge of and responsiveness to the baby's individual patterns of feeling and behavior. To be attuned is to acknowledge the child as a separate yet utterly dependent being, and to be able to enter into a variety of cooperative activities—feeding, bathing, changing, playing, lulling to sleep, stimulating when bored, soothing when overstimulated—that depend for their success and pleasure on getting on the child's wavelength, via *imaginative identification*.

In the early days the mother stands for the whole world—her face, her feel, her warmth, her smell, her capacity both to satisfy and frustrate. Gradually the child begins to turn outward, to encounter James's (1890) "buzzing booming" world of sensations with which she is bombarded, to discover for herself the place and the people—father, grandparents, siblings, friends—that are hers. The relationship with the mother usually provides the primary platform from which this outward turning can occur, although it is a job that fathers, grandparents and others can also do. The primary caregiver provides the secure base that makes it safe to begin to explore the world. At around 7 months of age an important change occurs when the child begins to distinguish those she knows from those she does not. Stranger anxiety makes her turn inward to the mother in the face of novel faces and sounds. As her confidence grows, working collaboratively with the mother, she uses visual cueing to check whether a new situation is safe or not.

Gradually the child will extend her radius of exploration away from the secure base, returning abruptly when threatened, tired, or ill. Of course the mother is much more than a secure base, also providing food, warmth and playful enjoyment. A key feature of the secure base is separation protest. Any attempt to part the child from the caregiver at times of stress will provoke furious protest, clinging, searching, and if separation is prolonged, bitter despair. It was the heart-rending recording of these responses in his films of children going into the hospital that Bowlby made with the Robertsons that made his ideas so widely known, and led to a radical change in attitudes toward parental visiting in children's wards.

Bowlby at times gave the impression that the recipe for happiness was the complete avoidance of such separations and therefore of the need for protest. It is now clear that pain, occasional desperation, and loss are universal phenomena in childhood; as mentioned in Part I, Bradley (1991) posits a "basic misery" to stand alongside Erikson's (1968) "basic trust." Babies fuss, cry, suffer colic, won't sleep, refuse food, get cold and wet, just as much as they smile, coo, giggle, gurgle, feed passionately, sleep satiatedly, and sweep us adults off our feet with their adorableness. It is not the absence of unhappiness that is important but how it is responded to and resolved. Bion (1962) saw the mother's role as that of containing such unhappiness, being unfazed by it, holding it inside herself, acknowledging it, and "detoxifying" it. As has been repeatedly emphasized throughout this book, the acceptance of healthy protest, without retaliation, while retaining the capacity to set state- and phase–appropriate boundaries—for example, putting the child to bed when she is obviously tired—is a vital ingredient leading to secure attachment.

Ainsworth and her followers established the major categories of anxious attachment between caregivers and their charges. Once established, these dyadic patterns of attachment tend to persist—patterns that carry through into adolescence and adult life and affect the ways in which we make sense of and ascribe meaning to our world. It seems likely that secure attachment is mediated by brain opioids: levels of these substances are lower in nonattached primates than in those securely attached to caregivers. De Zulueta (1994) links the increasing prevalence of self-injury, addiction, and social violence with insecure attachment and the desperate search for endogenous opiate release through the repetition—actually or in symbolic form—of traumatic events in childhood.

These findings suggest significant links between the private space of the family and infant–parent bonds on the one hand, and the public domain on the other. A particular social order inscribes itself through the security or otherwise of its children. The capacity of parents to provide security for their children will depend in part on the felt security of their world: the labor market, housing, health, and welfare. When their children grow up, if they have primarily internalized an insecure model of the world, they will perceive the public domain as inherently insecure, and respond to political strategies that chime with those feelings of insecurity. Insecurity breeds insecurity, and vice versa.

Attachment is not something that is grown out of once adulthood is achieved. We seek and try to maintain a secure base throughout life. If a secure base is not available, then an insecure one is better than no base at all. Faced with stress or threat, adults seek out their intimate attachments no less vigorously than a separated infant. Our capacity to be autonomous and deal with anxiety is dependent on an internal secure base comprising attachment, a gestalt of experiences, affects, and beliefs, which Kraemer (1992) calls the "attachment icon." The typical patterns of attachment—secure, avoidant, ambivalent, disorganized— seem to correlate with the way in which young adults approach intimate relationships. While two-thirds are relatively comfortable with their partners and can cope with closeness and separation, some find real intimacy intensely threatening, while others are made anxious or traumatized by any hint of distance or separation. We can easily image how political perceptions may also be colored by attachment models. Right-wing views can be related to avoidance, as Adorno argued in his characterization of the authoritarian personality. Some left-liberal policies have an ambivalent feel, based on unmetabolized aggression, perpetuating rather than helping to overcome dependency. The emergence of extreme political disaffection and banditry can perhaps be related to the increasing prevalence of disorganized patterns of relationship in childhood.

POLITICAL IMPLICATIONS

Can we use these by now familiar ideas and findings to illuminate contemporary political debate? I will comment schematically on five key areas: violence in society, community, the environment, gender, and nationhood.

Social Violence and Democracy

Bowlby was a passionate advocate of democracy, which he saw as an extension of the benign patriarchy he approved of in family life—responsive parents, prepared to listen to and take seriously the views of their children. His was essentially an enlightenment view of man as inherently good, cooperative, and free, perverted by social insecurity and defective parenting. For him violence was a response to trauma in early life, a manifestation of separation protest, or, in de Zulueta's (1994) phrase, "attachment gone wrong." He saw the capacity to express healthy protest and to have it listened to as a mark of a well-functioning family.

If the state is to be seen as a "good parent," then it needs to take its citizens seriously, to be attuned to the reality or their lives and their needs. Violence in the family arises when adults dehumanize children, failing to see them as capable of feeling pain or having separate minds. Respect for people begins in the cradle. Political yobboism—viewing citizens as "scum," "scroungers," "rent-a-crowd," "animals"—contributes to the very violence it deplores, since the greater the alienation from a secure base, the more unresponsive and unattuned the "parent," the greater will be the tendency to avoidance and unprovoked violence. Here too perhaps we see how narrative style reflects attachment patterns, the typical unelaborated argot of yobboism being a direct expression of avoidant attachment.

Bowlby did not perhaps realize the full extent to which destructive violence could overwhelm both individuals and societies. He resisted the Kleinian vision of envy and hatred as inherent properties of the human infant, no less than love and gratitude. But with the disadvantage of our late twentieth century hindsight we can see that any social philosophy that fails to take account of these dark forces is incomplete. Even within a more environmentalist vision, psychosocial trauma can, via the neurobiological mechanisms mentioned, lead to "wired-in" destructiveness at an early age that is hard to eradicate by simple ameliorist measures.

The basis of much of political life is institutionalized splitting: all that is bad is attributed to one's political opponents, the Devil's party, all goodness appropriated to one's own side. Democracy is important not because it enables this defensive splitting to be overcome—that can only happen when the badness becomes located in some external "enemy" (currency speculators, terrorists, the Russians)—but because it acknowledges the need to contain both sides of the split. Her majesty's opposition is no less vital than Her majesty's government. Whether the idealization of Her majesty is also required is another question. A parochial but psychologically important question for Britain and Australia is whether republicanism should be seen as one more step on the road to political maturity, or the expression of a ruthless and punitive superego that unrealistically insists they do away with the childish dependency implicit in clinging to a monarchy.

Community

Our hominid ancestors lived in groups, based on the need for protection, foraging, and nurture. Within those groups were to be found not only cooperation and mutuality but also dominance hierarchies and at times intense competition for resources. Humphrey (1992) has suggested that the ability to "read" one another's intentions and to distinguish between authenticity and cheating, between altruism and self-seeking, would have contributed significantly to survival among these "natural psychologists." Chance (1988) distinguishes between agonistic (i.e., competitive) and hedonistic or cooperative modes of relating, both of which are present in abundant potential within our psychological makeup.

A government that wanted to enhance agonistic behavior and destroy a sense of community could develop a clear strategy, based on ethology. First, it would encourage large status differentials, since it has been shown that dominance behavior increases among monkeys where competition for resources (food, sexual availability) are greatest (Gilbert 1989). Second, it would diminish as far as possible the potential for reciprocal altruism. Reverse Robin Hoodism—taxing the poor to give to the rich—means that there is less and less possibility for a sense of mutual advantage.

Third, it would ignore as far as possible the needs of the weakest in society. Cooperation depends on a sense of positive self-esteem. This is enhanced by resource holding potential—material possessions, which characterizes Galbraith's (1994) comfortable two-thirds of Western societies—and by what Gilbert (1989) calls attention holding potential. We crave recognition as well as goods. A state that turns a blind eye to the needy, that is not attuned to their feelings and aspirations, will also evoke agonistic rather than cooperative behavior. Finally such a government must never smile, smiling being one of the most potent methods of switching on community and switching off competition, or if it does smile it must ensure that it is not a genuine one, since we are biologically programmed to distinguish the ersatz smile from the real thing. If we believe in cutthroat competition and devil-take-the-hindmost as the route to salvation, by following these four precepts we shall be well on the way to achieving our nirvana.

Hutton's (1994) "forty-thirty-thirty" society (40 percent of whom are secure in their employment, 30 percent employed but only on insecure short-term contracts, and 30 percent poor and generally unemployed) or Galbraith's (1994) contented elites are built around insecure attachment, in which the possibility of community is constantly undermined by the struggle for resources, which includes security itself. Secure parents can provide a secure base for all their children, dealing fairly and bringing out the unique potential of each. The inherent inequality of Western societies means that the state often appears only to support the most disadvantaged, much as parents may appear always to side with the youngest and weakest of their offspring. When the state is weak—like when a parent's back is turned—this may unleash triumphal victimization of the weak by the strong.

THE ENVIRONMENT

Attachment theory is a *systemic* theory in that it sees the individual not in isolation, but in reciprocal relationship first to a primary attachment figure, then to subsidiary attachment figures within the family, then to wider society, of whose workings politics is a major expression. Each level of these concentric circles can provide security or insecurity for that which it contains. Thus, as I have argued, does social insecurity via joblessness, homelessness, and hopelessness percolate down to personal feelings of insecurity and resultant anger and destructiveness.

Until fairly recently the left tended to ignore the silent outer circle of this system—the environment—except, perhaps, via nostalgic arcadian communitarian yearnings far removed from the cloth cap and the barricade. Yet the ultimate secure base has to be the Earth, which sustains and nourishes us. Silent, the planet is a perfect vehicle for projection; we idealize our Earth-mother, while at the same time despoiling it, pouring our poisonous feelings of hatred and disappointment concretely into its folds and recesses. Capitalism, urbanization, and the mobility of people in search of resources has broken the intimate bond between person and place, so, like a military bomber command, we can attack alien locations so long as they are felt as *not-me*. But modern science, as well as giving us the potential to destroy this final attachment, also enables us to understand the Earth as a whole, as opposed to our little corner of it, giving us an ecological perspective from which to unite in mutual solidarity to secure a Mother Earth whose children we all are.

Behind this polemic lies a serious point about attachment and postmodernism. Attachment starts as the link between a particular parent and child in a specific house, apartment, or hostel in a town, suburb, or village. As development proceeds, attachment style becomes internalized as a template, fantasy, or internal working model for all intimate relationships. "Me and you" is transformed into "I and thou," "my home" becomes "our world." Our piecemeal, pluralistic postmodern existence can be integrated at this higher level, providing sufficient maturation of its citizens takes place, which is why education and support for children must be near the top of any political agenda that also takes the environment seriously.

Gender

No discussion of attachment theory would be complete without some consideration of gender. There is some irony in the fact that, despite his vilification from some feminist critics, Bowlby's central mission was the rehabilitation of childhood and the valuation of parenthood as a vital contribution to society. To recapitulate:

> Man and woman power devoted to the production of material goods counts as a plus in all our economic indices. Man and woman power devoted to the production of happy, healthy, and self-reliant children in their own homes does not count at all. We have created a topsy turvy world. [Bowlby 1988, p. 2]

In this late passage he is careful to say *man and* woman power, whereas in his early writings he was mainly concerned with women's role in bringing up children. The impact of his best-selling *Child Care and the Growth of Maternal Love* (Bowlby 1953) was ambiguous; it helped to raise the status of those delivering child care, and undoubtedly transformed pediatric practice, but a generation of working mothers felt guilty about leaving their children, and even those who did not felt bad about their inability to live up to the high standards of devotion Bowlby seemed to advocate. Winnicott (1958) with his sanctioning of "good-enough" mothering was the great liberator.

I have already suggested that large status differentials trigger agonistic rather than cooperative-hedonistic behavior, and this applies to status differences between men and women as well as between classes and different income groups. This does not just mean equal pay, opening up our political system to women, good maternity benefits, and so on, important though these are. It also means exposing the fantasies that underlie what Sayers (1995) calls "the man who never was," in a "patriarchal—but father absent" (Leupnitz 1988) society. It requires us to take account of the immense psychological as well as material damage that has resulted from mass unemployment, and a structurally insecure labor market, which means that men are deprived of their traditional roles and source of self-esteem as workers and providers. Depression and apathy or outbursts of destructive rage are typical responses to this collapse of a secure base and accompanying sense of self-worth. The reality of this inner destruction has somehow to be acknowledged within the political system: to be faced, symbolized, its story told, and mourned. How to do this while at the same time instilling hope is a formidable task for our political leaders.

Nationhood

Michael Ignatieff (1994) ends his magnificent foray into contemporary nationalism with the pessimistic conclusion:

> I began the journey as a liberal and I end as one, but I cannot help thinking that liberal civilisation—the rule of laws not men, or argument in place of force, of compromise in place of violence—runs deeply against the *human grain* and is only achieved and sustained by the most unremitting struggle against *human nature*. The liberal values—tolerance, compromise, reason—remain as valuable as ever, but they cannot be preached to those who are mad with fear or mad with

vengeance. . . . What's wrong with the world is not nationalism itself. Every people must have a home, every such hun-
ger must be assuaged. What's wrong is the kind of nation,
the kind of home that nationalists want to create. . . . A
struggle is going on . . . between those who still believe that
a nation should be a home to all, and that race, colour, religion, and creed should be no bar to belonging, and those who
want their nation to be home only to their own. It's a battle
between the civic and the ethnic nation. I know which side
I'm on. I also know which side, right now, happens to be win-
ning. [p. 189, my italics]

A battle, perhaps, between secure and insecure attachment.
The stumbling blocks in this argument are the phrases *human
nature* and *the human grain*. Liberalism is easily caught between an
ironic relativistic stance—whose practical expressions are pluralism, devolution, and an openness to self-deconstruction—and the
wish to proclaim liberal values as universals (Rorty 1991). Science,
as one of the highest expressions of liberalism, can help to tease
out what is intrinsic to human nature, and what, in contrast, is
socially derived. Attachment theory suggests that the potential for
both insecure and secure attachment exists within the human repertoire, and can point to the kinds of conditions in which one or
the other is likely to predominate.

The nation is as fictional and as necessary a notion as the self.
Both are composite entities, comprising diversity often subordi-
nated and repressed for the sake of survival. Psychiatry recognizes
borderline personality organization in which split and uncoordi-
nated aspects of the self—good and bad, destructive and hopeful—
struggle for recognition and integration. I have suggested in this
book that the orgins of borderline personality organization can be
traced in part at least to (a) lack of parental attunement, (b) lack of
metabolism of rage and protest, and (c) failure to recognize the
child as an experiencing being. The state has similarly to hear and
find some way to integrate the legitimate aspirations of its component members, with their regional, ethnic, and class- and gender-
based diversity. If the state acts like the parent of an ambivalent

child it will unpredictably intrude on and then neglect these voices, leading to a failure to respect boundaries or real differences. If it behaves like the parent of an avoidant child it will turn a deaf ear and try with increasing state power to quell expressions of discontent, leading in turn to disillusionment and sporadic violence. Nationalistic movements behave like insecurely attached individuals, clinging desperately to outmoded values, while projecting and attacking the weaker disowned part of the self in "the enemy."

The Sicilian writer Gesualdo Bufalino (quoted in Holmes 1993, p. 208) writes:

> Now I know this simple truth: that it is not only my right but my duty to declare myself a citizen of Everywhere as well as of a hamlet tucked away in the Far South between the Iblei Mountains and the sea; that it is my right and duty to allow a place in my spirit for both the majestic music of the universe and that of the jet gushing from a fountain in the middle of a little village square, on the far southern bastions of the West.

The village square and Everywhere; from the parish pump to One World. A new political system has to be fashioned that will accommodate both these attachments—the one concrete and specific, the other abstract and universal, that can connect local and global security in a meaningful way. The Northern Irish leader John Hume, a politician central to the 1994 cease-fire in Northern Ireland, gave an exemplary example of this new perspective (which could be seen as an example of nonattachment in the political sphere) when, in discussing the peace process in Northern Ireland, he made the very obvious but politically taboo point that which side you were on in the conflict depends entirely on the accident of your birth.

CONCLUSION

Nostalgic perhaps for his days as a neurologist, Freud described psychoanalysis and government as belonging to the "impossible professions"—because "one can be sure beforehand of achieving unsatisfying results" (Freud 1937a, p. 4). But if psychotherapy is hard work, politics is surely harder. To try to change the world is more formidable a task than merely interpreting it. Perhaps psychotherapy can provide some of the theoretical basis for political choice, if only by making policy makers more aware of the unconscious assumptions about human relationships upon which they base their decisions.

Politics is based on phenomena psychotherapists all too easily recognize as ways of dealing with anxiety: splitting, projection, idealization, and denial. Omnipotence versus real potency, acceptance of reality versus hopelessness, and the need for change versus manic change as a way of denying pain vie for dominance. Helplessness and confusion underlie many of our aspirations and efforts, both personal and political. Perhaps politicians are much less able to influence events than they would have us (and themselves) believe. Perhaps, like psychotherapists, the best they do is to try to create a climate or a setting in which certain kinds of outcomes are more or less likely to happen. Perhaps they should retain a degree of nonattachment about their work. That is not to say that there are moments when a line has to be drawn, a stand has to be taken, a decisive lead given. But for much of the time the style and manner of government are as important as its content, just as the style of psychotherapizing or parenting are crucial determinants of outcome. A psychologically informed politics would include the findings of attachment theory among its basic principles: respect for persons, the capacity to listen, acknowledgment of pain, acceptance of the need for legitimate expressions of anger, and above all the provision of a secure base for all citizens, the precondition for exploration, growth, and maturation.

References

Ainsworth, M. (1969). Object relations, dependency and attachment: a theoretical review of the mother–infant relationship. *Child Development* 40:969–1025.

———— (1982). Attachment: retrospect and prospect. In *The Place of Attachment in Human Behaviour*, ed. C. M. Parkes and J. Stevenson-Hinde. London: Routledge.

Alvarez, Al (1971). *The Savage God.* London: Penguin.

Alvarez, Anne (1992). *Live Company.* London: Routledge.

Andrews, G. (1993). The essential psychotherapies. *British Journal of Psychiatry* 162:447–451.

Aponte, H. (1985). The negotiation of values in therapy. *Family Process* 24:323–338.

Appelbaum, A. (1989). Supportive therapy: a developmental view. In *Supportive Psychotherapy: A Psychodynamic Approach*, ed. L. Rockland, p. 166–167. New York: Basic Books.

Balint, E. (1993). *Before I Was I.* London: Free Association.

Balint, M. (1957). *The Doctor, His Patient and the Illness.* London: Butterworth.

———— (1959). *Thrills and Regressions.* London: Hogarth.

———— (1968). *The Basic Fault.* London: Tavistock.

Bartholomew, K. (1990). Avoidance of intimacy: an attachment perspective. *Journal of the Society for Personal Relations* 7:147–178.

Bateman, A., and Holmes J. (1995). *Introduction to Psychoanalysis: Contemporary Theory and Practice.* London: Routledge.

Bateson, G. (1973). *Steps Towards an Ecology of Mind.* London: Paladin.

Beck, A., and Freeman, A. (1990). *Cognitive Therapy of Personality Disorders.* New York: Guilford.

Becket, W. (1992). *Art and the Sacred.* London: Rider.

Benjamin, J. (1989). *The Bonds of Love.* London: Virago.

Benoit, D., and Parker, K. (1994). Stability and transmission of attachment across three generations. *Child Development* 65:1444–1456.

Bergin, A. (1980). Psychotherapy and religious values. *Journal of Consulting and Clinical Psychology* 48:95–105.

——— (1991). Values and religious issues in psychotherapy and mental health. *American Psychologist* 46:394–403.

Bergin, A., Stinchfield, R., Gaskin, T., et al. (1988). Religious life-styles and mental health: an exploratory study. *Journal of Counseling Psychology* 35:91–98.

Bettelheim, B. (1960). *The Informed Heart.* New York: Free Press.

Bion, W. (1962). *Learning from Experience.* London: Heineman.

——— (1978). *Second Thoughts.* London: Heineman.

Birtchnell, J. (1993). *How Humans Relate.* New York: Praeger.

Black, D. (1993). What sort of thing is religion? A view from object relations theory. *International Journal of Psycho-Analysis* 73: 613–628.

Bloch, S. (1995). Supportive psychotherapy. In *Introduction to the Psychotherapies*, ed. S. Bloch, pp. 201–216. Oxford: Oxford University Press.

Bloch, S., Hafner, J., Harari, E., and Szmukler, G. (1994). *The Family in Clinical Psychiatry.* Oxford: Oxford University Press.

Bollas, C. (1987). *The Shadow of the Object.* London: Free Association.

Boszormenyi-Nagy, I., et al. (1991). Contextual therapy. In *Handbook of Family Therapy*, vol. 2, eds. A. Gurman and D. Kniskern, pp. 220–232. New York: Brunner.

Bowlby, J. (1951). *Maternal Care and Mental Health*. Geneva: WHO Monograph Series No 2.

———— (1953). *Child Care and the Growth of Maternal Love*. London: Penguin.

———— (1958). The nature of the child's tie to his mother. *International Journal of Psycho-Analysis* 39:350–373.

———— (1960). Separation anxiety. *International Journal of Psycho-Analysis* 41:89–113.

———— (1961). Processes of mourning. *International Journal of Psycho-Analysis* 42:317–340.

———— (1969). *Attachment*. London: Penguin

———— (1973). *Separation*. London: Penguin

———— (1979a). On knowing what you are not supposed to know and feeling what you are not supposed to feel. *Canadian Journal of Psychiatry* 24:403–408.

———— (1979b). *The Making and Breaking of Affectional Bonds*. London: Tavistock.

———— (1980). *Loss*. London: Penguin.

———— (1988). *A Secure Base*. London: Routledge.

———— (1990). *Charles Darwin*. London: Hutchinson.

———— (1991). The role of the psychotherapist's personal resources in the therapeutic situation. *Tavistock Gazette* (Autumn).

Bowlby, J., Young, R., and Figlio, K. (1986). An interview with John Bowlby. *Free Associations* 6:36–64.

Bradley, B. (1991). *Infant Minds*. Cambridge, UK: Polity Press.

Brazelton, B., and Cramer, T. (1991). *The Earliest Relationship*. London: Karnac.

Bretherton, I. (1991a). Pouring new wine into old bottles: the social self as internal working model. In *Self Processes and Development*, ed. M. Gunnar and L. Sroufe. Hillsdale, NJ: Erlbaum.

———— (1991b). Roots and growing points of attachment theory.

In *Attachment Across the Life Cycle,* ed. C. M. Parkes, J. Stevenson-Hinde, and P. Marris, pp. 9–32. London: Routledge.

Brown, D., and Pedder, J. (1993). *Introduction to Psychotherapy*, 2nd ed. London: Routledge.

Brown, H. (1987). The impact of suicide on therapists in training. *Comprehensive Psychiatry* 28:101–112.

Bruner, J. (1986). *Actual Minds, Possible Worlds.* Cambridge, MA: Harvard University Press.

Byng-Hall, J. (1995). *Rewriting Family Scripts.* New York: Guilford.

Campbell, D., and Hale, R. (1991). Suicidal acts. In *Textbook of Psychotherapy in Psychiatric Practice,* ed. J. Holmes, pp. 287–306. Edinburgh: Churchill-Livingstone.

Casement, P. (1985). *On Learning from the Patient.* London: Tavistock.

Cavell, M. (1994). *The Psychoanalytic Mind.* Cambridge, MA: Harvard University Press.

Chance, M., ed. (1988). *Social Fabrics of the Mind.* London: Erlbaum.

Chasseguet-Smirgel, J. (1985). *Creativity and Perversion.* London: Free Association.

Chemtob, M. (1988). Patients' suicides: frequency and impact on psychiatrists. *American Journal of Psychiatry* 145:224–228.

Chodorow, N. (1978). *The Reproduction of Motherhood.* Berkeley, CA: University of California Press.

Colthart, N. (1993). *How to Survive as a Psychotherapist.* London: Harvester.

Craik, K. (1943). *The Nature of Explanation.* Cambridge, UK: Cambridge University Press.

Crittenden, P. (1988). Relationships at risk. In *Clinical Implications of Attachment,* ed. J. Belsky and T. Nezworsky. New York: Erlbaum.

Crown, S. (1988). Supportive psychotherapy: A contradiction in terms? *British Journal of Psychiatry* 152:266–269.

Cryan, E., Kelly, P., and McCaffrey, B. (1995). The experience of patient suicide among Irish psychiatrists. *Psychiatric Bulletin* 19:4–7.

Davies, H. (1980). *William Wordsworth*. London: Weidenfeld & Nicolson.

de Zulueta, F. (1994). *From Pain to Violence*. Northvale, NJ: Jason Aronson.

Doane, J., and Dramond, D. (1994). *Affect and Attachment in the Family*. New York: Basic Books.

Donne, J. (1624). *Collected Poems and Prose*. London: Nonesuch, 1992.

Eagle, M. (1984). *Recent Developments in Psychoanalysis*. New York: McGraw-Hill.

Eisenberg, L. (1986). "Mindlessness" and "brainlessness" in psychiatry. *British Journal of Psychiatry* 148:497–508.

Eliot, T. (1952). *The Cocktail Party*. London: Faber.

——— (1959). *Four Quartets*. London: Faber.

——— (1975). *Selected Prose*, ed. F. Kermode. London: Faber.

Elkin, I., Shea, M., Watkins, J., et al. (1989). NIMH treatment of depression collaborative research programme: general effectiveness of treatments. *Archives of General Psychiatry* 46:971–982.

Ellenberger, H. (1970). *The Discovery of the Unconscious*. New York: Basic Books.

Erickson, M. (1993). Rethinking Oedipus. *American Journal of Psychiatry* 150:411–416.

Erikson, E. (1968). *Identity: Youth and Crisis*. New York: Norton.

Fahy, T., and Wessely, S. (1993). Should purchasers pay for psychotherapy? *British Medical Journal* 307:576–577.

Fairbairn, R. (1952). *Psychoanalytic Studies of the Personality*. London: Routledge.

Ferenczi, S. (1932). Confusion of tongues between adults and children. In *The Assault on Truth*, ed. J. Masson. London: Penguin, 1985.

——— (1955). *Further Contributions to the Theory and Technique of Psychoanalysis*, ed. M. Balint. London: Hogarth.

Fonagy, P. (1991). Thinking about thinking: some clinical and theoretical considerations in the treatment of a borderline patient. *International Journal of Psycho-Analysis* 72:639–656.

——— (1993). Psychoanalytic and empirical approaches to developmental psychopathology: Can they be usefully integrated? *Journal of the Royal Society of Medicine* 86:577–581.

Fonagy, P., Steele, M., Steele, H., et al. (1991). The capacity for understanding mental states: the reflective self in parent and child and its significance for security of attachment. *Infant Mental Health Journal* 12:201–218.

——— (1994). The theory and practice of resilience. *Journal of Child Psychology and Psychiatry* 35:231–257.

Forster, E. M. (1910). *Howards End*. London: Penguin.

——— (1925). *Two Cheers for Democracy*. London: Hutchinson.

Frank, J. (1986). Psychotherapy: the transformation of meanings. *Journal of the Royal Society of Medicine* 79:341–346.

Freud A. (1936). *The Ego and the Mechanisms of Defence*. London: Hogarth.

Freud, S. (1911). Formulations on the two principles of mental functioning. *Standard Edition* 12:215–227.

——— (1912). The dynamics of transference. *Standard Edition* 12:99–112.

——— (1914). On narcissism. *Standard Edition* 14:67–102.

——— (1923). The ego and the id. *Standard Edition* 19:3–66.

——— (1924). Neurosis and psychosis. *Standard Edition* 19:149–156.

——— (1926). Symptoms, inhibitions and anxiety. *Standard Edition* 20:75–175.

——— (1933). New introductory lectures on psycho-analysis. *Standard Edition* 22:3–182.

——— (1937a). Analysis terminable and interminable. *Standard Edition* 23:209–253.

——— (1937b). Constructions in analysis. *Standard Edition* 23:255–269.

——— (1940a). An outline of psychoanalysis. *Standard Edition* 23:141–208.

―――― (1940b). Splitting of the ego in the process of defense. *Standard Edition* 23:271–278.

Gabbard, G. (1992). Psychodynamic psychiatry in the "decade of the brain." *American Journal of Psychiatry* 149:991–998.

Galbraith, J. (1994). *Culture of Contentment*. London: Penguin.

Gallwey, P. (1991). Social maladjustment. In *Textbook of Psychotherapy in Psychiatric Practice*, ed. J. Holmes. Edinburgh: Churchill-Livingstone.

―――― (1993). *The Concept of a Person: Sanity and Insanity in Thinking and Behaviour.* Unpublished manuscript.

Gardner, M. (1981). *The Mind's New Science*. London: Penguin.

Garland, C. (1991). External disasters and the internal world. In *Textbook of Psychotherapy in Psychiatric Practice*, ed. J. Holmes. Edinburgh: Churchill-Livingstone.

Gergen, K. (1985). The social constructionist movement in psychology. *American Psychologist* 40:266–275.

Giddens, A. (1992). *Intimacy and the Search for Self*. Oxford: Polity.

Gilbert, P. (1989). *Human Nature and Suffering*. London: Erlbaum.

Gill, M. (1951). Ego psychology and psychotherapy. *Psychoanalytic Quarterly* 20:62–71.

Glover, E. (1931). The therapeutic effect of inexact interpretations: a contribution to the theory of suggestion. *International Journal of Psycho-Analysis* 12:397–411.

Goldberg, S., Muir, R., and Kerr, J., eds. (1995). *John Bowlby's Attachment Theory: Clinical, Historical and Social Significance.* New York: Academic Press.

Grant, S., Holmes, J., and Watson, J. (1993). Guidelines for psychotherapy training as part of general professional training. *Psychiatric Bulletin* 17:695–698.

Greenberg, J., and Mitchell, S. (1983). *Object Relations in Psychoanalytic Theory*. London: Harvard University Press.

Greenson, R. (1967). *Technique and Practice of Psychoanalysis*. New York: International Universities Press.

Grosskurth, P. (1986). *Melanie Klein: Her World and Her Work*. Cambridge, MA: Harvard University Press.

Grossman, K., and Grossman, K. (1991). Attachment quality as an organiser of emotional and behavioural responses in a longitudinal perspective. In *Attachment Across the Life Cycle*, ed. C. M. Parkes, J. Stevenson-Hinde, and P. Marris. London: Routledge.

Grotstein, J. (1990). Introduction. In *Psychotic Anxieties and Containment,* by Margaret Little. Northvale, NJ: Jason Aronson.

———— (1992). Reflections on a century of Freud: some paths not chosen. *British Journal of Psychotherapy* 9:181–187.

Grunbaum, A. (1984). *The Foundations of Psychoanalysis.* Berkeley: University of California Press.

Gunderson, J., and Sabo, A. (1993). The phenomenological and conceptual interface between borderline personality disorder and PTSD. *American Journal of Psychiatry* 150:19–27.

Haldane, D. (1993). Personal communication.

Haldane, D., and Trist, E. (1992). Obituary: Jock Sutherland. *British Journal of Medical Psychology* 65:1–4.

Hamilton, V. (1982). Narcissus and Oedipus. London: Routledge. (Reprinted 1995, London: Karnac.)

———— (1985). John Bowlby: an ethological basis for psychoanalysis. In *Beyond Freud*, ed. J. Reppen. New York: Analytic Press.

———— (1994). *Oedipus and Narcissus*, 2nd ed. London: Routledge.

Harman, C. (1992a). Introduction. In R. L. Stevenson's *Essays and Poems*. London: Everyman.

———— (1992b). Introduction. In *The Strange Case of Dr. Jekyll and Mr. Hyde*, by R. L. Stevenson. London: Everyman.

Harris, M., and Waddell, M. (1991). *The Chamber of Maiden Thought.* London: Routledge.

Hart, B. (1912). *The Psychology of Insanity.* Cambridge, UK: Cambridge University Press.

Hartland, S. (1991). Supportive psychotherapy. In *A Textbook of Psychotherapy in Psychiatric Practice*, ed. J. Holmes. Edinburgh: Churchill-Livingstone.

Hazan, C., and Shaver, P. (1994). Attachment as an organisational framework for research on close relationships. *Psychological Inquiry* 5:1–22.

Heard, D., and Lake, B. (1986). The attachment dynamic in adult life. *British Journal of Psychiatry* 149:430–438.

Herman, J., Perry, C., and Kolk, B. (1989). Childhood trauma in borderline personality disorder. *American Journal of Psychiatry* 146:490–495.

Hinde, R. (1982). *Ethology*. London: Fontana.

Hinshelwood, R. (1989). *A Dictionary of Kleinian Thought*. London: Free Association Books.

———— (1991). Psychodynamic psychiatry before World War I. In *150 Years of British Psychiatry*, ed. G. Berrios and H. Freeman. London: Gaskell.

———— (1995). Psychoanalysis in Britain: points of cultural access 1893–1918. *International Journal of Psycho-Analysis* 76:135–152.

Hobsbaum, E. (1961). *The Age of Extremes*. London: Joseph.

Hobson, P. (1993). *Autism and the Development of Mind*. Hillsdale, NJ: Erlbaum.

Hobson, R. (1985). *Forms of Feeling: The Heart of Psychotherapy*. London: Tavistock.

Holmes, J. (1992). *Between Art and Science: Essays in Psychotherapy and Psychiatry*. London: Routledge.

———— (1993). *John Bowlby and Attachment Theory*. London: Routledge.

———— (1994a). Clinical implications of attachment theory. *British Journal of Psychotherapy* 11:62–76.

———— (1994b). Psychotherapy—a luxury the NHS cannot afford? More expensive not to treat. *British Medical Journal* 309:1070–1071.

———— (1994c). Psychotherapy and its relationships. *Current Opinion in Psychiatry* 7:213–215.

———— (1995a). Meaning and mechanism in psychiatry. In *Philosophical Aspects of Psychiatry*, ed. R. Griffiths. Cambridge, UK: Cambridge University Press.

———— (1995b). Supportive psychotherapy: the search for positive meanings. *British Journal of Psychiatry* 167:439–445.

———— (1995c). Something there is that doesn't love a wall. In

John Bowlby's Attachment Theory: Clinical, Historical and Social Significance, ed. S. Goldberg, R. Muir, and D. Kerr. New York: Academic Press.

———— (1996). Values in Psychotherapy. *American Journal of Psychotherapy* (in press).

————, ed. (1991). *A Textbook of Psychotherapy in Psychiatric Practice.* Edinburgh: Churchill-Livingstone.

Holmes, J., and Crown, S. (1996). Long term individual psychotherapy. In *The Psychotherapies,* 3rd ed., ed. S. Bloch. Oxford: Oxford University Press.

Holmes, J., and Lindley, R. (1989). *The Values of Psychotherapy.* Oxford: Oxford University Press.

Holmes, R. (1985). *Footsteps.* London: Penguin.

Horowitz, M. (1988). *Introduction to Psychodynamics.* London: Routledge.

Horowitz, M., Marmar, C., Weiss, D., et al. (1984). Brief psychotherapy of bereavement reactions: the relationship of process to outcome. *Archives of General Psychiatry* 41:438–448.

Humphrey, N. (1992). *A History of the Mind.* London: Chatto.

Hutton, R. (1994). *The State We are In.* London: Faber.

Iga, M. (1993). Japanese Suicide. In *Suicidology: Essays in Honour of Edwin Schneiderman,* ed. A. Leenaars. Northvale, NJ: Jason Aronson.

Ignatieff, M. (1994). *Blood and Belonging.* London: Vintage.

James, W. (1890). *Principles of Psychology.* New York: Basic Books.

Jaspers, J. (1963). *General Psychopathology,* trans. J. Hoenig and M. Hamilton. Manchester, UK: Manchester University Press.

Kahane, M. (1968). Suicide among patients in mental hospitals: a study of the psychiatrists who conducted their psychotherapy. *Psychiatry* 3:32–43.

Karasu, B. (1993). Depression: the relative merits of pharmacotherapy and psychotherapy. *Current Opinion in Psychiatry* 6:184–190.

Karen, R. (1994). *Becoming Attached.* New York: Warner.

Kelly, T., and Strupp, H. (1992). Patient and therapist values. *Journal of Consulting and Clinical Psychology* 60:34–40.

Kernberg, O. (1984). *Psychoanalytic Treatment of Personality Disorders.* New York: Academic Press.

Khan, M. (1958). Introduction. In *Through Paediatrics to Psychoanalysis,* by D. Winnicott. London: Hogarth.

King, P. (1989). The activities of British psychoanalysis during the Second World War. *International Review of Psycho-Analysis* 16:15–33.

Klein, M. (1940). Mourning and its relation to manic-depressive states. In *The Writings of Melanie Klein. Vol. 1: Love, Guilt, and Reparation.* London: Hogarth.

——— (1961). *Narrative of Child Analysis.* London: Hogarth.

——— (1967). *Collected Writings, Vol. 3,* ed. R. Money-Kyrle. London: Hogarth.

Klerman, G., Weissman, M., Rounsaville, B., and Chevron, E. (1984). *Interpersonal Therapy of Depression.* New York: Guilford.

Kohon, G., ed. (1986). *The British School of Psychoanalysis: The Independent Tradition.* London: Free Association Books.

Kohut, H. (1977). *The Restoration of the Self.* New York: International Universities Press.

——— (1984). *How Does Psychoanalysis Cure?* Chicago: University of Chicago Press.

Kraemer, G. (1992). A psychobiological theory of attachment. *Behavioural and Brain Sciences* 15:493–541.

Kuhn, T. (1962). *The Structure of Scientific Revolutions.* New York: Academic Press.

Lacey, H. (1986). An integrated behavioural and psychodynamic approach to the treatment of bulemia. *British Journal of Bulemia and Anorexia Nervosa* 1:19–26.

Laing, R. (1961). *The Divided Self.* London: Penguin.

Langs, R. (1978). *The Listening Process.* New York: Jason Aronson.

Langsley, D., and Yager, J. (1988). The definition of a psychiatrist: eight years later. *American Journal of Psychiatry* 145:469–475.

Lasch, C. (1979). *The Culture of Narcissism.* New York: Norton.

Laufer, M., and Laufer, E. (1984). *Adolescence and Developmental Breakdown.* London: Yale University Press.

Lazarus, A., and Messer, S. (1988). Clinical choice points: behavioural versus psychoanalytic interventions. *Psychotherapy* 25: 59–70.

Leff, J., and Vaughn, C. (1983). *Expressed Emotion in Families*. New York: Guilford.

Leiman, M. (1995). Early development. In *Cognitive Analytic Therapy: Developments in Theory and Practice*, ed. A. Ryle. Chichester: Wiley.

Leupnitz, D. (1988). *The Family Interpreted*. New York: Basic Books.

Levenson, P. (1985). Interpersonal theory. In *Models of the Mind*, ed. A. Rothstein, pp. 68–92. New York: International Universities Press.

Levi, P. (1958). *If This Be a Man*. London: Paladin.

Lewin, K. (1950). *The Psychoanalysis of Elation*. New York: Norton.

Lewis, A. (1979). *Later Papers*. Oxford: Oxford University Press.

Linehan, M. (1993). *Cognitive-Behavioural Treatment of Borderline Personality Disorder*. New York: Guilford.

Linehan, M., Armstrong, H., Suarez, A., et al. (1991). Cognitive-behavioural treatment of chronically parasuicidal borderline patients. *Archives of General Psychiatry* 48:1060–1064.

Lomas, P. (1987). *The Limits of Interpretation: What's Wrong with Psychoanalysis*. London: Penguin.

London, P. (1984). *The Modes and Morals of Psychotherapy*. New York: Norton.

Lorenz, K. (1953). *King Solomon's Ring*. London: Methuen.

Luborsky, L. (1984). *Principles of Psychoanalytic Psychotherapy: A Manual for Supportive-Expressive Treatment*. New York: Basic Books.

MacMurray, J. (1957). *The Self as Agent*. London: Faber.

Main, M. (1991). Metacognitive knowledge, metacognitive monitoring, and singular vs. multiple models of attachment. In *Attachment Across the Life Cycle,* ed. C. Parkes et al. London: Routledge.

——— (1995). *Clinical aspects of attachment: the work of Mary Main.* Lecture given at conference, University College, London.

Main, M., and Goldwyn, R. (in press). Adult attachment scoring and classification system. In *Systems for Assessing Attachment*

Organisation Through Discourse, Behaviour and Drawings, ed. M. Main. Cambridge: Cambridge University Press.

Main, M., and Weston, D. (1982). Avoidance of the attachment figure in infancy. In *The Place of Attachment in Human Behaviour*, ed. C.M. Parker and J. Stevenson-Hinde. London: Routledge.

Malan, D. (1979). *Individual Psychotherapy and the Science of Psychodynamics*. London: Butterworth.

Mallinckrodt, B., Gantt, D., and Coble, H. (1995). Attachment patterns in the psychotherapy relationship. *Journal of Counselling Psychology* 42:307–317.

Maltsberger, J., and Buie, D. (1974). Countertransference hate in the treatment of suicidal patients. *Archives of General Psychiatry* 30:625–633.

Marx, K. (1848). *The Communist Manifesto*. London: Lawrence & Wishart, 1952.

Mead, M. (1962). A cultural anthropologist's approach to maternal deprivation. In *Deprivation of Maternal Care*. Geneva: WHO.

Meares, R. (1993). *The Metaphor of Play*. Northvale, NJ: Jason Aronson.

Menninger, K. (1958). *Theory of Psychoanalytic Technique*. London: Imago.

Miller, A. (1987). *Timebends*. London: Hutchinson.

Miller, K. (1985). *Doubles*. Oxford: Oxford University Press.

Mitchell, S. (1988). *Relational Concepts in Psychoanalysis*. Cambridge, MA: Harvard University Press.

Molnos, A. (1984). The two triangles are four: a diagram to teach the process of dynamic brief psychotherapy. *British Journal of Psychotherapy* 1:112–125.

Murray, L., and Cooper, P. (1994). Clinical applications of attachment theory and research: changes in infant attachment with brief therapy. In *The Clinical Application of Ethology and Attachment Theory*, ed. J. Richter. London: Association for Child Psychology and Psychiatry.

New, C., and David, M. (1985). *For the Children's Sake*. London: Penguin.

O'Dowd, T. (1988). Five years of heart-sink patients in general practice. *British Medical Journal* 297:528–536.

Orlinsky, D., Grawe, K., and Parks, B. (1994). Process and outcome in psychotherapy—*noch einmal*. In *A Handbook of Psychotherapy and Behaviour Change*, 4th ed., ed. S. Garfield and A.Bergin, pp. 270–378. Chichester: Wiley.

Parker, G. (1983). Parental "affectionless control" as an antecedent to adult depression. *Archives of General Psychiatry* 40:956–960.

Parkes, C., Stevenson-Hinde, J., and Marris, P., eds. (1991). *Attachment Across the Life Cycle*. London: Routledge.

Pedder, J. (1986). Attachment and a new beginning. In *The British School of Psychoanalysis: The Independent Tradition*, ed. G. Kohon, pp. 295–308. London: Free Association.

———— (1995). Personal communication.

Phillips, A. (1987). *Winnicott*. London: Fontana.

Pine, F. (1986). Supportive psychotherapy, a psychoanalytic perspective. *Psychiatric Annals* 16:527–529.

———— (1994). The interpretive moment. *Bulletin of the Menninger Clinic* 48:54–71.

Pines, M. (1991a). The development of the psychodynamic movement. In *150 Years of British Psychiatry*, ed. G. Berrios and H. Freeman, pp. 206–231. London: Gaskell.

———— (1991b). A history of psychodynamic psychiatry in Britain. In *Textbook of Psychotherapy in Psychiatric Practice*, ed. J. Holmes, pp. 31–56. Edinburgh: Churchill-Livingstone.

Pinkser, H. (1994). The role of theory in teaching supportive psychotherapy. *American Journal of Psychotherapy* 48:530–542.

Popper, K. (1968). *The Logic of Scientific Discovery*. London: Hutchinson.

Post, R. (1992). Transduction of psychosocial stress into the neurobiology of recurrent affective disorder. *American Journal of Psychiatry* 149:999–1010.

Quinodoz, J.-M. (1993). *The Taming of Solitude*, trans. P. Slotkin. London: Routledge.

Rayner, E. (1991). *The Independent Mind in British Psychoanalysis.* London: Free Association.

———— (1992). John Bowlby's contribution. *Bulletin of the British Psychoanalytic Society*, pp. 20–32.

Reik, T. (1948). *The Inner Experience of a Psychoanalyst.* New York: Farrar, Straus.

Reps, P. (1971). *Zen Flesh, Zen Bones.* London: Penguin.

Rey, H. (1994). *The Schizoid Mode of Being.* London: Free Association.

Rieff, P. (1979). *Freud: the Mind of a Moralist*, 3rd ed. London: University of Chicago Press.

Rilke, R. (1964). Departures. In *Selected Poems*. London: Penguin.

Riviere, J. (1936). On the genesis of psychical conflict in earliest infancy. *International Journal of Psycho-Analysis* 17:265–277.

Roazen, P. (1973). *Freud and His Followers.* London: Penguin.

Roberts, G. (1992). The origins of delusion. *British Journal of Psychiatry* 161:298–308.

Rockland, L. (1987). A supportive approach: psychodynamically oriented supportive therapy—treatment of borderline patients who self mutilate. *Journal of Personality Disorders* 1:350–353.

———— (1989). *Supportive Psychotherapy: a Psychodynamic Approach.* New York: Basic Books.

———— (1992). *Supportive Psychotherapy for Borderline Patients.* New York: Guilford.

———— (1993). A review of supportive psychotherapy, 1986–1992. *Hospital and Community Psychiatry* 44:1053–1060.

Rokeach, M. (1973). *The Nature of Human Values.* New York: Free Press.

Rorty, R. (1991). *Contingency, Irony, and Solidarity.* Cambridge, UK: Cambridge University Press.

Rose, S. (1993). *The Making of Memory.* London: Minerva.

Roustang, F. (1980). *Dire Mastery*, trans. N. Lukacher. Baltimore: Johns Hopkins University Press.

Russell, G., Szmuckler, G., Dare, C., and Eisler, I. (1987). An evaluation of family therapy in anorexia nervosa and bulimia nervosa. *Archives General Psychiatry* 44:1047–1056.

Rustin, M. (1991). *The Good Society and the Inner World*. London: Verso.

Rutter, M. (1981). *Maternal Deprivation Reassessed*. London: Penguin.

————— (1985). Resilience in the face of adversity: protective factors and resistance to psychiatric disorder. *British Journal of Psychiatry* 147:598–611.

————— (1995). Clinical implications of attachment concepts: retrospect and prospect. *Journal of Child Psychology and Psychiatry* 36:549–571.

Rycroft, C. (1985). *Psychoanalysis and Beyond*. London: Chatto.

Ryle, A. (1990). *Cognitive Analytic Therapy: Active Participation in Change*. Chichester: Wiley.

—————, ed. (1995). *Cognitive Analytic Therapy: Developments in Theory and Practice*. Chichester: Wiley.

Sandler, J. (1986). Reality and the stabilising function of unconscious fantasy. *Bulletin of the Anna Freud Centre* 9:177–194.

Sayers, J. (1995). Consuming male phantasy: feminist psychoanalysis retold. In *Psychoanalysis in Contexts*, ed. A. Elliott and S. Frosh, pp. 123–141. London: Routledge.

Schneiderman, E. (1993). *Suicide as Psychache: A Clinical Approach to Self Destructive Behavior*. Northvale, NJ: Jason Aronson.

Segal, H. (1957). Notes on symbol formation. *International Journal of Psycho-Analysis* 38:391–397.

————— (1991). *Dream, Phantasy and Art*. London: Routledge.

Shafer, R. (1992). *Retelling a Life*. New York: Basic Books.

Shapiro, D. (1995). Finding out how psychotherapies help people change. *Psychotherapy Research* 5:1–21.

Shapiro, D., and Firth, J. (1987). Prescriptive versus exploratory therapy: outcomes of the Sheffield psychotherapy project. *British Journal of Psychiatry* 151:790–799.

Shepherd, M. (1979). Psychoanalysis, psychotherapy and health services. *British Medical Journal* 3:1157–1559.

Singer, P. (1994). *How Are We to Live*. London: Mandarin.

Skynner, R. (1976). *One Flesh: Separate Persons*. London: Constable.

Slavin, M., and Kriegman, D. (1992). *The Adaptive Design of the Human Psyche*. New York: Guilford.

Smail, D. (1988). Psychotherapy: deliverance or disablement. In *Ethical Issues in Caring*, ed. G. and S. Fairbairn, pp. 162–172. Avebury, UK: Gower.

Spence, D. (1982). *Narrative Truth and Historical Truth: Meaning and Interpretation in Psychoanalysis*. New York: Norton.

———— (1987). *The Freudian Metaphor*. New York: Basic Books.

Steiner, J. (1985). The interplay between pathological organisations and the paranoid-schizoid and depressive positions. *International Journal of Psycho-Analysis* 68:69–80.

———— (1993). *Psychic Retreats*. London: Routledge.

Stern, D. (1985). *The Interpersonal World of the Infant*. New York: Basic Books.

Stevenson, R. L. (1886). *The Strange Case of Dr. Jekyll and Mr. Hyde*, ed. C. Harman. London: Everyman, 1992.

Stiles, W., Shapiro, D., and Elliot, R. (1986). Are all psychotherapies equivalent? *American Psychologist* 41:165–180.

Stolorow, R., Brandshaft, B., and Atwood, G. (1987). *Psychoanalytic Treatment, an Intersubjective Approach*. Hillsdale, NJ: Analytic Press.

Storr, A. (1992). John Bowlby. *Munks Roll*. London: Royal College of Physicians.

Strachey, J. (1934). On the nature of the therapeutic action of psychoanalysis. *International Journal of Psycho-Analysis* 15:127–159.

Sullivan, H. (1953). *Interpersonal Theory of Psychiatry*. New York: Norton.

Sutherland, J. (1966). The psychotherapeutic clinic and community psychiatry. *Bulletin of the Menninger Clinic* 30:338–350.

———— (1980). The British object relations theorists. *Journal of the American Psychoanalytic Association* 28:829–860.

———— (1991). *Fairbairn's Journey to the Interior*. London: Free Association Books.

————, ed. (1971). *Towards Community Mental Health*. London: Tavistock.

Sutherland, J., and Fitzpatrick, G. (1944). Some approaches to group problems in the British army. *Sociometry* 6:205–217.

Symington, N. (1994). *Emotion and Spirit*. London: Karnac.

Symington, J., and Symington, N. (1996). *Bion*. London: Routledge.

Szasz, T. (1969). *The Ethics of Psychoanalysis*. New York: Dell.

Taylor, K. (1969). Prokaletic measures derived from psychoanalytic techniques. *British Journal of Psychiatry* 115:407–419.

Trevarthen, C. (1984). Emotions in infancy: regulators of contacts and relationships with persons. In *Approaches to Emotion*, ed. K. Scherer and P. Ekman. Hillsdale, NJ: Erlbaum.

——— (1987). Mind in infancy. In *The Oxford Companion to the Mind,* ed. R. Gregory. Oxford: Oxford University Press.

Truax, C., and Carkhuff, R. (1967). *Towards Effective Counselling and Psychotherapy*. Chicago: Aldine.

Valliant, G. (1977). *Adaptation to Life*. Boston: Little, Brown.

Vygotsky, L. (1962). *Thought and Language*. Cambridge, MA: MIT Press.

Wallace, E. (1988). What is "truth"? Some philosophical contributions to psychiatric issues. *American Journal of Psychiatry* 145:137–147.

Wallerstein, R. (1986). *42 Lives in Treatment: A Study of Psychoanalysis and Psychotherapy*. New York: Guilford.

Walls, G. (1989). Values and psychotherapy: a comment on "Psychotherapy and Religious Values." *Journal of Consulting and Clinical Psychology* 48:640–641.

Warn, M., and Carlson, E. (1996). Associations among adult attachment representations, maternal sensitivity, and infant-mother attachment in a sample of adolescent mothers. *Child Development* (in press).

Watts, D., and Morgan, G. (1994). Malignant alienation. *British Journal of Psychiatry* 164:11–15.

Werman, D. S. (1984). *The Practice of Supportive Psychotherapy*. New York: Brunner/Mazel.

Weston, D. (1992). The cognitive self and the psychoanalytic self: Can we put ourselves together? *Psychological Inquiry* 3:1–13.

White, D., and Epston, D. (1990). *Narrative Means to Therapeutic Ends*. New York: Norton.

Whitehead, A. (1958). *An Introduction to Mathematics*. Oxford: Oxford University Press.

Winnicott, D. (1958). Hate in the countertransference. In *Through Paediatrics to Psychoanalysis: Collected Papers.* London: Hogarth.

———— (1965). The capacity to be alone. In *The Maturational Process and the Facilitating Environment*, pp. 29–36. London: Hogarth.

———— (1971). The use of an object. In *Playing and Reality*, pp. 101–111. London: Penguin.

Winston, A., Pinsker, H., and McCullogh, L. (1986). A review of supportive psychotherapy. *Hospital and Community Psychiatry* 37:1105–1114.

Wordsworth, W. (1954). *Collected Poems.* Oxford: Oxford University Press.

Zukier, H., and Pepitone, A. (1984). Social roles and strategies in prediction: some determinants of the use of base rate information. *Journal of Personality and Social Psychology* 47: 342–356.

Credits

Many of the chapters in this book started life as lectures and then became journal articles. Chapter 1 was part of the first joint Royal College of Psychiatrists and British Psychological Society Psychotherapy Sections meeting on attachment in 1995. Chapter 2 was first delivered at a conference on John Bowlby's work in Toronto in 1993, and parts of it appear in Holmes 1994a and 1995c. Chapter 3 (which also appears as Holmes 1995b) and Chapter 5 emerged from an invitation to speak at the Australian and New Zealand College of Psychiatrists annual meeting in 1995. Chapter 4 began as the inaugural Sutherland Trust lecture in Edinburgh in 1993. Chapter 6 was delivered at a conference on suicide at St. Georges's Hospital London in 1994. Chapter 7 began as a lecture to the Royal Philosophical Society (Holmes 1995a), and as a talk at the Scottish Section meeting of the Royal College of Psychiatrists in 1994. Chapter 8 emerged from a symposium on ethics in psychotherapy, edited by Sidney Bloch for the *American Journal of Psychotherapy* (Holmes 1996). Finally, the Epilogue came out of a conference at the Tavistock Clinic on attachment and society in 1995 organized by Sebastian Kraemer and Jane Roberts.

Index

ABOUT THE AUTHOR

Jeremy Holmes, MD, MRCP, FRCPsych, trained in science, medicine, and psychiatry at King's College Cambridge, University College Hospital London, and at the Maudsley Hospital. A consultant psychiatrist and psychotherapist in North Devon, England, he is currently a senior clinical lecturer at Bristol University Medical School. His research interests are in attachment theory and the treatment of personality disorder, and in the provision of an integrated psychotherapy service as part of general psychiatry. Dr. Holmes lectures widely in the UK and internationally, and has published seven books and over sixty papers on psychotherapy.